BABY YOU'RE A RICH MAN

STAN SOOCHER

BABY YOU'RE A RICH MAN

Suing the Beatles for Fun & Profit

ForeEdge

ForeEdge

An imprint of University Press of New England

www.upne.com

© 2015 Stan Soocher

All rights reserved

Manufactured in the United States of America

Designed by Eric M. Brooks

Typeset in Parkinson Electra Pro by Passumpsic Publishing

For permission to reproduce any of the material in this book,
contact Permissions, University Press of New England, One Court
Street, Suite 250, Lebanon NH 03766; or visit www.upne.com

Library of Congress Cataloging-in-Publication Data

Soocher, Stan.

Baby you're a rich man: suing the Beatles for fun and profit /
Stan Soocher.

    pages   cm

ISBN 978-1-61168-380-6 (cloth: alk. paper)—

ISBN 978-1-61168-813-9 (ebook)

1. Beatles—Trials, litigation, etc. 2. McCartney, Paul—
Trials, litigation, etc. 3. Lennon, John, 1940-1980—Trials,
litigation, etc. 4. Harrison, George—Trials, litigation, etc.
5. Starr, Ringo—Trials, litigation, etc. I. Title.

ML421.B4S653   2015

782.42166092'2—dc23   2015003397

5 4 3 2 1

What was it — I paused to think —

what was it that so unnerved me in the

contemplation of the House of Usher?

○ EDGAR ALLAN POE,
○
○ "The Fall of the House of Usher"
○
○
○
○
○
○
○
○
○
○
○

CONTENTS

Illustrations follow page 110.

INTRODUCTION

A disheveled Allen Klein stood in the narrow hallway of the New York state court auxiliary building in lower Manhattan's Tribeca district. For several days now, in the summer of 1998, dressed in what appeared to be the same wrinkled white suit, the Beatles' former manager attended a music royalty case that pitted the 1960s Ronettes vocal group against Klein business associate Phil Spector. Klein's ABKCO Industries administered the licensing of the sound recordings that Phil Spector produced, including those by the Ronettes and their lead singer, Spector's former wife Ronnie. At the trial, Klein testified on Spector's behalf and even paid the record producer's legal costs.

But during a recess in the proceedings, Allen Klein talked in the court hallway not about the music-royalty dispute at hand but what was likely his favorite music business topic: his 1969 renegotiation of the Beatles' recording contract with Capitol Records. The Capitol contract had come with an exceptionally high 25 percent artist royalty rate and a pro-artist Beatles-to-Capitol licensing arrangement. Klein got the agreement only a few months after he became the Beatles' manager, and it gave him considerable bragging rights in light of the many business missteps the Beatles had already made in their careers. These included problems caused by the business naïveté of their prior manager, Brian Epstein, and the group's struggle to launch their own business empire, Apple Corps.

Of course, Klein greatly benefited from the management commissions he took from the Beatles' elevated royalty rate under the renegotiated Capitol deal. But in the Ronettes/Spector recess, Klein spoke animatedly about his bright, shining Beatles achievement as if he was the world's greatest artists' advocate.

In fact, Allen Klein had a long history of tangling with artists he represented — as manager or recording-contract wizard — such as the Rolling Stones and Herman's Hermits. Klein was involved in so many court cases that journalists often mistakenly referred to him as a "lawyer." (He wasn't one.)

The main focus of this book is on legal disputes that arose during Klein's time as the Beatles' manager and during the several years that followed. From 1969 through the mid-1970s, the Beatles' personal, creative, and business affairs were dominated by a convergence of forces and lawsuits that led to both the formal end of the band and the individual members establishing their solo identities. The court cases revealed inside details on the Beatles' management intrigues, the band's breakup, and the challenges faced particularly by the litigation-prone John Lennon and George Harrison in adjusting to their post-Beatles artistic and personal lives.

Though some of these cases are among the most famous in music history, in researching court archives I found a number of documents from thirty-five or more years ago still in their original staples, apparently unbent by prior copying. Original inked signatures of John Lennon, George Harrison, Yoko Ono, Brian Epstein, Allen Klein, and many of the judges on court orders popped up on these primary sources. (Documents signed by Paul McCartney and Ringo Starr that I researched were on photocopies of the originals or stored on microfilm.)

Paul McCartney — who was set on having his lawyer in-laws, Linda McCartney's father, Lee Eastman, and her brother, John, guide the Beatles — had famously rejected Allen Klein, whom Paul didn't trust, from the outset. Klein was the reason Paul sued the other Beatles in December 1970 to end the band's partnership, though Allen continued to handle business for Lennon, Harrison, and Starr until they terminated his management relationship with them in March 1973.

By then, Klein had embedded himself so deeply into the Beatles' affairs that it would take years — and a bitter batch of lawsuits — for John, George, and Ringo to oust him from their lives.

◦ ◦ ◦ ◦ ◦ To understand the Beatles' relationship with Allen Klein, it's essential to first look at their relationship with Brian Epstein. His entry into the Beatles' lives is where this book begins, by examining Epstein's management idiosyncrasies, key agreements he procured for them, and the major Beatles-related litigation of his management tenure — the court fight against London party maven Nicky Byrne and his business partners, to whom Epstein's NEMS Enterprises had granted the exclusive worldwide rights to license Beatles merchandise, in a deal that embarrassingly lost the Beatles tens of millions of dollars. (To be fair, the unparalleled popularity of the Beatles made Epstein among the first to face many such mammoth music-business issues.)

Epstein also had to worry about competition from Allen Klein, who made it no secret in the mid-1960s that he had set his sights on becoming the Beatles' manager. Epstein became "scared," Klein claimed, after he heard that Allen told the press, "I was going to have the Beatles one day."

Klein's opportunity arrived just over a year after Brian's August 1967 death from a drug overdose. Klein entered the Beatles' business orbit at a crucial time. In 1969, the freewheeling, spendthrift atmosphere at Apple Corps, and overly idealistic altruism of the Beatles for funding new artists and ideas, had the band's London headquarters teetering on collapse.

John Lennon, in particular, was persuaded that Allen Klein could save Apple.

"People were very scared of him to start with — and some still are — but that's probably good," Lennon said in 1969. "He's swept out all the rubbish and the deadwood, and stopped it being a rest-house for all the world's hippies."

Lennon's embrace of the cost-conscious Klein reflected a more widespread shift in the attitude of artists of that era, as the music business evolved into the massive industry it became in the 1970s. Author Johnny Rogan noted in his history of UK music management, *Starmakers and Svengalis*, that this growth opened the door to an "influx of accountants, solicitors and anonymous agencies" as artists "began searching for business-oriented managers."

Allen Klein's aggressive, loud, and often crude style certainly was a far cry from the genteel personality the Beatles were used to with Brian Epstein, whose adoring dedication and promotional ability was essential in bringing worldwide fame to the band. Epstein's keen attention to the details of his clients' personal and business lives was driven by his vision of what the Beatles' image should be. The street-tough Klein, on the other hand, was more concerned with maximizing financial gain from his artists' business endeavors — usually to fill his own pockets.

Klein's agenda was hindered beginning in March 1971, however, by Paul

McCartney's successful bid to have an English court appoint a receiver to watch over the Beatles' finances. Allen nevertheless maintained close relationships — both good and bad — with the other Beatles, particularly John and George. He enthusiastically offered financial and production support for George's August 1971 Madison Square Garden benefit concerts — the first major rock industry event of its type — to aid starving refugees during a civil war in Bangladesh. But the concerts' noble mission was tainted when the Internal Revenue Service came knocking for taxes from the event's income, because Klein had failed to make sure the proper charity tax-exemption forms were filed before the shows took place.

When George was sued for copyright infringement over his song "My Sweet Lord," Allen offered him advice and retained defense counsel for George. But during the litigation, Klein went behind Harrison's back to buy the rights from plaintiff Bright Tunes Music to collect copyright damages from George — a phase of the case that would go on for more than twenty years. Under the pretext of offsetting a small tax burden on Klein's ABKCO music company, Allen separately sued George in an attempt to seize ownership of most of the other songs George had written.

Klein's mixed-bag relationship with John Lennon was just as influential. This included Allen loaning expense funds to, and sometimes traveling with, John and Yoko in their quest for physical custody of Yoko's daughter from a prior marriage. Also, Allen testified in support of John at a 1972 federal immigration hearing over the U.S. government's effort to deport Lennon from the United States — purportedly for John's 1968 drug conviction in England but in actuality for his outspoken opposition to the Vietnam War. But after Lennon later dropped him as manager, Klein acted as a "spoiler" in trying to manipulate the outcome of a settlement John reached with the notorious music mogul Morris Levy, who had sued the Beatles' Apple Records claiming that "Come Together" infringed on a Chuck Berry song that Levy's publishing company owned.

Eventually, Klein's Beatles incursions led him to being convicted for tax evasion. In renegotiating the Beatles' recording deal with Capitol Records in 1969, he procured a provision for the band's Apple Records to receive a large number of free copies of Beatles releases — ostensibly to help promote the product — that Capitol Records shipped to ABKCO's New York office. Caught red-handed with the cash in his hand from under-the-counter sales of the promotional copies to record distributors, Klein argued that his promotion director Pete Bennett, who made the actual sales, was trying to frame him. The cash-for-copies scheme wasn't new to the corruption-prone music industry, but it definitely confirmed the prescience of Paul McCartney's from-the-start refusal to trust Klein.

During the tax-evasion proceeding, Assistant U.S. Attorney Robert N. Shwartz said, that if Klein "only cheated the Beatles on their royalties or only cheated Capitol on money they were entitled to make had they sold these [promotional] records to the distributors instead of [Pete] Bennett and Klein . . . we wouldn't be here today, no federal crime."

Of course, the gravity of Allen Klein's modus operandi is a matter of perspective. When he was asked about his music business instincts, "Would you do anything short of killing?" he unhesitatingly replied, "Yeah, I think so."

PART ONE

CAN'T BUY ME LOVE

1 · Dripping with Enthusiasm

Brian Epstein coordinated most aspects of the Beatles' career from the time he became their manager in 1962. But the band enforced a hands-off policy when it came to their music, so Brian rarely stopped by Beatles recording sessions. One day in the spring of 1967, however, while the Beatles were working on the *Sgt. Pepper's* album, an excited Epstein showed up at Abbey Road Studios in London to tell them he had just sealed a deal for the band to be Britain's cultural representatives on *Our World* — an international live TV broadcast expected to attract hundreds of millions of viewers.

Brian "looked around the room expectantly. I almost thought he was getting ready to take a bow," Beatles' recording engineer Geoff Emerick recalled. "To his utter dismay, the group's response was . . . to yawn."

"Well, Brian," John Lennon said, "that's what you get for committing us to doing something without asking first."

Epstein stormed out of the studio, but the truth was that the Beatles resented Brian announcing the *Our World* news to them as "a fait accompli. They were at a point where they wanted to take control of their own career," Emerick said.

For the Beatles' June 25, 1967, international TV performance, John Lennon did pen the peace anthem "All You Need Is Love," which Brian Epstein called "an inspired song and they really wanted to give the world a message. The nice thing about it is that it cannot be misinterpreted."

Lennon's message to Epstein at that Abbey Road session certainly had been just as clear: Brian's marketing and promotion skills and unswerving commitment to the Beatles' career may have been crucial in bringing the Beatles to the top of the entertainment industry, but his tenure for guiding the day-to-day details of their activities was winding down. Epstein's involvement with the Beatles had been decreasing ever since the band stopped touring in 1966.

(During that 1966 tour, there had been assassination threats by a right-wing faction when the band performed in Japan; the band was roughed up and barely escaped intact in an airplane after Philippines first lady Imelda Marcos claimed they failed to honor an invitation [which the Beatles said they hadn't known about] to attend a palace reception; and security concerns increased for the Beatles' us shows following protests and death threats over John Lennon's statement that the Beatles were more popular than Jesus.)

Beset by a growing list of business and personal problems and unshakeable insomnia, the once meticulous, reliable Epstein was getting lost in a haze of drugs and alcohol. But Epstein's management of the Beatles had made pioneers both out of him and the band, as they laid the groundwork for what would become the modern music industry, one that operated on an international level. This, and the fact that the Beatles were the first artists Epstein represented, meant he managed on a learning curve. The result was Epstein made major mistakes — most tellingly in the handling of the Beatles merchandise business — that left his effectiveness open to question and had him worried the Beatles might leave him when his initial management-contract term with them ended in the fall of 1967.

Tony Bramwell, who worked for Epstein's management company, confirmed that Brian, "stammered and stuttered when he mentioned it, was abnormally distressed, convincing himself that they weren't going to sign up again because they loathed him. Going through months of paranoia, he looked for reasons and forlornly asked the question, 'Don't they like me anymore?'"

o o o o o In the early days, Liverpool club owner and talent agent Allan Williams "was our first 'manager,'" John Lennon said, though Williams mostly acted as the Beatles' booking agent. It was Williams, owner of the popular Blue Angel and Jacaranda clubs in Liverpool, who procured crucial early gigs for the Beatles, including in Hamburg, Germany, in 1960. McCartney described Williams as "a little Welshman with a little high voice — a smashing bloke and a great motivator, though we used to take the mickey out of him."

But Brian Epstein was the Beatles' first fully dedicated manager. Epstein was born on September 19, 1934, to a well-to-do Jewish family who operated a retail furniture business in north Liverpool, England. Brian, his father,

Harry, his mother, Queenie, and younger brother, Clive, were a close-knit unit who observed religious holidays and maintained a Kosher home. Brian even called his parents "Mummy" and "Daddy" when he was an adult.

But, "Brian was artistic, temperamental, volatile, mercurial, flamboyant," the Epsteins' next-door neighbor, attorney Rex Makin, said. "He didn't fit into his background."

Brian instead had a troubled childhood. He wasn't interested in academics and spent his formative years moving from school to school. "Eppy" was drawn more to the theater world than to intramural sports, and at one point, to his family's dismay, wanted to be a dress designer. Immaculately dressed and soft-spoken, in a precise, sophisticated manner, Brian started working as a salesman for his family's furniture business in 1950. But in 1952, he was drafted into the Royal Army Service Corp. "I venomously hated nearly everything about the army," Brian complained. The military stint didn't last long. He was discharged on "medical grounds" after arriving back at the London barracks in Regent's Park from a night out on the town, dressed above his private's rank in an officer's uniform.

Brian did return home to Liverpool, but four years later enrolled in the Royal Academy of Dramatic Arts (RADA) back in London. Despite his love of theater, he didn't fare well as an actor, though, and left RADA prior to completing his first year. While there, Brian, who was gay, (then illegal in England), was ensnared in a highly embarrassing situation. In April 1956, he was arrested for "persistently importuning" an undercover officer at a public restroom at a London transit station. Brian claimed the officer initiated the incident, but the reality was that the aspiring actor often engaged in homosexual trysts, usually with rough, macho types who sometimes beat him up. His Liverpool friend Joe Flannery recalled that Brian showed up at Joe's house one night in a white shirt tuned bright red with blood from a "rough trade" beating.

Brian said, "When I left RADA, I was determined to throw myself into the family business and make an increasing and lifelong success of it." The Epsteins sold pianos and sheet music in their North End Music Stores, which initially was one outlet adjacent to their furniture shop, and when they expanded the family business by opening a furniture and appliance store on Great Charlotte Street in downtown Liverpool, they included a record department in that location that Brian developed into a thriving operation.

The Epsteins soon launched a third record store that Brian managed, this one on Whitechapel Street in downtown Liverpool. There in the fall of 1961, the twenty-seven-year-old record retailer found himself scrambling to meet strong demand for the German Polydor label single "My Bonnie" by British singer Tony Sheridan, who was backed on the disc by the "Beat Brothers." Only, Epstein's customers were asking for "My Bonnie" by the Beatles, a Liverpool band renamed the Beat Brothers by Polydor for the Sheridan release. The Beatles had recorded the single under a contract with German artist/producer Bert Kaempfert, who signed them when they were playing club dates in Hamburg. But, "Bert K et al thought the Beatles were TOO BLUSEY! [*sic*]" John Lennon said. "That's why we ended up as Sheridens' [*sic*] backing group."

On the morning of November 9, 1961, Epstein arrived at the NEMS Great Charlotte Street location to tell his personal assistant Alistair Taylor that "he'd seen this poster at the bottom of Mathew Street advertising The Beatles 'direct from Hamburg,' and of course Mathew Street is where the Cavern Club was," Taylor recalled.

The music venue was located in a dark, dank basement only a couple of hundred yards from the music store. "So we decided to go see them during our lunch hour," Taylor continued. "It was an awful club. There was condensation running down the walls and it smelt. There were these four guys onstage in black leather, wearing what we call bomber jackets today, black trousers, black T-shirts, and they were so loud. There was smoking onstage and they were joking with the girls in the audience and it was just like, 'Oh my God, what are we sitting here watching?'"

According to Taylor, "It took about half-an-hour for Brian to decide to manage them. We went for lunch and he asked me my opinion first, and I said I thought they were awful but there was something there. He said, 'They are awful but I think they're fabulous.' And then he suddenly said, 'What do you think about me managing them?' And it was as quick as that."

○ ○ ○ ○ ○ Brian Epstein had a habit of becoming keen on new projects, then dropping them just as quickly. But whether Epstein was sexually attracted to the Beatles or thrilled by discovering a new business interest, artist management became his new central focus — though he later admitted the Beatles was "a Liverpool group that I had actually heard of some time

before." Brian had seen them hanging out in his music store listening to records, and NEMS sold issues of the local *Mersey Beat* music newspaper, for
which Brian was writing a record-review column. The cover of the July 20,
1961, issue had announced the Bert Kaempfert deal: "Beatles Sign Recording Contract."

John Lennon, Paul McCartney, George Harrison, and their then drummer Pete Best needed new guidance when Epstein approached them. A
dispute had arisen between the band and Allan Williams, who claimed the
Beatles stiffed him on his commission for booking them at the Top Ten
Club in Hamburg. "I told John Lennon [they] would never fucking work
again," Williams recalled. "At that time, there were 300 groups in Liverpool
who were as good or better than the Beatles," the bitter Williams claimed.

Brian Epstein clearly disagreed. In his initial management negotiations
with the Beatles, on December 3, 1961, he promised them a significant
jump in touring profile and to get them a recording contract with a major
label. Impressed, the Beatles inked an initial contract with Epstein on January 24, 1962.

Brian, though, didn't sign the management agreement that day. "I signed
my name as a witness to Brian's signature," Alistair Taylor said. "It made
me look a right fool." Epstein claimed, "I had given my word about what
I intended to do, and that was enough. I abided by the terms and no one
ever worried about me not signing it." Tony Bramwell, a Beatles childhood
friend and Epstein management aide, noted "such was their utter faith in
Brian that they never read a single contract he gave them to sign."

Brian did sign a five-year management contract with the Beatles on October 2, 1962, three days before the release of the group's first Parlophone
single, "Love Me Do." He said the agreement gave NEMS Enterprises, the
management company he founded in June 1962, expansive "authority to negotiate and to enter into all contracts on their behalf relating to all aspects of
their professional interests and careers throughout the world." This wasn't
unusual for personal management contracts, though Epstein convinced the
Beatles to give him 25 percent of gross weekly income that exceeded £200,
a commission at the high end of what managers got paid. (Epstein's management commission was 15 percent for up to £100 in Beatles' weekly gross
income and 20 percent for up to £200 in weekly gross income.) Epstein
softened this by giving the Beatles a 10 percent stake in NEMS Enterprises.

Though he hated to delegate work to others, Brian claimed he practiced a transparent management style with his artists. "I'm very careful, desperately careful not ever to exploit them," he said. "Even if they don't want to know about a certain contract or a certain fee or something, it's my duty to inform them even though they may throw the bit of paper away on which I tell them." But even though the Beatles implicitly trusted Epstein, they were somewhat skeptical because they "always had disrespect and disregard for anyone in authority, anyone in control of the purse strings—they were basically suspicious of everybody," the band's recording engineer Geoff Emerick noted.

○ ○ ○ ○ ○ By the time Brian and the four Beatles all signed the management agreement, his relentless campaign to make them a worldwide phenomenon was in full swing. "I did everything that I could, you know, *everything*; shouted from the rooftops," Brian said. "He would kill for them," the Rolling Stones' early manager Andrew Loog Oldham added. "He could be quite tough. He represented his act 24/7."

The dapperly dressed Epstein immediately set out to reshape the Beatles image, to attract a mainstream audience beyond local Liverpool tastes. He ordered the band members to clean up their onstage language and dress in formal, matching outfits that reflected Epstein's tidy style.

On January 1, 1962, Brian Epstein got the Beatles into a Decca Records studio in London to tape an audition. But the label passed on signing the band, which performed a set of light pop standards chosen by Epstein that failed to highlight the Beatles' dynamic stage sound. (In February 1962, Brian obtained German producer Bert Kaempfert's consent to let the Beatles out of their limited four-tracks-per-year recording contract with him.)

That didn't stop the tenacious Epstein, who continued to pound the pavement for his act by going from one London record company to another looking for a label deal. But the rookie manager made his work more difficult because he was using the recordings the Beatles made during the band's unsuccessful audition for Decca Records as a calling card at the other labels.

Only producer/executive George Martin from the Parlophone comedy and jazz label showed serious interest in the Beatles. Epstein got Martin interested enough in the Decca audition tapes that Martin wanted to make his own test recordings of the Beatles, which were done at Abbey Road Studios on June 6, 1962. "It was love at first sight. That may seem exaggerated, but the fact is that we hit it off straight away," Martin said about his first studio session with the Beatles.

Alistair Taylor had a more cynical take on Parlophone's interest in the band. He claimed Epstein, whose thriving record stores were an important retail account for Parlophone's parent label EMI, forced the label's hand by "threaten[ing] to withdraw his business from EMI if they didn't" sign the Beatles. "EMI took them on sufferance because Brian was one of their top customers," Taylor said. "I saw Brian in tears, literally, because Martin promised to phone back, and day after day went by and George Martin was never available, always 'in a meeting.'"

In July 1962, Martin and Parlophone signed the Beatles to a recording contract with an initial one-year term, to be counted from June 6, 1962, with three one-year options that the label could exercise to bind the band until 1966. But Parlophone wasn't contractually obligated to fund more than six Beatles tracks per year, the equivalent of three singles, which was the dominant consumer format at that time. Parlophone also had the right to require the band to "repeat any performance for the purpose of producing . . . a perfect record."

In exchange, Epstein and the Beatles got the label's standard artist royalty of one penny per single sold (half a penny for US single sales), which manager and band split five ways. The Parlophone deal wasn't unusual for a new recording act, though to George Martin—who received a flat fee from EMI, rather than a producer's royalty, from his early studio work with the Beatles—it demonstrated that "EMI was as mean with its artists as with its permanent staff."

The Parlophone contract did increase the Beatles' royalty rate by 25 percent (one-quarter of a penny) for each of the subsequent one-year terms. But the Beatles later became "very critical of [Epstein's] handling of their contract—the one to which I originally signed them," Martin said. "That had not been his fault. He had been in no position to argue" with the label about his largely unknown band "and he knew it."

○ ○ ○ ○ ○ After the Beatles' debut Parlophone single, the Lennon/McCartney original "Love Me Do," made it to the British Top 20 in October 1962, the Beatles began a string of number one hits on the UK charts with

"Please Please Me" in February 1963. But it was the band's wildly success-ful October 13, 1963, appearance on the popular British TV series *Sunday Night at the London Palladium* that cemented the dominance of what the press dubbed "Beatlemania" in the United Kingdom.

The pandemonium at the theater was so great, "The Beatles were pris-oners in the Palladium, unable to go out. Even their parents, who had been given tickets for the show, were unable to come backstage and see them because they could never have got through the crush," stage-door guard George Cooper said.

Screaming, aggressive fans were now commonplace at Beatles events, but Epstein was still largely untested in the entertainment industry, though eager to learn. Walter Hofer, a US attorney for NEMS, recalled of his first meeting with Epstein, during Epstein's pre–Beatles Invasion trip to New York City in November 1963, "From the beginning he was full of questions. How did American TV work? How did the radio stations work?" But, Hofer said, "While he was in town, I gave a cocktail party for him, which was a disaster. No one had ever heard of Brian Epstein."

Despite his limited industry experience, Brian quickly caught on to ne-gotiating commendable concert fees once the Beatles broke through on the US charts and with their wildly popular February 1964 TV appearances on *The Ed Sullivan Show*. NEMS chief executive officer Geoffrey Ellis said Epstein "did everything he could to find out what was the highest fee ever paid at each given venue — very likely that for Elvis Presley — and then sim-ply demanded double. Generally, he got it."

Yet, the accelerated pace of the Beatles' fame coupled with the variety of issues presented by the sheer scale of Beatlemania quickly overwhelmed Epstein. NEMS Enterprises' Tony Bramwell admitted the "trouble was, for a long time Brian didn't know what was best. He might have given the ap-pearance of being coolly in control, but he was floundering all the way to the top."

This was seen during the Beatles' US tour in the summer of 1964, when Epstein failed to take the simple step of making sure the required Internal Revenue Service foreign-withholding tax forms were filled out in advance of the shows. The result was some nerve-wracking, last-minute intrigue. Attorney Tom Levy, who worked for Epstein's US lawyer Walter Hofer in 1964, recalled, "Walter came into my office one afternoon and asked, 'You have anything that you can't get out of this afternoon?' I said, 'Yeh, but . . .' He said, 'I want you to go to Kansas City. We need to get some documents completed for the Beatles so they can get tax clearance. They're leaving the U.S. next week.'"

When Levy arrived at the Muehlebach Hotel, the Beatles and Epstein's Kansas City headquarters for their September 17, 1964, concert, he headed upstairs to the band members' suite, where they signed the IRS forms for Levy to forward to a tax specialist. Such matters were so new to the Beatles that "Lennon couldn't tell the difference between a lawyer and an accountant," Levy said. The Beatles were returning to England on September 21, but their passports were needed to complete the IRS process. "I collected the passports, immediately got on a plane back to New York City and was back in the office by eight the next morning." The four famed Brits thus were temporarily left without the primary required ID to pass through customs for their return home, though the Beatles did made it back to England on schedule.

(But after the 1964 North American tour, the IRS placed a hold on a large portion of the $2.8 million that the Beatles earned from their US concerts. The British government claimed it had the right to levy the tour earnings under a British/US tax treaty. However, with the Beatles' tour income so high, the IRS got a US court to escrow $1 million of that money while the two countries sorted out the income tax issue. "The money has got to be paid to someone in tax," Epstein said, "and Washington and London are trying to decide who'll scoop the lot." But the United States continued to hold these funds prior to the band's 1965 US tour, nearly causing those shows to be scuttled. In January 1965, a Beatles spokesperson acknowledged that Epstein said, due to the tax issue, "no American visits could be considered," though the Beatles did tour the United States that year, too.)

∘ ∘ ∘ ∘ ∘ There was plenty of evidence that Brian Epstein was more intrigued by the creative side than intricacies of the financial side of the projects he negotiated. "I'm not a commercial person really. I'm a frustrated actor," he said. "It may be a fault of mine in the business that I'm not ruthless enough."

In one example, journalist Sean O'Mahony approached him, after the Beatles' "Please Please Me" was a number one UK hit, to discuss founding

The Beatles Monthly Book magazine. Though Epstein went into the nego-tiation with an upper hand, he offered to split magazine's revenues 50/50 with the start-up publisher O'Mahony. When O'Mahony countered with an offer to Epstein and the Beatles of just 33⅓ percent, Epstein snapped it up, despite the fact that the Beatles were the only reason the publication, which soon was selling 350,000 copies per issue, even existed. It was the promotional value of *Beatles Monthly* that meant more to Epstein than seizing on it as a source of income.

In another instance, Brian Epstein negotiated for only a small share of the net revenues from the Beatles' first movie *A Hard Day's Night*. United Artists, the film's studio, had instructed its producer Walter Shenson, "Just make sure there are enough new songs for a soundtrack album and don't go over budget." Shenson went into the negotiations ready to offer Epstein and the Beatles 25 percent of the movie's profits. However, before the film pro-ducer put the offer on the table, the inexperienced Brian insisted on getting 7½ percent as if he wouldn't accept less. Shenson happily accepted what was a bargain for United Artists. (United Artists later increased the Beatles' profit share in *A Hard Day's Night* to 20 percent.)

However, neither the *Beatles Monthly* deal nor the outcome of the United Artists negotiation compared to the catastrophic financial impact of Epstein's licensing of the Beatles' worldwide merchandising rights. In fact, he handled the matter so poorly that the Rolling Stones' early manager/producer Andrew Loog Oldham concluded it "was Brian's most embar-rassing failure as a businessman." The merchandising litigation became the most protracted legal dispute involving Beatles rights to arise during Brian Epstein's time as Beatles' manager. By the time it was over, it would gener-ate three tons of court papers.

2   "Start a Scream Team!"

O n February 9, 1964, hours after the Beatles' landmark first US appearance on *The Ed Sullivan Show*, Nicky Byrne sat sipping champagne at the Oak Bar in the Plaza Hotel, where the Beatles were staying, next to New York City's Central Park. Byrne was president of Seltaeb Inc. ("Beatles" spelled backward), which owned the right to license Beatles merchandise in the United States. Over his drink, he confidently predicted that during the next year US teenagers would buy $50 million worth of Beatles merchandise. But the Seltaeb president coyly claimed it "would be cheeky to predict" how much of the merchandise income would actually go to the Beatles.

Two months prior, on December 4, 1963, Seltaeb's English-based parent company Stramsact had signed an agreement with NEMS Enterprises, the UK company run by Beatles manager Brian Epstein. The agreement gave Stramsact, in which Nicky Byrne was a partner, an initial five-year term for controlling Beatles worldwide merchandise licensing. Stramsact (which NEMS chief executive officer Geoffrey Ellis said was an anagram for "Smart Acts") soon licensed over one hundred different Beatles products and, on January 30, 1964, granted exclusive North American rights to its US subsidiary Seltaeb. But within a year, NEMS would sue Seltaeb and Stramsact for failing to pay NEMS its share of Beatles merchandise revenues. Seltaeb and Nicky Byrne would in turn accuse NEMS of issuing overlapping merchandise licenses that conflicted with the exclusive rights NEMS promised Stramsact.

For now, though, with Beatlemania skyrocketing its way into American culture, US companies clamored to sell anything Beatles-related to the British band's rabid fans. There were Beatles facemasks, Beatles "Flip Your Wig" board games, and Beatles "Krunch Coated" ice-cream bars. Seltaeb-licensee Lowell Toy Company had back orders for 500,000 Beatles wigs, at a retail price of $3 each. The company that licensed the right to sell Beatles spinners on sticks even named itself Beatle Twigs Inc.

In one three-hour period, exclusive US apparel licensee Reliance Manufacturing, which paid Seltaeb a $100,000 advance, received orders for 60,000 Beatles sweatshirts. It took Reliance only three days to sell one million Beatles T-shirts. Reliance also launched a Beatles-influenced "Youthquake" Mod apparel line through its sublicensee Puritan Fashions. The promotion offered consumers a bonus recording of the specially composed song "Youthquake" by the Skunks on Mercury Records. And Reliance affiliate Fashion Sportswear opened a "Beatles" showroom in midtown Manhattan.

According to Reliance president Miles Rubin, by mid-February 1964 his company's wholesale revenues from Beatles merchandise, including hats, pajamas, pants, and tennis shirts, reached $1.4 million. "We had almost a tongue-in-cheek attitude when we first got into this," Rubin said, "but it turned out to be the biggest promotion in our 60 years in business."

○ ○ ○ ○ ○ On February 6, 1964, the day before the Beatles' historic US arrival at Kennedy International Airport in New York, Remco Industries obtained an exclusive merchandise license from Seltaeb to manufacture and distribute Beatles dolls in the United States and Canada. Remco, based in Harrison, New Jersey, was an internationally successful merchandise operation with annual sales of $21 million. The company described itself as "widely recognized among department and variety store chains, retail buying offices, toy and doll jobbers, wholesalers and individual retail stores, as well as competitors, suppliers and consumers as one of the leaders in its field."

Remco president Saul Robbins said the merchandise license his company got from Seltaeb gave the toy manufacturer the right to make Beatles "dolls and parts of dolls and particularly the heads of dolls . . . be shaped as likenesses, caricatures and other resemblances of The Beatles." The company hired puppeteer Paul Ashley, who had worked on the *Captain Kangaroo* TV series, to help design its Beatles items, which were rush-released to stores by the end of February. The dolls that Ashley and Remco developed were four-and-one-half-inch-high, mop-topped vinyl depictions of John, Paul, George, and Ringo, each featuring that Beatle's signature. The black/magenta/turquoise boxes the dolls were packaged in implored buyers to: "Start a scream team with your own GEORGE, JOHN, RINGO and

PAUL! Keep the Liverpool Lovables close at hand. In your room for private swooning. By the record player or radio. In your car. YEAH! YEAH! YEAH!"

Marketing materials Remco sent its retailers invited the vendors to "Ride the Landslide!" The flyers proclaimed Beatles dolls were, "Just the jolt the toy business needs to turn the fastest profit you've ever known! Get in on the hysteria that's gripping the young market like nothing you've ever seen!"

Remco spent a total of more than $350,000 for the licensing rights from Seltaeb and for manufacturing and promoting its Beatles dolls, which quickly generated more than half a million dollars in revenues. Pending orders were worth millions of dollars more. Saul Robbins noted his company's Beatles collectibles were so popular that the "rate and enthusiasm of orders which Remco has been receiving" resulted in its manufacturing capabilities being "geared to the maximum."

The seasoned toy executive believed, however, that Beatles dolls were a fad. "The promotional nature of the property here involved has a life span which may be extraordinarily short and compact," he said. "Remco's opportunity to realize upon its great investment and risk will have to be in the immediate present."

○ ○ ○ ○ ○ In the midst of the escalating number of licensed goods, however, a flood of unauthorized Beatles merchandise was invading US stores, too. To warn away doll bootleggers, Remco Industries, for example, bought advertisements in the *Wall Street Journal,* and in the trade magazines *Toys and Novelties* and *Toy and Hobby World.* The ads warned, "Remco is the only manufacturer with these rights and will protect them vigorously!"

Brian Epstein's NEMS Enterprises had already sued bootleg merchandisers based in Blackpool and Manchester, England. On February 16, 1964, attorney Paul Marshall, whose New York firm represented EMI Records, to which the Beatles were signed, told the *New York Times* that he was looking into as many as sixty US "Beatlegging" cases, from California to Rhode Island. In one case, Seltaeb obtained an injunction against a clothing manufacturer that made items bearing the name "Beetles." Even Gimbel's, a major New York City department store, sold unofficial "bug wigs."

Goldberger Doll Manufacturing, in Brooklyn, New York, was one among those working on producing "knockoff" Beatles goods. Remco president Saul Robbins claimed Goldberger's doll prototype was so similar to Remco's official ones "that Remco's own customers cannot tell the difference." Robbins worried once "the Goldberger 'YEAH, YEAH' or BEATLE doll hits the market, the entire Remco BEATLE program may be dealt a fatal blow."

Remco and NEMS sued Goldberger Doll on April 24, 1964, in the US District Court for the Eastern District of New York in Brooklyn. The lawsuit alleged copyright infringement for copying "substantial material" from Remco's Beatles dolls, and unfair competition for making lower-priced, "substantially inferior" goods that were likely to cause confusion as to who really manufactured them.

But Goldberger Doll contended it wasn't manufacturing counterfeit Beatles goods. Goldberger vice president Lawrence Doppelt claimed that Goldberger was instead producing a "banjo doll," a reference to the guitar the doll held in its hand. Still, Doppelt had given Remco George Harrison and John Lennon dolls to Goldberger's product designer, with instructions "to make a doll that was similar," but featuring "something original, something different."

Remco's suit against Goldberger Doll was assigned to Brooklyn federal district judge George Rosling, a sixty-three-year-old grandfather who personified the generation gap between adults and the fan frenzy the Beatles fueled. Judge Rosling convened a hearing at the Brooklyn federal courthouse on May 6, 1964, to consider Remco's motion for a preliminary injunction to stop Goldberger's production.

"I didn't think when I got this job I'd be playing with dolls," Rosling quipped in the proceeding. To him, this case was about "capitaliz[ing] on the fact that quartets from abroad with conservative clothing and peculiar hairdos were making the little girls squeal, possibly when signs were lifted up, out of sight of the viewer of television, 'Scream now.'"

The judge and his wife had watched the Sunday, May 3, edition of *The Ed Sullivan Show*, when Gerry & the Pacemakers, another British Invasion group that Beatles manager Brian Epstein managed, appeared on the program. "I said, 'Did they get a haircut?'" Rosling noted of the Pacemakers' shorter coifs. "There were four 'Liverpudlians.' I don't know whether they were licensed by the Beatles. I doubt it. They had the same mandolins or banjos [referring to the Pacemakers' guitars], the same accompaniment of squeals. They didn't stand alongside of each other [as the Beatles did].

They stood in sort of a quadrangular effect . . . and the hair didn't come down as far, and the hair was blonde."

"Well, they didn't shake their hips as much as the Beatles do," Mrs. Rosling had commented.

"No, they don't follow Elvis Presley to that extent," Judge Rosling agreed.

Expressing skepticism, at the court hearing, about the copyrightability of Beatles-doll elements, Rosling stressed to Remco's attorney Alan Latman, a well-known copyright-law specialist, that the Goldberger defendants had "selected the one thing that seems to be the hallmark" of American mania for British Invasion musicians, "this ancient, disheveled hairdo that represents what people wore generally before there were barbers and scissors. . . . [It] is not original with the Beatles at all."

But Latman claimed Goldberger "took much more." He argued that the face on Goldberger's doll was a composite of Remco's Harrison and Lennon items. Rosling opined, however, "There is the look in that face [on the Goldberger doll], the lips are turned upward and so on, of what we in this country hope is the fact that we are smart, we are smarter than the rest of the world. And the expression in the Beatles is of — well, it's closer to [ventriloquist Edgar Bergen's slow-thinking dummy] Mortimer Snerd, as I recall him, then it is to Einstein."

But Judge Rosling's disdain for Beatlemania aside, on May 14, 1964, he granted Remco's request for the preliminary injunction. To prevent "great and irreparable injury" to Remco's business and help protect its investment, Rosling barred Goldberger from manufacturing or selling "a doll approximately five inches tall, representing a male figure wearing a dark suit and exhibiting a 'mop' haircut associated with the musical group known as the Beatles."

Goldberger filed an appeal to Rosling's ruling, but on July 3 its defense counsel David Kirschstein announced, "Settlement papers have been drawn up and are in the process of being signed." In the settlement deal, Goldberger agreed to pay an undisclosed sum to Remco Industries and NEMS Enterprises. In addition, Goldberger stipulated it would destroy or hand over to Remco any of its banjo doll materials, and permanently stop manufacturing the disputed item.

The Goldberger matter would soon be eclipsed, however, by the nasty dispute that was developing between the Beatles' management company and its official worldwide Beatles merchandise licensor.

3 "Outrageous Irrelevancies & Distortions"

The Beatles' record releases may have topped the British charts beginning with "Please Please Me" in February 1963, but according to Tony Bramwell, an executive at NEMS Enterprises, which managed the Beatles, it was after the band's smash October 1963 appearance on the popular British TV series *Sunday Night at the London Palladium* that NEMS received a flood of requests to issue licenses for rights to sell Beatles merchandise. "[W]e were besieged by requests from manufacturers who wanted to sell everything . . . even some dreadful black nylon wigs that would scare horses," Bramwell said.

But with no experience in what was still — other than for Elvis Presley — a largely untapped music-business revenue stream, Brian Epstein needed immediate legal advice. He wrote London attorney David Jacobs on October 14, seeking representation "generally on all matters" regarding the Beatles and other artists signed to NEMS. (The other acts included Cilla Black, Gerry & the Pacemakers, and Billy J. Kramer with the Dakotas.) Jacobs, a flamboyant London solicitor who wore garish makeup, counted Marlene Dietrich, Judy Garland, and Liberace among his many famous clients. Like Epstein, he was part of the London entertainment scene's gay community.

The only specific type of advice Epstein sought in his letter to Jacobs was for merchandise deals. Or as Rolling Stones' manager Andrew Loog Oldham put it, "Overwhelmed by licensing requests he could not evaluate, Brian kicked the ball over to" Jacobs. But Jacobs, like Epstein, knew little about music merchandising. This was made clear by the modest £2,000 Jacobs's office negotiated on behalf of NEMS that allowed Mobil Oil to hand out Beatles photos at Mobil's service stations across Australia. And there were the small royalty percentages of only 5 to 10 percent that Jacobs obtained for NEMS in the two- and three-year licenses he negotiated with companies that wanted to manufacture and distribute merchandise depicting the Beatles. These deals included, for example, the sweaters advertised in the program book for the Beatles' November–December 1963 UK tour as "designed specially for Beatles people by a leading British manufacturer with a top quality two-tone Beatle badge." Ten percent wasn't an unusually rare royalty for a merchandise licensor to receive from its licensees' sales, but with Beatlemania in full swing in the United Kingdom, Jacobs had the clout to negotiate a much higher percentage of the wholesale price that NEMS' Beatles merchandise licensees charged their retail outlets.

David Jacobs's law office became the administrative headquarters for the Beatles' burgeoning merchandise business, which by now was a host of products such as Beatles wallpaper, ottomans, metal trays, chewing gum, bedspreads, toy guitars, and "Ringo Rolls" sold at a Liverpool bakery. John Lennon "used to pop in from time to time and take a few prototypes home with him for [his son] Julian or even for his own attic playrooms," Tony Bramwell recalled, "but he was the only [Beatle] who took any interest in the mass of stuff." However, the time needed to monitor the licenses that NEMS issued quickly outstripped Jacobs and NEMS' capabilities. So Brian Epstein asked Jacobs to enlist an outsider for that purpose. Tony Bramwell recalled, "David came up with Nicky Byrne, a young man in the Chelsea set, on the basis that he gave fabulous parties and his [ex-]wife ran a fashionable boutique, so he knew a little about sales."

Upon hearing from Jacobs, the twenty-something Byrne and five of his young friends formed the merchandise-rights company Stramsact. Byrne's primary business experience came from operating the Condor music club in London's Soho section, but like Epstein and Jacobs, he had no real knowledge of entertainment merchandise or what Stramsact's share from merchandising revenues should be. For the December 4, 1963, contract Stramsact entered into with NEMS, Byrne's lawyer advised him, "Write in what percentage you think you should take on the deal." "So I put down the first figure that came into my head," Byrne said, which was a 90 percent lion's share of the licensing fees and royalties to be sent in by the Beatles merchandise licensees that Stramsact signed. "To my amazement, David Jacobs didn't even question it," Byrne recalled.

By comparison, the deal that Elvis Presley's manager, Colonel Tom Parker, negotiated in 1956 for the worldwide rights to Elvis merchandise split the third-party licensing income equally between Parker/Presley and the Hank Saperstein merchandising company. But NEMS did reserve the right to reasonably object to any merchandise items "calculated or likely to lower the reputation of The Beatles in the mind of the public." This was a primary concern for Brian Epstein, who, Tony Bramwell recalled, "was concerned that poor-quality items, dolls that split and trays that rusted, would be very bad for his boys' image."

The Beatles themselves were entitled to little income under the Stramsact contract. This can be seen from the royalty statement in which Stramsact's US affiliate Seltaeb calculated what it owed NEMS from February 1 to June 30, 1964. The merchandise royalties that Seltaeb owed NEMS Enterprises from the first, intense months of North American Beatlemania totaled $79,623.66 from North American merchandise licenses, minus NEMS' UK withholding-tax liability of $24,818.79. Of the remaining $54,804.87 NEMS took a management commission from the Beatles of 25 percent of gross. When the $41,103.65 balance was split four ways, each Beatle was owed a mere $10,275.91.

Still, the first royalty check that Nicky Byrne gave Brian Epstein in February 1964, for $9,700, amounted to nearly four times what the Beatles were paid to appear on *The Ed Sullivan Show*. But this paled in comparison to "Nicky Byrne's personal income alone, [which] Brian estimated, could add up to five million dollars," NEMS executive director Peter Brown recalled. "Brian was sick. *They had given it away!* An incomprehensible sum signed away [to Stramsact] for nothing! He wondered what the Beatles would say when they found out." Epstein was so worried, Brown said, that he "couldn't think of it without wanting to vomit."

To make the playing field more level, NEMS and Stramsact revised their 1963 contract. In a June 5, 1964, "Heads of Agreement" Stramsact got greater worldwide licensing rights, but NEMS stepped up to a more realistic, though not generous, share of income from Beatles merchandise sales. Going forward from May 1, 1964, NEMS had a right to 45 percent of gross merchandise revenues, with 55 percent going to Stramsact. However, the amended agreement didn't quell growing tensions between Brian Epstein's and Nicky Byrne's companies. Epstein complained, "Royalty statements from Seltaeb to Stramsact [and thus to NEMS] were always late and always in relatively small sums."

The bad blood between NEMS Enterprises and Stramsact-Seltaeb erupted into lawsuits NEMS filed in both US and UK courts.

⚬ ⚬ ⚬ ⚬ ⚬ Brian Epstein's US counsel Walter Hofer initially represented NEMS in its New York litigation. Epstein met the Manhattan-based Hofer through the Beatles' UK music publisher Dick James. Hofer had a thriving entertainment practice (including in one case representing future Beatles' manager Allen Klein). Hofer's firm quickly became known as "the House the Beatles built" and even provided space for the Beatles Fan Club. It was a training ground for young lawyers who grew into successful music practitioners. "Walter had a considerable practice, but he oversold his clients on what he was able to accomplish," claimed Tom Levy, a law associate for Hofer in 1964 who later served as legal counsel to brothers Jean and Julian Aberbach, partners in Elvis Presley's music-publishing companies.

The case that Walter Hofer filed on behalf of NEMS Enterprises, in New York County Court, alleged Seltaeb, Nicky Byrne, and Byrne's business partners breached their obligations to NEMS. NEMS claimed that Seltaeb had "willfully and deliberately failed and refused" to make royalty payments since September 1964. The December 11, 1964, civil suit filing further asserted the defendants had done so by illegally conspiring among themselves to keep the monies owed NEMS. In addition to $500,000 in damages, NEMS wanted its contractual relationship with Seltaeb declared void and Seltaeb to be placed in the hands of a financial receiver.

But Louis Smigel, an attorney from Hofer's office, claimed the answers Seltaeb filed with the court in response to NEMS' suit were "so replete with blatant lies and outrageous irrelevancies and distortions as to make a proper reply virtually impossible."

Nicky Byrne blasted back. He claimed NEMS was attempting "to grab everything for itself," that the goal of NEMS' lawsuit was "by one fell swoop, it would finally destroy Seltaeb." Byrne and Seltaeb launched counterclaims for fraud and breach of contract, and sought $5.165 million in damages, plus interest. Seltaeb contended NEMS was withholding the approvals Seltaeb needed for new licensing deals, while at the same time granting merchandise licenses independent of Seltaeb and Stramsact. Some of the licenses that NEMS issued allegedly overlapped with each other, while others allegedly conflicted with merchandise licenses that Seltaeb and Stramsact already granted, such as for Beatles jewelry — at least twelve separate license grants — scarves, aprons, brushes, bath soap, talcum powder, perfume, badges, eyeglasses, and puzzles.

But Brian Epstein swore that by June 1964 NEMS stopped issuing its own merchandise licenses. According to Walter Hofer's office, NEMS now forwarded any licensing inquiries to Seltaeb. One, for example, was from a chemical laboratory in Los Angeles that wanted to know the royalty rates for US rights "to franchise both a candy bar and an ice cream bar with a 'Beatle' label or wrapper. These wrappers to be redeemed for color pictures of the group of any individual boy.'"

Still, Nicky Byrne warned about the damaging fallout from the NEMS/ Seltaeb litigation. "Large retailers and manufacturers confronted with even one conflict do not wish to do any further business with Seltaeb," he said. NEMS chief executive officer Geoffrey Ellis confirmed "that manufacturers who had been considering applying for licenses for their own proposed Beatles products took flight and decided not to go ahead, for fear of becoming involved in the legal tangle. The Beatles thus lost a considerable amount of potential income." Both J. C. Penney and Woolworth backed out of deals with Seltaeb worth a total of $78 million for each company to set up Beatles counters at hundreds of their store locations.

○ ○ ○ ○ ○ It was an "intense animosity" between Brian Epstein and Nicky Byrne that fueled much of the NEMS/Seltaeb fight. Byrne went so far as to buy compromising photos from a press paparazzo of Epstein partying in his hotel room with a group of male hustlers that Byrne could now use against him if necessary. As for harsh words being slung around by Byrne about him, Epstein protested, "A great many heated and intemperate statements have been made in this litigation by defendant Byrne about me, many bordering on libel."

NEMS' allegations against Byrne were highly personal too, including that he was siphoning off merchandise revenues for himself that should otherwise go to NEMS. "This made Brian Epstein furious," Geoffrey Ellis said, "and eventually he demanded that something be done to control the licensing and curb the excesses." Epstein wasn't the only one who thought Byrne was living too high a lifestyle. Byrne's business associates complained to NEMS that Byrne "promptly usurped all corporate profits to himself," including by "running up of huge bills at hotels and restaurants"; renting chauffeured limousines "for weeks on end"; employing "female companions and other social acquaintances at exorbitant salaries"; and accruing nearly $2,000 a week in hotel bills for Byrne's "girlfriends kept at the Drake Hotel."

Epstein additionally claimed that Byrne's management of Seltaeb was "horrendous," citing how Byrne "arbitrarily refused" to finalize licensing deals "unless large advances, which Byrne needed for his personal extravagances were made, instead of long-term pay outs more advantageous to Seltaeb." Epstein charged Byrne used some of these monies for a "private venture" to "purchase the contracts of various artists and singers." The real reason behind Byrne's counterclaims against NEMS, Epstein believed, was that "he does not have the money with which to pay the royalties which are due" NEMS and "is probably of the opinion he has nothing to lose."

∘ ∘ ∘ ∘ ∘ On December 4, 1964, two of Nicky Byrne's Seltaeb partners sued him in New York state court. They were Lord Peregrine Eliot, the tenth Earl of St. Germans whose self-professed pastime was "mucking about," and Malcom G. Evans (not to be confused with Beatles confidant Mal Evans) from the management staff of UK-based Rediffusion TV. Eliot and Evans were alarmed, too, at Byrne's handling of Seltaeb. Seltaeb's May 1964 balance sheet had listed $98,847 in liabilities but only $108,844 in total assets. Thus, at the height of Beatlemania, the US licensor for Beatles merchandise possessed a positive financial balance of just $9,997.

Eliot and Evans charged that, in a recent five-month period, Byrne siphoned off $100,000 of Seltaeb's Beatles merchandise earnings, sometimes by submitting "petty cash vouchers at will for fictitious people." Eliot and Evans revealed Byrne had written so many overdraft checks that Seltaeb's bank had asked the company to move its accounts elsewhere. All this, the partners' lawsuit warned, placed "the continued existence" of Seltaeb "in jeopardy."

None of this convinced the New York court to oust Byrne. Instead, in February 1965 Byrne won a ruling that allowed him to continue to operate the shaky merchandise firm.

But there was the parallel case that Brian Epstein's company filed against Stramsact in the High Court of Justice in London. On December 31, 1964, the English court ordered Stramsact to account to NEMS within four weeks for any outstanding merchandise monies. The royalty statement that Stramsact submitted to NEMS, however, covering February through December 1964, equaled only a relatively pitiful $159,401 in US dollars.

○ ○ ○ ○ ○ Back in New York, NEMS' action against Seltaeb became bogged down by Brian Epstein's refusal to be deposed by Seltaeb. (One party in a lawsuit may depose an opposing party under oath as part of the evidence "discovery" process that occurs after a lawsuit is filed.) Epstein, who occasionally had bouts of glandular fever, attributed his obstinacy in part to health concerns that made him unable to travel from England to New York. But Nicky Byrne claimed, "Epstein has been, and continues to come, to New York City very frequently. He is in good health. There is nothing brought forward which would indicate it would be a hardship for him to come here for examination before trial in this lawsuit."

However, Brian Epstein had an additional, more relevant, reason for not wanting to sit for a deposition in the litigation: his purported ignorance of the details of NEMS' relationship with Seltaeb, which he had delegated to NEMS lawyer David Jacobs. Epstein admitted he was "probably not as qualified to answer all the questions which may be put to me." This was the opposite of what he claimed in the April 1964 copyright infringement suit that NEMS and its Beatles merchandise licensee Remco Industries had filed against Goldberger Doll. In an affidavit in that case, Epstein stated, "I am familiar with all the facts and pertinent documents relating to all licenses, grants, authorities, and commitments made and authorized by NEMS."

The New York state judge in the NEMS/Seltaeb litigation wasn't pleased with Epstein. After the Beatles' manager failed to submit to a deposition by January 14, 1965, and then by an April 8, 1965 extension, Justice George Carney threw out NEMS' complaint in May by declaring this "cannot be tolerated."

○ ○ ○ ○ ○ Justice Carney, however, did let Nicky Byrne and Seltaeb proceed with their counterclaims against NEMS. But NEMS received some needed good news in October 1965 when the New York Appellate Division decided it would be unfair to force NEMS to drop its case. The appellate court instead let Epstein's company refile its claims against Seltaeb.

The amended complaint that NEMS filed raised new allegations involving the unauthorized release of Beatles recordings. Ed Rudy was a nationally broadcast radio journalist for Radio Pulsebeat News who had traveled with the Beatles throughout their first US trip in February 1964. In spring 1964, the Rudy-affiliated Freedom Now Ltd. marketed an album of his Beatles interviews titled *The American Tour with Ed Rudy*. The renegade record label hadn't obtained the Beatles' consent for the album release but claimed it had a license from Seltaeb.

Walter Hofer sent Freedom Now a cease-and-desist letter, but after settlement talks proved fruitless, the Beatles filed suit in New York state court to enjoin further distribution of the Rudy album. The Beatles won the injunction on July 20, 1964, though Hofer complained that "six months later we discovered that the Rudy record was still being sold."

In the NEMS/Seltaeb litigation, NEMS now charged Seltaeb with failing to tell Beatles management about the Freedom Now arrangements. Walter Hofer claimed Seltaeb had "issued a license to Rudy in an area not even remotely connected with an *authorized* licensing power" from NEMS and "proposes *to go into competition with the Beatles* and their phonograph record companies."

o o o o o But by now the demands of the NEMS/Seltaeb case had Walter Hofer floundering. "For all his business and negotiating skills," Geoffrey Ellis noted, "Walter Hofer was not experienced in litigation and his reports to me of the progress of the proceedings in the New York courts were not particularly encouraging."

Most tellingly, on November 1, 1965, the New York state court granted a default judgment against NEMS that made Brian Epstein's company liable for Seltaeb's $5 million in counterclaims. The court again cited Epstein's failure to sit for a deposition. His US business and social partner, attorney Nat Weiss, heard about the ruling by chance when he was at the state courthouse on a different legal matter. Weiss phoned Epstein in England to deliver the news. "It's *terrible*. It's a *nightmare!*" Weiss warned.

Weiss was able to convince Epstein to immediately travel to New York. Brian took along David Jacobs and Geoffrey Ellis to strategize on how to save NEMS' case. Weiss recommended they bring famed trial lawyer Louis Nizer's firm into the litigation. Blaming himself for the Beatles merchandise fiasco, Epstein personally paid Nizer's firm a $50,000 retainer fee.

On November 24, 1965, the firm of Phillips, Nizer, Benjamin, Krim and Ballon formally replaced Walter Hofer as NEMS' counsel in the Seltaeb litigation (though Hofer continued to work on other Beatles legal matters). Louis Nizer assigned the case to Englishman Simon Rose, a lawyer in the Phillips Nizer firm who maintained a British image by wearing a bowler hat when he was in Manhattan. But the still-stubborn Brian Epstein continued to refuse to be deposed; this time he based his excuse on a diagnosis from a London doctor who attested that the Beatles' manager was "suffering from Infective Hepatitis" and had to "be confined to his household" in England "because of the damage to his liver." (Seltaeb claimed that Epstein "had left his home on several occasions" and "was out several nights during that time.")

Epstein finally was deposed in January 1966, in sessions held over several days. During the sessions, antagonism between Simon Rose and Seltaeb's counsel Jerome Katz grew so foul that Epstein's deposition was held before a judicial referee at the Bar Association of the City of New York and at the state courthouse in lower Manhattan, instead of what was typically at the office of a suit party's law firm.

As Epstein had feared, he performed poorly in answering Seltaeb's questions, because, as Geoffrey Ellis noted, "he had to admit that he knew virtually nothing of the numerous contractual arrangements, in Britain or America, which were the basis of the dispute. He also had to admit that his knowledge of the accounts and financial affairs of the merchandising was sketchy, to say the least."

○ ○ ○ ○ ○ Nicky Byrne and Seltaeb had their own worries about the case. They were concerned about the outcome of their claim that NEMS issued conflicting merchandise licenses that affected Seltaeb's rights. Byrne and Seltaeb argued the evidence was clear enough that the point could be decided by the judge without a trial. "There is no honest distinction between a 'Beatle Booster Pin' and a 'Beatle Metal Badge,'" Nicky Byrne insisted to the court. But in May 1966, the state judge decided a trial was needed to dig deeper for a one-on-one comparison of whether the disputed goods were "sufficiently similar" to establish that NEMS breached its merchandising contract with Seltaeb.

With nearly $100 million in damage claims between them and an uncertain trial result for each, NEMS and Seltaeb carved out a settlement. It ended up a relative bargain for NEMS, which agreed to pay Seltaeb less than £100,000 to end their dispute. NEMS and Seltaeb filed the case discontinuance notice in the New York court on June 30, 1967.

After the NEMS/Seltaeb dispute was over, Nicky Byrne moved to the Bahamas, where Seltaeb reincorporated to minimize its US tax liability. Walter Hofer continued to practice entertainment law until 1983, when he died at his desk of a heart attack amidst accusations that he had embezzled money from his clients. David Jacobs, who had negotiated NEMS' merchandising rights grants to Seltaeb's UK parent company Stramsact, was found dead on December 15, 1968, hanging in the garage of his south England home in Sussex. The coroner concluded Jacobs, who recently suffered a nervous breakdown, committed suicide, though the reason remained a mystery.

As for Brian Epstein, after the NEMS/Seltaeb dispute was over, he coughed up $85,000 out of his personal funds to cover the balance of NEMS' legal fees. By then, Epstein was depressed and becoming more isolated from the Beatles, who were setting up a new business of their own, Apple Corps, without him. Geoffrey Ellis had "no doubt at all" that the Seltaeb litigation contributed significantly to Brian's fragile mental state.

The Beatles formed their own merchandise company, Maximus Enterprises, in 1967. But with the band entering a less pop and more inventive phase, the stampede for Beatles merchandise had subsided from its frenzied Beatlemania peak. Paul McCartney lamented about the Beatles' early merchandise deals, "We got screwed for millions."

He didn't hesitate to point a finger in saying so. "It was all Brian's fault. He was green. I always said that about Brian. Green."

4 · The Reign Ends

By 1967, Brian Epstein faced a growing set of personal problems. He had attempted suicide in 1966, following an incident in which he was robbed and blackmailed by an errant boyfriend named Dizz Gillespie during the Beatles' final US tour. In May 1967, Brian entered the Priory Hospital in London to improve his failing health, the result of depression and a long-running battle with insomnia that he had fought with large doses of sedatives. Then in July, his father Harry died suddenly from a heart attack. Despite all this, Brian's "biggest fear was of ever letting the Beatles down in any way whatsoever," said Peter Asher, of the British pop duo Peter & Gordon and brother of Paul McCartney's mid-1960s girlfriend, actress Jane Asher.

The fact was, Brian Epstein had become obsessed with the likelihood that the Beatles would terminate his management contract with them when its initial five-year term ended on September 30, 1967. He had previously sought out business partners for his NEMS Enterprises management company — in February 1966 merging with the Vic Lewis Organization, a major British booking agency, and at the start of 1967 announcing that Cream and Bee Gees manager Robert Stigwood was the new comanaging director of NEMS. But Brian intended to continue to manage the Beatles and singer Cilla Black, with whom Epstein was particularly close, while Stigwood concentrated on bringing in new talent to NEMS.

The Beatles had formalized their internal operations in May 1963 with articles of association for The Beatles Ltd. Now, however, the band members indeed were preparing to take greater control of their business affairs away from Epstein.

"Brian's reign was ending," confirmed Paul McCartney, who took the artistic lead in pushing the Beatles to their 1967 projects, the *Sgt. Pepper's* album and *Magical Mystery Tour* movie. "To begin with, we needed the man in the Ford Zodiac to get us recording contracts and to make sure we wore the right clothes. But by 1967, a lot of things were escaping his grasp."

To Brian's credit, in January 1967 he managed to deliver a major business victory to the Beatles, when he completed renegotiating their recording contract with EMI. The amended agreement was a nine-year deal that greatly increased the band's royalty — to 10 percent of EMI's wholesale price to dealers, with a bump to 15 percent for sales exceeding 100,000 of a single and 30,000 of an album. The rate went up to 17.5 percent for sales in North America, after returned records and taxes were deducted. The new contract required the Beatles to record five albums, for a total of seventy tracks, during the first five years but gave the band the freedom to decide whether to record at all during the last four years of the EMI agreement.

However, Epstein glaringly failed to obtain key benefits that the Rolling Stones' manager Allen Klein got for his band when he recently negotiated their updated deal with Decca Records: a significant advance payment ($1.25 million for the Stones), plus a 25 *percent* artist royalty rate. The Beatles' superstar status would have justified EMI giving them a deal like the one Klein obtained from Decca for the Stones and the advance money would have been especially comforting at a time when the Beatles' finances were sagging, following the missed opportunity to capitalize on Beatles merchandise sales and their decision to stop performing live after 1966.

But the new EMI agreement had an enormous silver lining from Epstein's perspective. Under the renegotiated arrangement, Epstein's NEMS Enterprises would take a 25 percent management commission from the Beatles' record royalties, even if Brian was no longer able to, or simply decided not to, actively manage the Beatles. Still, Tony Bramwell concluded this "gnawed at his conscience because in his heart he knew he had conned them."

○ ○ ○ ○ ○ Epstein's US business partner and close friend Nat Weiss said Brian was willing to decrease his Beatles management commission from 25 percent down to 15 percent. But like Paul McCartney, George Martin believed "it was inevitable" that Epstein "would have shortly lost the Beatles." Martin noted, "Brian, by his own design, had become too fragmented and the Beatles were too selfish to ever have someone like that."

The Beatles also needed a new corporate entity in which to place their income and help lower their sky-high individual tax rates. Though they were beginning to unravel as a music group, in an April 19, 1967, agreement the band formed The Beatles & Co., a partnership with a ten-year term. Each Beatle owned 5 percent of the partnership and Apple Corps, the new name of The Beatles Ltd., owned 80 percent. John, Paul, George, and Ringo in turn each owned 25 percent of Apple Corps, with most group-related income — though not for songwriting — equally shared among the band members. This included solo projects.

Despite this long-range plan, the growing frictions among the Beatles themselves didn't bode well for a secure group future. Keyboardist Billy Preston, who first played a Beatles studio session on January 22, 1969, recalled, "George Harrison wanted me to stop by Apple Records. I came over, and they were recording and filming *Let It Be*. There wasn't much bickering in the studio, because they were concentrating on music. But when we'd break for lunch, they'd start to talk about business. . . . I was surprised to learn they'd gotten ripped off so many times."

The question of whether Brian Epstein would continue to manage the Beatles was answered forever when he died on August 27, 1967, at his home in London. The coroner ruled the cause was an accidental overdose of drugs. "On the bedside table were his bottles of pills. There were about half a dozen of them," said NEMS executive Alistair Taylor. "Brian took a lot of pills. He needed pills to get him up in the morning, pills to get him to sleep, pills to calm him down and pills to get him through the day."

After Epstein's death, Paul McCartney said, "John got particularly frightened. I think he thought, 'Right, this is it. This is the end of the Beatles,' and it kind of was."

PART TWO

FOR THE BENEFIT OF MR. K

5 "Charismatic, Arrogant – American"

For the first year after Brian Epstein passed away, the Beatles managed Apple Corps with their own staff, but the company was poorly run and hemorrhaged huge amounts of money. "Since Brian died, we've sort of been torn apart," Ringo Starr said. "We have to look after ourselves and do everything Brian did. . . . If I wanted to be a businessman, I would never have taken up drums."

Paul McCartney noted, "Brian's death opened the floodgates. It gave other people the possibility to come in," especially after John Lennon told reporters in the fall of 1968 that the Beatles were in dire financial straits. The news caught the eye of Rolling Stones' manager Allen Klein. The bellicose New Yorker had set his sights on the Beatles even when Brian Epstein was alive. But in 1969, John Lennon said, "[W]e *were* in a mess, and only my saying it to the press . . . enabled Klein to hear about it, and come over."

Indeed, it wasn't long until Klein took over management of the Beatles' business empire, with enthusiastic support from Lennon, George Harrison, and Ringo Starr, but over the virulent objections, and then a lawsuit, from Paul McCartney. Allen Klein's entry into the Beatles' lives ended up being the death knell for the most popular music group of all time.

○ ○ ○ ○ ○ John Lennon and Allen Klein had a lot in common. Both had been raised with similar childhood insecurities. By the age of five, John was "abandoned by his father and, effectively, his mother too," John's first wife Cynthia said. John's father, Alf "Fred" Lennon, was a drifter seaman who rarely spent time with his wife, Julia, and his son. After Julia became pregnant by another man while Fred was at sea, Fred offered to bring up the child, but Julia's father pressured her into putting the baby up for adoption. In 1946, Fred asked John whether he'd rather live with Julia or him. John chose Julia and didn't see the elder Lennon from 1946 to 1964, when Fred contacted John after the Beatles became famous.

Independent and unconventional, Julia shuffled her son among family members. She moved in with a boyfriend, Bobby Dykins, and gave birth to their two daughters. John, meanwhile, was brought up by his strict Aunt Mimi Smith (Julia's sister) and easygoing Uncle George at their home, "Mendips," in Liverpool's suburban Woolton neighborhood. John and Julia, however, developed a closer relationship during John's teen years, when she bought him his first guitar. In 1956, he formed a "skiffle" group named the Quarrymen that was the seed for the Beatles. (Skiffle style is a blend of folk, country, and blues played on crude instruments.) Tragically, in July 1958, Julia was hit and killed by a car driven by a drunken off-duty policeman while she walked from Aunt Mimi's house to a nearby bus stop.

Allen Klein was also deeply affected as a child by family instability. The youngest of four children, the "moody and sensitive" Klein was born on December 18, 1931, in Newark, New Jersey. His mother died of cancer when he was nine months old. When he was four years old, his "insecure and ineffectual" father, a Kosher butcher with a modest income, placed him and two of his three older sisters in the local Hebrew Orphanage and Sheltering Home. The young Allen's father rarely visited the facility where corporal punishment was common, but after remarrying when Allen was ten, he brought his son home.

After graduating from high school in 1950, the short, stout Allen Klein spent two years in the US Army, where he underwent shock treatment for anxiety. In 1956, he received a degree in accounting from Upsala College in East Orange, New Jersey. The same year, he met his future wife, Betty. "I went on vacation to celebrate my graduation, I met her, and she lived in New York, and I lived in New Jersey, and I was traveling back and forth," Allen recalled. "So I got a job in New York working for an accounting firm to clerk. I wanted to get married, and it was difficult to get married on $60 a week. So I decided to go into business for myself."

Like Allen, Don Kirshner was a student at Upsala College, though he lived in the Bronx, New York, near Betty. "He was going with a girl in Newark and I was coming to New York to meet my wife," Allen said, "and we kept crossing each other as I was going home and he was coming back." Kirshner — who soon developed into a music impresario through his involvement in the careers of the artists Bobby Darin, Connie Francis, Neil Sedaka, and Neil Diamond, among others — urged Klein to work in the music business.

In 1957, Allen found work at an accounting firm that audited record companies on behalf of music publishers. After marrying Betty in 1958, he formed Allen Klein & Co., an accounting and management firm for entertainers, later changing the name to ABKCO. To strengthen his company's credentials, he hired Henry Newfeld, a certified public accountant (Klein wasn't) and an assistant, Joel Silver, who also had an accounting background.

Klein's first big entry into the music industry came when he injected himself into a successful audit of record royalties owed Bobby Darin, who Klein met through Don Kirshner. Klein personally delivered the $100,000 check from Capitol Records to Darin, who gratefully had Allen renegotiate his Capitol contract into a deal that was so beneficial to Darin that he acquired the lucrative Trinity Music publishing company, which owned rights to Darin's tunes along with other hits of the day.

Klein's auditing ability attracted other big name clients to him, like pop and R & B singer Sam Cooke. Beginning in 1957, Cooke had charted major hits like "You Send Me," "Cupid," and "Chain Gang." But he "was not in very good financial position," Klein recalled. "The first time I met him was at a concert in Philadelphia," in the spring of 1963, when Allen rented the State Theatre to put on concerts with disc jockey Jocko Henderson, who hosted similar shows at the Apollo Theater in New York City's Harlem neighborhood.

Henderson signed Sam Cooke to headline the Philadelphia show. Klein claimed he and Cooke, who became the first major artist Allen managed, hit it off right away. "[We] just seemed to have a — you know, a simpatico between us," recalled Allen, who was eager to expand his music business role beyond royalty bookwork.

Sam Cooke initially retained Klein to conduct an audit of Sam's royalty account with RCA Records. After Klein uncovered $150,000 in unpaid royalties due Cooke from RCA, Cooke made him his personal manager. Klein then renegotiated Cooke's recording contract with RCA into an innovative artist's deal that became Klein's trademark. Under the September 1, 1963, "buy-sell" arrangement for Sam, Klein created Tracey Ltd. (named after Sam's daughter Tracey) into which RCA would pay the royalties it owed the artist. The "buy-sell" feature was that Tracey Ltd. "bought" Cooke's recordings from RCA, then "sold" them back under a license that gave RCA the distribution rights. (RCA manufactured the product at its plants.) "This was completely unheard of — for an African-American to have artistic self-determination and economic self-determination," Klein spokesperson Bob Merlis said about Cooke's buy-sell deal. The arrangement was also a forerunner to the buy-sell agreement Klein negotiated for the Beatles with Capitol Records in 1969.

Klein's commission from Cooke was as follows: Cooke received 4.5 percent (a ballpark royalty for recording artists in the early 1960s), and Klein separately received 1.5 percent, of suggested retail price from RCA. Then, "on his music publishing I got 10 percent." Klein said. "And [I got] nothing on his performance income on the road and the total guarantee [of $450,000 over four years] got from RCA was all Sam Cooke's, so that if no records were sold at all my one and a half percent meant nothing." But the true nature of the rights weren't in Sam's favor, because Klein structured Tracey so that he, not Cooke, was the real owner of the company. Or, as Andrew Loog Oldham, the Rolling Stones' early manager, remarked, "Allen would get you back your kingdom, then pocket the keys." Unfortunately, Sam Cooke's music-making days ended in December 1964, when he was shot to death under mysterious circumstances by a motel manager in Los Angeles.

In 1964, Allen Klein began negotiating recording contracts for other artists. First, for heartthrob singer Bobby Vinton, whom Klein also now managed, he renegotiated a more favorable contract with Epic Records. Allen also negotiated contracts for artists he didn't manage. He procured a buy-sell deal with Epic Records for Dave Clark, whose British Invasion band the Dave Clark Five competed successfully on the charts against the Beatles.

From Dave Clark, Klein received a flat fee of about $90,000 and from Bobby Vinton a percent of the guarantee (though none from Vinton's subsequent 1969 Epic contract). Klein's standard fee for negotiating these contracts was an ongoing right to 20 percent of the artist's record royalties.

In one deal, Allen negotiated a five-year agreement for British hit producer Mickie Most with CBS Records, for whose Epic label Most produced folk-rock singer Donovan, British pixie Lulu, and the blues-rocking Yardbirds as well as one of its former lead guitarists, Jeff Beck, who founded his own band. Klein also negotiated a buy-sell contract with Warner Bros. for the North American rights to recordings by another British Invasion band, the Kinks, and worked with Donovan's manager Ashley Kozak in securing Donovan's contract with Epic.

Allen Klein made a controversial acquisition in 1967 that Paul McCartney later used to challenge Klein's credibility as Beatles manager. In July 1967, Klein purchased the Cameo-Parkway record catalog, which was built out of Philadelphia in association with Dick Clark and the TV series *American Bandstand*. The Cameo-Parkway label included dance hits by Chubby Checker, the Orlons, and Dee Dee Sharp. But for several months in 1968, the US Securities and Exchange Commission banned Cameo-Parkway from over-the-counter trading on the American Stock Exchange owing to the record label's financial losses in recent years. Klein claimed the losses occurred before he acquired the company, not because of "any dishonest or improper conduct on my part."

∘ ∘ ∘ ∘ ∘ In 1965, Allen Klein maneuvered his way into the Rolling Stones' lives. Their manager, Andrew Loog Oldham, had first met Klein the year before, to pursue an ownership interest for the Stones in an R & B song Klein controlled, Bobby Womack's "It's All Over Now," which in 1964 became the band's first UK number one hit. Oldham explained, "Our habits then were that if we had recorded an outside tune I would go around knocking on the doors of the various publishers going, 'Could be a single, but we want a piece.' Klein was sitting there asking [me] all the right questions like: 'Do I want to be a millionaire?' and 'Do the Stones want to be famous?' Yes."

Impressed, Oldham introduced Mick Jagger and Keith Richards to Klein. Richards recalled of his first meeting with Klein, "In walks this little fat American geezer, smoking a pipe, wearing the most diabolical clothes. But we liked him, he made us laugh and at least he was under 50. There was a new deal with Decca and Andrew told us Klein was a fantastic cat for dealing with those people, which we couldn't do."

Oldham and the Stones brought Klein in as a business advisor in 1965. As noted in the preceding chapter, Allen negotiated a highly favorable artists' deal for its time with the Decca label that included a $1.25 million advance and a record royalty of 25 percent of wholesale price. For this, Klein was entitled to 20 percent of the Stones' royalties, "although the Stones didn't pay me any money on record royalties, it came out of Andrew Oldham's" share, Klein said. "They had an arrangement where he got half and they got half. Out of the total 100 percent, my company received 20 percent of the gross, all of which came out of Andrew Oldham's one-half." Oldham made the concession as he said he "got heavily into drugs, and I was in no shape to contribute much to the Stones."

But a dispute arose between Klein and the Stones because Decca had forwarded the record contract advance to a new US company of Klein's, Nanker Phelge Music *Inc.*, rather than the Stones' preexisting Nanker Phelge Music *Ltd.* in England. Klein claimed the advance money was to be released to the Stones once the band's recording income under the Decca deal reached that amount. Oldham accused Klein of using the US Phelge Music company as "a vehicle for diversion" of the Stones' assets, but Klein was able to negotiate a settlement with Oldham that was highly advantageous to Klein: He agreed to pay Oldham $1 million to buy out Oldham's management contract with the Rolling Stones in 1967. Oldham reportedly did this without discussing it with the Stones. The Stones, however, had been pleased by Klein when he showed up in an English court in June 1967 to offer moral support to Mick Jagger and Keith Richards, who were being tried on drug charges.

Allen Klein was now the Rolling Stones' new manager. But Mick Jagger's girlfriend Marianne Faithful (who Oldham had also managed) said that over time, "Mick really hated him. I had never known Mick to hate anyone like that. It all began when Mick suspected that Allen wasn't giving him a fair shake on the accounting" for the Rolling Stones' record sales.

The Stones fired Klein in 1970 and sued him the following year for misrepresentation. But they were so determined to move on to new ventures without him that they agreed to a settlement giving Klein the lucrative ownership rights to the Stones' early recordings and music publishing. In a 1984 suit to try to get the rights back, an exasperated Mick Jagger testified in New York federal court, "What did he want from us? Apart from the moon, I don't know." But the result of that Stones suit was that Klein's ABKCO retained the rights to the band's recordings and music publishing through the 1971 *Sticky Fingers* album.

○ ○ ○ ○ ○ The Rolling Stones weren't the first artists who Allen Klein clashed with in court. In a forerunner to the Stones' — and later the Beatles'

— bitter litigations with Klein, as early as 1965 British Invasion teeny-boppers Herman's Hermits sued Klein and one of his companies, in this case for copyright infringement. The clean-cut, five-member group from Manchester, England, featuring former child actor Peter Noone on lead vocals, had inherited a sizeable chunk of the Beatles' preteen and teen fan base as the Beatles' music, with angst-ridden songs like John Lennon's "I'm a Loser" and "Help!," outgrew a strictly pop focus. Herman's Hermits scored its first US hit in 1964 with "I'm Into Something Good." The record was produced by Mickie Most, with whom the Hermits signed a long-term agreement. A series of Top 40 hits followed, including the number one hits "Mrs. Brown You've Got a Lovely Daughter" and "I'm Henry the VIII, I Am" in 1965.

To increase their income, Herman's Hermits formed Hermusic Ltd. to publish the band members' original songs and to acquire compositions from other writers. Five of these tunes, including "I Know Why" and "Don't Try to Hurt Me," were produced by Mickie Most for Herman's Hermits — via a deal Most had with Klein's Reverse Producers Corp. — as single B-sides and album cuts. As an enticement to use Hermusic's compositions, Herman's Hermits were willing to give Allen Klein a discounted first-use license of 1.5 cents per song. (Under copyright law, songwriters and publishers controlled the right to consent to and negotiate a song-licensing fee for first publication of their works. Once published, anyone could get a "compulsory license" for a "mechanical" use of that song on a sound recording in exchange for paying a statutory licensing fee, which in the 1960s was 2 cents for each track sold.)

In September 1965, however, Hermusic sued Most, Klein, Klein's Reverse Producers Corp., and Pete Bennett, the promotion director at Klein's main music company ABKCO Industries. Though Reverse claimed it had reached an oral agreement with the band's company to use the compositions, it never obtained written licenses from Hermusic, which alleged copyright infringement. Plus, the Hermits now wanted a 2-cent song royalty per track.

Attorney Marty Machat, who later became Phil Spector's lawyer and business adviser, represented Allen Klein in the litigation. Hermusic sought a minimum of $100,000 in unpaid royalties as well as an award of the defendants' profits for use of the Hermusic songs. But Klein claimed the fact that Herman's Hermits had performed on the disputed tracks gave Reverse an implied license to sell the song recordings.

In April 1966, the US District Court for the Southern District of New York granted a pretrial judgment in favor of Peter Noone and the Hermits. But Reverse failed to comply with a court order for it to submit detailed manufacturing, distribution, and income statements by July 15, 1966. Hermusic attorney Robert C. Osterberg charged that Reverse was using "every dilatory device and resort[ed] to every conceivable untenable contention to impede and obstruct" his clients.

A court-appointed master agreed that Reverse's intransigence "completely stopped all forward progress in this matter." The federal court found Klein's company in contempt, though the case dragged on until March 1972, after Herman's Hermits' hit-making years were over. The parties settled the litigation, with neither side recouping its court costs from the other.

But the Hermits/Klein grudge match didn't end there. As late as 2008, the surviving band members accused ABKCO of underpaying them recording artist royalties going back to 1966. The group's Chimeron LLC sued ABKCO — which had acquired Mickie Most's production contract with the Hermits — in Los Angeles Superior Court but agreed to drop the case after Klein's company said it would let Chimeron conduct a royalty audit. Herman's Hermits accountants Prager & Fenton calculated the band was owed $539,272 in accrued record royalties. According to Herman's Hermits' lawyer Barry Slotnick, however, "The minute the audit report was submitted to ABKCO, the company filed suit in New York for a declaration that it didn't owe Herman's Hermits any money."

In the surprise action filed in New York federal court in April 2010, the year after Allen Klein died, ABKCO — by then honchoed by Allen's son, Jody — claimed it accounted to the Hermits for royalties through 1973. But with no US hits since the 1960s, the band's recording income was "drastically diminished." Barry Slotnick said that when Hermits lead singer Peter Noone had occasionally asked Allen Klein about royalties, Allen would refer to a $465,000 guarantee MGM had obligated itself to pay Herman's Hermits in telling Noone, "You're unrecouped!"

Chimeron filed a breach-of-contract counterclaim against ABKCO in New York. But ABKCO cited New York's six-year statute of limitations for such claims in asking the federal court to limit Chimeron's recovery. Barry Slotnick noted, however, that "the truly bizarre" underlying agreement that Herman's Hermits signed with Mickie Most in the 1960s failed to include a customary accounting provision that said the producer would account to and pay the artist every six months. This helped Herman's Hermits, Slotnick said, because "ABKCO was never in breach until after we formally asked for an audit, which allowed us to go back almost to the inception of the contract in seeking royalties."

A trial began in the ABKCO/Chimeron case in January 2012. In the courtroom, the still-boyish Peter Noone described Allen Klein as a "nice guy, charismatic, arrogant — American," which made the jury laugh. But Noone admitted he often publicly described Klein as a "scumbag." The jury awarded Chimeron $150,000, to which Judge William H. Pauley III added 9 percent in interest, for a total of $475,701. ABKCO appealed to the US Court of Appeals for the Second Circuit, but in February 2013 the Second Circuit affirmed the jury's findings.

"We didn't even get a song out of you," Judge Pauley had said as Peter Noone finished his trial testimony. "It might have to be on the next run," Noone joked back.

6 "Don't You Want It Now?"

n May 1968, John Lennon and Paul McCartney sat for a joint interview with *Newsweek* magazine, as part of their campaign to publicly launch the Beatles' utopian, artist-oriented Apple Corps Ltd. During the interview in a New York hotel suite, McCartney "sipped beer, flicked ashes on the rug" and told *Newsweek*, "We're in the happy position of not needing any money." "The aim of this company isn't a stack of gold teeth in the bank," Lennon concurred about Apple Corps' goal of providing artists with opportunities outside the conventional music business structure. To symbolize its independent approach, Apple convened an initial US board meeting in a boat that circled the Statue of Liberty in New York Harbor.

But Lennon admitted he lacked practical business sense. When his accountants told him how much he was worth, "I wrote it down on a bit of paper. But I've lost the bit of paper." Lennon just didn't pay close attention to income details. "I don't go around reading record royalty statements," he said. "Somehow, I am given the money, and hopefully it ends up in my bank account."

Paul McCartney said the Beatles' original goal for Apple was to be an "umbrella where people can do things in the way they want." Paul added, "When we get Apple going big, we'll do that with our feet up. You can have business meetings which are an uplift not a bringdown."

Apple Corps' hopes for a thriving artists' haven soon turned into economic chaos. In 1967, the fledgling enterprise opened business offices upstairs from its short-lived Apple Boutique clothing store on 75 Baker Street in central London. By June 1968, Apple purchased its most famous location, the five-story townhouse at 3 Savile Row in London's upscale Mayfair section. This is where the Beatles last public performance, the band's January 1969 lunchtime rooftop show, took place.

There were few financial controls at Apple Corps, however. Booze, drugs, and fancy food flowed freely, and hippies and Hells Angels camped out in its offices. Apple Corps lost money on most of the artists it signed, and visitors and employees walked away at will with office equipment, furniture, and artwork. Apple executive Peter Brown claimed, "The largesse of the Beatles, combined with the willingness of those who benefited from it, bordered on organized crime."

Apple Corps held weekly business meetings, but Pete Shotton, Apple Boutique's manager and John Lennon's best childhood friend, said, "These get-togethers were rarely anything more or less than a surrealistic farce. John would arrive high on LSD, Paul would immerse himself in his inveterate doodling, and Ringo would literally fall asleep in the corner. Only George made much of a show of listening attentively to the dreary recitation of statistics."

"Apple was a complete fiasco, and it cost them millions," Beatles record producer George Martin said. "From the start, and this is not speaking with hindsight, I took a jaundiced view of the whole proceedings, because I could see the awful way it was going, and that it was doomed from the outset."

John Lennon attributed the failing Apple to Brian Epstein's death. "Brian's death left us on our own," John said. "He handled the business and we find it hard to." The Beatles desperately sought new business advice. At first, they retained attorneys Lee Eastman and John Eastman, the father and brother of Paul McCartney's soon-to-be-wife Linda Eastman. Lee Eastman, a first-generation American of Russian Jewish descent, was a prominent New York attorney who represented top names in the visual arts and music-publishing worlds. Capitol Records lawyer Charles Tillinghast described him as "hardheaded, sophisticated, and energetic." According to Paul McCartney, Lee was "very patriarchal. Linda would try and avoid him on the street if she was with one of her long-haired friends because he wouldn't approve."

Lee Eastman groomed his son John, who sported a John Kennedy–like appearance, for a career in entertainment law. "I think [Lee] wanted a kind of Kennedy dynasty thing," Paul said. "I remember when I first met John Eastman, I asked him, 'What do you want to do? What's your ambition in life?' He said, 'To be the president of the United States of America,' . . . [The Eastmans] were very preppy. Very aspirational." (Lee Eastman died in 1991. Today, John's son Lee Eastman II is a lawyer at Eastman & Eastman and works closely on McCartney legal matters, including overseeing Paul's MPL music companies.)

But Paul admitted about the other Beatles' view of the senior Lee, "Obviously everyone worried that because it was my father-in-law, I'd be the one he'd look after. Quite naturally, they said, 'No, we can't have him.' So in the end it turned out to be Klein."

∘ ∘ ∘ ∘ ∘ With his keen interest in representing lucrative British Invasion artists, Allen Klein had targeted the top act, the Beatles, as management clients even when Brian Epstein was alive. But when EMI managing director Len Wood told Epstein that Klein "seemed to be interested in looking after the Beatles," Epstein didn't seem worried. NEMS staffer Tony Bramwell said Epstein had seen a press story as early as 1966 that reported on "John and Paul meeting secretly with the Stone's voracious manager" Klein, a meeting Bramwell said never happened and "was a Klein publicity leak — probably planted by Andrew Loog Oldham in the growing sense of competitiveness between the Stones and the Beatles."

But Manchester, England, booking agent Danny Betesh said that in the mid-1960s he and Epstein talked about Klein "at some length; he always thought Klein was a big threat to him." Betesh well knew Klein's aggressive nature. He had won a nasty battle against Klein, who was trying to take over management of Peter Noone, the lead singer of Herman's Hermits, from Betesh's Kennedy Street Enterprises.

In 1964, Epstein and Klein had met face-to-face, in London, to discuss the possibility of Sam Cooke opening the Beatles' 1964 US summer tour. During the meeting, Klein offered to help with handling the Beatles' finances. NEMS executive Peter Brown recalled "Klein said that he heard the Beatles' low royalty rates from EMI were 'for shit' and that he could renegotiate their contracts. Brian was royally offended at the suggestion that someone else should do his job for him, and he had Klein shown to the door."

Allen Klein's opportunity with the Beatles didn't come until after Epstein died. "It was like I was clairvoyant. I was driving across a bridge out of New York and I heard on the radio that Epstein had died and I said to myself, 'I got 'em.' Who else was there?"

John Lennon first met Klein in December 1968, at the London sound stage where the Rolling Stones were filming their superstar video production *Rock and Roll Circus*. Afterward, in his campaign to become the Beatles' manager, Klein placed a series of phone calls to Apple trying to reach Lennon. A December 1968 article in *Disc and Music Echo* in which Lennon worried that the Beatles were nearly broke lent an air of urgency to Klein's appeal for Lennon to meet with him to talk Beatles business.

After postponing a couple of times, John and his wife, Yoko Ono, visited Klein on January 27, 1969, for dinner and an evening of discussion at Klein's suite at London's upscale Dorchester Hotel. Earlier that day, the Beatles had worked under makeshift conditions at Apple Corps headquarters on Savile Row recording the song "Get Back." That night at the Dorchester, the well-prepared Klein made a show of his substantial knowledge of John's music and Yoko's conceptual art. "I think he's a sentimental old Jewish mommy," Lennon purred afterward about Klein.

At the Dorchester meeting, Lennon said to Klein, "Look, the Eastmans are the exclusive representative of the Beatles. So we can't talk about that. Would you be willing to represent Yoko and me?" "I was really trying to re-main — not appear very anxious," Klein recalled, "and I said, 'Well, I think we should sleep on it tonight.' And he said, 'What's the matter, don't you want it now?'"

Klein claimed the eager Lennon phoned him a few hours later to seal a management deal with the Beatles. "And I was sleeping. I got up," Klein said. "And that's how it began." Lennon noted later, however, "It was plain to me that Klein came to London expressly to offer his management ser-vices to the Beatles." (Yoko retained Klein as her manager, too, including for her music-publishing company, Ono Music.)

John and Yoko's relationship with Klein grew into a close personal bond. The Lennons bought Klein a Rolls Royce; Klein, who liked to dress down in mock-turtleneck sweaters and sneakers, reciprocated with an expensive watch for John from a high-end London jewelry store. Despite the Beat-les' idealistic promise to give aspiring artists easy access to Apple's finan-cial support, John admitted, "Apple was/is a capitalist concern." In hiring Klein, "We brought in a capitalist to prevent it sinking (with the Beatles on board)."

But Nat Weiss said, "Klein was the primary beneficiary in any deal he ever made." George Harrison's wife, Pattie Boyd, recalled when Mick Jag-ger learned the Beatles were considering Klein as manager, Mick phoned Apple executive Peter Brown warning "the Beatles should not meet with Klein because he could not be trusted." Brown put together a meeting for

Jagger to tell this to the Beatles. But, Pattie said, "John, in his perverse way, invited Klein to be there too. Mick left."

John Lennon now quickly convinced George Harrison and Ringo Starr that Allen Klein should oversee the Beatles' business affairs. According to George, "[T]here was no alternative, really. There was nobody managing Apple. It was wasting away all this money, and nobody had any ability to be a business manager in our party. We needed somebody at that time."

John Eastman said, however, "Neither ABKCO nor Klein were acceptable to McCartney. McCartney, from the beginning, refused to allow ABKCO or Klein to act on his behalf in any capacity and vigorously objected to their acting in any capacity with respect to The Beatles or any of their companies."

Paul added, "We were kind of all in it together, and it wasn't really 'til Allen Klein came in that we got really divisive and started getting our own lawyers and stuff. 'Cos he divided us. It was basically him that divided us. I didn't see the strength of this guy other than he was a great chatter."

On January 27, 1969, John Lennon wrote EMI Chairman Sir Joseph Lockwood that Allen Klein was now looking after his business affairs. Lennon wrote similar letters to Brian Epstein's brother Clive Epstein at the renamed NEMS Enterprises, Nemperor Holdings Ltd. (derived from the nickname Beatles publicist Derek Taylor had given Brian Epstein: the "Emperor" of NEMS), Northern Songs publisher Dick James — who published the Beatles songs — and Beatles' accountant Harry Pinsker. According to the *Times* in London, Klein's associations with the Beatles and the Rolling Stones made him "the most powerful man in pop music," though one known for "brutal methods" and "shady dealings."

In a letter submitted to a sentencing judge in 1979, following a tax evasion trial against Klein involving Beatles records, his psychiatrist determined that underpinning this, "Allen tends to be masochistic and self-defeating and is his own worst enemy." Despite Klein's notorious reputation, the psychiatrist said Allen was "loyal and decent to people regardless of how he has been mistreated by them."

○ ○ ○ ○ ○ Allen Klein entered the Beatles' lives just as several key business matters were converging. In addition to how to effectively operate Apple Corps, the ownerships of both Nemperor Holdings and Northern Songs were in flux. Queenie and Clive Epstein, Brian's mother and brother, controlled 90 percent of Nemperor, which still had a 25 percent right to Beatles record royalties and all other income under the late Brian Epstein's agreement with the band. When the Beatles learned that the financial firm Triumph Investment Trust had made a £1 million offer to the Epsteins for Nemperor, Paul McCartney asked Lee Eastman to come right away to England to advise the Beatles. But Lee sent son John Eastman, whom Tony Bramwell recalled as "sharp, but young and the other three Beatles wanted someone with gravitas. They discussed it among themselves and came up with the conclusion that while Eastman Jr. might lack his father's status when put up against the big-city guns, he was all they had."

The Beatles already owned 10 percent of Nemperor through their deal with Brian Epstein. John Eastman urged them to acquire the balance. But at a meeting at Apple's Savile Row offices on the night of January 28, 1969, Klein advised all four Beatles to wait for more complete information on the state of the band's financial affairs. On February 1, Klein met with the Beatles again, with John Eastman present. Eastman thought the Beatles could afford Nemperor's £1 million price. He also wanted them to acquire Nemperor's 237,000 shares in Northern Songs. But Allen Klein was concerned the forthcoming record royalties from EMI that the Beatles planned to use to buy Nemperor would be heavily taxed and in effect double the purchase price. During the meeting, Eastman "launched an attack on my personal integrity," Klein complained, by bringing up the controversy that surrounded Klein's 1967 purchase of Cameo-Parkway. "He alleged I had a bad reputation in general."

Klein met with Clive Epstein, and Nemperor and Apple accountant Harry Pinsker on February 3. Clive agreed to wait three weeks to decide how to dispose of the Epsteins' company. Klein then looked into the Beatles financial history, including record royalties from Capitol-EMI, film revenues from United Artists, and income from the Beatles' US tours that had been booked through General Artists Corporation, a major US booking agency to which Epstein had signed his artists. Klein doubter Paul McCartney even signed a letter dated February 28, 1969, that directed Nemperor to make accessible to Klein the Beatles' contracts and "other material which he may request in connection with our affairs." Based on financial audits that a group of established, outside accounting companies, including the Beatles' accountants Bryce Hanmer, conducted at Klein's behest — also with Paul McCartney's approval — Klein concluded by mid-March that, unfortunately, the Beatles' companies owed more than they were worth.

○ ○ ○ ○ ○ Before the financial audits were completed, Allen Klein had received a frantic phone call from Apple Corps managing director Neil Aspinall on February 21, 1969. Aspinall told Klein that Queenie and Clive Epstein had already sold the family's majority interest in Nemperor, to Triumph Investment Trust. Klein claimed "the reason which sparked" the sale was a February 14 letter John Eastman sent Clive Epstein alluding to the "propriety" of Nemperor having a right to commission the Beatles record royalties for nine more years. Clive Epstein responded by demanding Eastman "please be good enough to let me know precisely what you mean by . . . 'propriety.'" Instead, at a hastily assembled strategy meeting at the Dorchester Hotel, Allen Klein, ABKCO vice president Harold Seider, John Eastman, the Beatles, and English lawyers from Joynson-Hicks & Co., which handled legal work for Klein, decided to terminate Nemperor's ability to collect income on behalf of the Beatles.

The Beatles instructed EMI to remit $2.4 million in pending record royalties directly to Apple Corps. Triumph and Nemperor tried to get London's High Court of Justice to block the payment. Triumph claimed the Beatles had "fallen under the influence" of Klein, who was being prosecuted in New York federal court for failing to pay employee withholding taxes. Jeremiah Harman, court barrister for Triumph and Nemperor, told the court, "There might be a grave danger that we would never recover" Nemperor's share of royalty monies EMI sent Apple. However, on April 1, 1969, the High Court denied Triumph's bid to have the Beatles funds held in escrow.

Allen Klein and the Beatles met with Triumph's managing director Leonard Richenberg to negotiate a settlement. The settlement terms allowed Nemperor to buy out the Beatles' 10 percent interest in the management company but required Nemperor to give up its 25 percent commission from Beatles' income. The Beatles in return paid £772,500 to Nemperor to cover commissions that could accrue through March 1972, and 5 percent of the Beatles' record royalties from April 1972 to January 1976.

But Paul McCartney later had second thoughts and balked at signing the settlement agreement. That caused Klein to barge into a Beatles recording session at Abbey Road Studios, where he demanded a clarification from McCartney. According to Klein, with George Harrison and Ringo Starr looking on, McCartney told Klein, "'That's ridiculous.' He got up and left the room. A few minutes later he came back (having evidently made a telephone call). He then said, 'It's all right. It's good now.' I understood that he must have instructed his lawyers to agree to the exchange of the documents."

The signed papers were finally handed to Triumph on July 9, 1969. But ill will persisted between Apple Corps and Triumph Investment Trust. This could be seen from a dispute over a modest amount of money due Apple, from distribution of the Beatles' 1967 film *Magical Mystery Tour*, under an October 1968 Apple/Nemperor agreement. The movie, with no major US distribution deal, wasn't a big moneymaker. ABKCO English attorney Peter Howard determined that as of February 14, 1969, Nemperor accounted for just $53,346.82 in film revenues, of which $25,000 was sent to Apple. By October 1969, Nemperor sent Apple an additional $25,000. But in July 1971, Apple's New York lawyers began drafting a lawsuit against Nemperor for additional money they believed Nemperor now owed the Beatles from the growing cult popularity of the *Magical Mystery Tour* movie.

Nemperor, however, wasn't doing well. Since its management settlement with the Beatles, it had failed to develop new artists with strong earnings power and the value of the management company dropped. Even its 3½ years' right to 5 percent of the Beatles record royalties didn't look that promising when it kicked in 1972, with neither Paul McCartney's latest release, *Wild Life* by his new offshoot band Wings, or John Lennon's June 1972 album, the politically charged *Some Time in New York City*, selling near previous Beatles' sales levels. Triumph ended up selling Nemperor to the Hemdale Group, a diversified UK entertainment company, for £250,000 in August 1972. At the time, Nemperor's net value was only £65,000.

∘ ∘ ∘ ∘ ∘ Music house Northern Songs formed in February 1963 as a publishing vehicle for John Lennon and Paul McCartney's compositions. Its cofounder, song plugger Dick James, had been recommended to Brian Epstein by Beatles producer George Martin, who produced hit records for James's earlier singing career. James impressed Epstein in their first meeting by picking up the phone and on the spot getting the Beatles their first major TV booking, on the nationally broadcast TV series *Thank Your Lucky Stars*.

James initially secured the rights to early Lennon/McCartney compositions like "Please Please Me" and "Ask Me Why" for his fledging publishing firm. When "Please Please Me" became a major UK hit, James started Northern Songs with business partner Charles Silver. Northern got copyright ownership of the songs Lennon and McCartney would write; Lennon and McCartney each received a 20 percent, and Brian Epstein's NEMS a 10 percent, equity interest in the new publishing company. As publisher, Northern was responsible for promoting Lennon and McCartney's songs for other artists to record and for monitoring and collecting the song royalties.

Today, composers are more likely to form their own publishing companies, then enter into agreements with established publishing houses. (In a copublishing deal, a songwriter can end up with 75 percent of a song's income.) But British songwriter Mitch Murray, who wrote hits for such UK artists as Gerry & the Pacemakers and Freddie and the Dreamers, said of Lennon and McCartney's deal, "It was a unique set-up at the time, there were no precedents in this country but it was sweeter than just a publishing contract because it gave the writers a bit of equity in the company." But a cynical George Harrison, who signed to Northern Songs in 1965, said, "I learned that people from the early days, people had come in the studio and stick [*sic*] a piece of paper under your nose, and you'd be — you'd have to sign it, and that was later we found out what publishing was."

To gain more favorable tax treatment, Northern Songs offered 1.25 million shares to the public in February 1965. The London-based *Investors Chronicle* winced, "The stock exchange seems to have lowered its barriers remarkably in order to allow this issue into the marketplace." But *Newsweek* reported, "Demand for the stock outran supply by four to one," and, as a result, underwriter Solomon & Co. was forced to suspend trading. "We honestly have no idea how many youngsters may, in their enthusiasm, have let their desire surpass their bank accounts," a Solomon spokesperson said of the avalanche of orders from Beatles fans.

After the stock sale, Lennon and McCartney's stock percentages in Northern Songs were reduced to 15 percent each, though those interests were each worth $1.54 million. Meanwhile, Lennon and McCartney formed Maclen Music Ltd., a holding company for their song income from Northern. (In September 1969, Maclen Music Ltd. sued Northern Songs for underpayment of royalties. Allen Klein explained, "It emerged that the amounts accounted for by Northern Songs as received from Maclen Music Inc. [a North American sub-publisher that Northern Songs set up with the confusingly same name — other than "Inc." — as the Lennon/McCartney UK Maclen Music Ltd.] are substantially lower than the amounts which ought to be received if Northern Songs licensed Maclen Music Inc. on normal commercial terms" to independent third parties.)

In early 1969, the Beatles owned 30.32 percent of Northern's ordinary stock. Individually, John Lennon had 694,000 shares, Paul McCartney had 751,500, Ringo Starr owned 40,000, the Beatles movie division Subafilms Ltd. owned 30,000 and George Harrison's wife, Pattie, owned 1,000 shares. But in March 1969, minority shareholder Associated Television Corporation (ATV), which was run by entertainment impresario Sir Lew Grade, increased its minority stake in Northern Songs to 35 percent. ATV had bought the shares owned by Northern managing director Dick James and chairman Charles Silver. James had been concerned that Lennon and McCartney might not extend their songwriting agreements with Northern. But "James had made his fortune on those two kids. I told him he was a bastard to sell to Grade," John Eastman said.

In an effort to gain control of Northern Songs, the Beatles cobbled together a counterbid group that offered to pay £2,125,000 for Northern Songs, though if they won they would have corporate ownership of an income stream that was highly taxed. Allen Klein said John Lennon brought the Northern Songs issue up to him as soon as the Beatles discussed Klein becoming their manager. It "was a very sore point with Lennon," Klein said. "And at that time I thought he was really speaking on behalf of" all four Beatles. "John Lennon had told me that he and Paul McCartney wanted me to . . . come to London and see what I could do to prevent ATV from successfully taking control of Northern Songs."

Klein went to the British banking firm Henry Ansbacher & Co. Ltd. for representation on the counterbid. Ansbacher agreed to provide £1,250,000 to fund the Beatles' bid and Klein's ABKCO put in 45,000 shares, valued at £750,000, that it owned in the US entertainment company MGM. To sweeten their offer, Lennon and McCartney promised Northern Songs the right of first refusal for their songwriting services for two years after their current songwriting agreement with Northern ended in February 1973. Meanwhile, the four Beatles entered into an agreement among themselves that gave the band members a right of first refusal for ten years if any of them decided to sell his shares of Northern Songs.

But according to Allen Klein, on April 18, 1969, Lennon "and I both considered just selling and doing it so that — and I think one of the things which brought it more in focus was that Lee Eastman was recommending that Paul McCartney — that no one in the group sell their shares at all and I was frightened by the potential possibility of [Lew] Grade getting 70 percent of the shares and the only other shareholders being Lennon and our group and we being minority shareholders. . . . [W]e would have had no leverage and we would have been in a terrible bargaining position." Other companies eyed Northern Songs, too. Early in May 1969, Warner Brothers–Seven Arts said that, in response to interest expressed by its Atlantic Records president Ahmet Ertegun, it would send representatives to London to meet with brokers representing a consortium of 15 percent of Northern's public shares.

On September 19, 1969, the Beatles met at Apple's London headquarters to discuss how to compose a board of directors for their hoped-for Beatles-controlled Northern Songs. John Eastman "insisted that Paul should have as many votes as the other Beatles put together," Klein said, though McCartney balked at the idea. Ringo Starr told Eastman, "Look, the more and more we talk, it seems like you're trying to split us, not keep us together." But news arrived during the meeting that ATV had purchased the consortium's 15 percent share, making ATV's capture of Northern Songs inevitable.

On November 18, the defeated Beatles agreed to sell their Northern Songs stock to ATV, but walked away with more than £3 million worth of ATV shares as payment. Allen Klein, who negotiated the Beatles stock sale through talks with Lew Grade, took credit for the higher per-share price of £2 ATV paid above its earlier offer of £1.85 per share for Northern Songs stock. ATV Music managing director Geoffrey Heath said, "Lennon and McCartney's biggest resentment was that they had gone into a deal to float Northern Songs and nobody advised them about having a 'poison pill' clause [at least in their agreement with Northern upon the public sale of shares of the publishing company in 1965] whereby, if the company got bought, their [songwriting] contracts would be cancelled." (Lennon and McCartney's songwriting contract with Northern Songs obligated them to deliver a minimum of six new songs per year through February 1973. But Allen Klein claimed he was responsible for getting the Beatles almost $10 million total from their sales of the Northern Songs stock to ATV and their 10 percent ownership interest in NEMS to Triumph Investment Trust.)

Paul McCartney offered this simple summary of the complicated music-publishing wars: "In March 1969, when I was on my honeymoon and John was doing his bed-in [with Yoko], Dick James sold the songs — while we were out of town. When we got back to town, we said, 'Dick! You can't do that!' He said, 'You want a bet?' And he was quite right. It's just the way these things go."

In the early 1980s, the financial fortunes of Sir Lew Grade's media and entertainment empire plunged, after his film division invested in a series of expensive flops like *Raise the Titanic*, about which Grade reportedly said, "It would have been cheaper to drain the Atlantic." ATV Music president Sam Trust recalled that Grade, in immediate need of an infusion of tens of millions of dollars, "called Lee Eastman and said he was offering" Northern Songs "to the 'boys,' meaning Lennon and McCartney, and the price was then only $30 million." Paul McCartney was eager to buy but reportedly couldn't come to an agreement with John Lennon's widow Yoko on the amount they should together pay for Northern Songs.

Eventually, it was the larger ATV Music, which included Northern Songs, that Lew Grade decided to sell. McCartney protested, "I'm not interested in buying his whole company. I just want my songs. Give me back my babies, Lew!" But in 1985, ATV Music was acquired by Michael Jackson for $47.5 million. Today, it is co-owned by Jackson's estate and Sony Corp., which paid Michael $90 million in 1995 for a 50 percent interest in what is now known as Sony/ATV Music Publishing and estimated to be worth more than $1 billion.

7 · "Each & Every Word"

The pitched battle between Klein and the Eastmans for the business soul of the Beatles engendered long-term ill will on all sides. John Eastman called Klein "the biggest bulltwaddler ever." In a letter drafted to Paul and Linda McCartney, John Lennon complained about "all the petty shit that came from your insane family/in-laws."

When it came to painting a public face on the bitter relationships, however, the Klein-controlled Apple Corps issued a homey press release stating: "Apple, Beatles, Eastman and Klein have over the past few months established a warm, workable relationship which is to their benefit."

When Allen Klein first took hold of Apple Corps' reigns, he claimed to have spent so much time on the Beatles' business that he confessed to Ringo Starr "the Rolling Stones complained to him that he was neglecting them for the Beatles." On May 9, 1969, Starr, John Lennon, and George Harrison signed a written agreement that Klein drafted (dated May 8), formally making ABKCO the exclusive business manager for "Apple Corps Ltd. on behalf of The Beatles and The Beatles Group of Companies." After McCartney refused to sign, Lennon raged around the Apple Corps offices shouting, "Fuck McCartney, that does it, I won't be writing any more songs with him."

ABKCO's contract obligated Apple Records to "pay for all future reasonable travel expenses and provide living quarters for all ABKCO personnel while in London, when travelling at our request." ABKCO was to receive a commission of 20 percent from all Beatles sources, except for 10 percent on Apple Records gross income, 10 percent on Harrison's and Starr's publishing income (increased to 20 percent in January 1970) and excluding preexisting Beatles record royalty rates. The contract, which had an initial three-year term, was cancelable by Apple or Klein at the end of any of one of those years but contained a clause that was highly unfavorable to the Beatles: Klein was entitled to his full commissions in perpetuity from "all agreements" the Beatles and their companies signed with third parties during the management term. (It's not unusual for a manager to have a right to post-management commissions from an artist, but these are usually for diminishing percentages over a limited post-term time.)

According to attorney Nat Weiss, Klein ran Apple "like Mussolini, making the trains run on time. Klein is a creature of instinct, who likes to intimidate you, just to see how far he can go." Apple staffer Chris O'Dell noted, "The Hells Angels' arrival at Savile Row in 1968 was only the first takeover of Apple — Allen Klein . . . waged the second and final battle for Apple's soul. So, in retrospect, maybe those three weeks when the Hells Angels took us hostage weren't really so bad."

Beatles engineer Geoff Emerick, who supervised the construction of Apple's in-house recording studio, recalled, "The short, round business manager would arrive every morning in one of Lennon's cars dressed in an ill-fitting polo-neck sweater and shapeless trousers. He'd spend most of the day up in his office, yelling at people on the phone."

Allen Klein immediately began an extensive housecleaning of Apple employees, though Neil Aspinall — who started as the Beatles' roadie in 1961, had acted as Apple Corps' manager since November 1967, and was "practically *married* to the Fabs" — survived the cuts. "Neil had a better idea of what the Beatles wanted than they did," said Peter Brown, who for a time ran Apple Corps with Aspinall. "He kept things going daily with these four disparate entities, who were not easy to agree on anything. Nobody else could get a decision out of them." (Aspinall served as Apple Corps' top executive until his retirement in 2007; he died from lung cancer in 2008.)

After the Nemperor and Northern Songs episodes, Allen Klein needed to achieve a major breakthrough for the Beatles. He saw his opportunity in upcoming renegotiations of the Beatles recording contract with EMI's US affiliate Capitol Records. The Beatles wanted separate recording contracts with Capitol and with EMI. At a May 7, 1969, meeting in London, EMI representatives told Klein and the Beatles that the record company wouldn't discuss contract changes until the Nemperor affair was resolved. With that done, EMI managing director Len Wood recalled Klein "wanted to cancel the 1967 [Beatles/EMI recording] contract and I told him he couldn't. Then he said he wanted to change it and I told him we'd be happy to change parts of it." But Klein "wouldn't agree to anything so I told him to get out." Klein later called Wood to apologize, though the EMI executive concluded Klein "was the most difficult man I ever had to deal with."

○ ○ ○ ○ ○ In July 1969, Allen Klein traveled with ABKCO in-house counsel Harold Seider to Los Angeles, where they discussed essential renegotiation terms with Capitol Records. But Klein claimed that during the renegotiation process, John Eastman "had been writing to Capitol to the effect that I had no right to negotiate on behalf of" McCartney, that "the whole negotiation was a waste of time," though Paul later acquiesced to Klein's handling of the contract talks.

Final drafting talks were held at ABKCO's offices in New York. Capitol legal department director Elliot Chaum, staff lawyer Charles Tillinghast, and outside counsel Payson Wolff traveled there from Los Angeles to face off against Klein, Seider, and ABKCO/Apple UK lawyer Peter Howard. Tillinghast recalled that the negotiations "seemed interminable, not because the issues were so complex or required much reinvention of old concepts, but just because so much time went by with so few decisions made, indeed so much time when we waited for Klein, who was busy elsewhere. Maybe he was inflicting on us his personal vision of water boarding, in this case drowning by boredom rather than by water."

Klein did occasionally stop by the ABKCO conference room the day that Capitol's lawyers labored inside drafting the contract revisions. According to Tillinghast, "I was only half-awake when, at 4:30 in the morning, Klein cheerfully entered the conference room, seemingly as fresh as the proverbial daisy, certainly a lot fresher than any of us felt, and suggested we all adjourn to a 'little place' he knew of that served wonderful French onion soup—twenty-four hours a day, apparently." It was in the Manhattan eatery, over the soup, that the Beatles contract discussions were concluded.

Under the amended record deal of September 1, 1969, the Beatles received a significant royalty uplift, from the existing 17½ percent rate to 25 percent of wholesale income from the sale of their records in the United States. The renegotiated agreement also included a buy-sell provision modeled after the one that Klein got for Sam Cooke with RCA Records in 1963. Under the Beatles' September 1969 "buy-sell" deal, which helped lower the Beatles' tax liability for recording-sales income, EMI gave the New York-based Apple Records Inc. the exclusive North American rights to manufacture and distribute Beatles product. Apple simultaneously licensed the US distribution rights to Capitol, which also did the actual manufacturing work under the agreement with Apple Records. (EMI, however, retained owner-ship of the copyrights in the Beatles recordings.)

John Lennon's view was that the revised agreement would bring renewed record label attention to the Beatles' recordings. Lennon said Klein "no-ticed that the Beatles had stopped selling records as they were doing around the world and he found out that it was because the record company simply wasn't bothering to push them. They thought that our records would sell themselves, and they were wrong. They don't. Klein's very good — he's going to make sure they stop sitting on the records and actually release them."

One wrinkle Klein acknowledged, though, was that "Capitol had the right, if an individual Beatle put out a record, [to] not have to accept it under the September 1, 1969, agreement as a Beatle record in satisfaction of certain obligations that the Beatles had under that agreement." Instead, Capitol could deem a Beatles solo album as accepted under an October 1, 1969, agreement that Klein negotiated with Capitol-EMI for Apple Records regarding non-Beatles artists signed to the Apple label. This, of course, was for a lower royalty than under the September 1, 1969, agreement for Beatles product.

George Harrison lamented what he saw as a renegotiation oversight, that "prior to the contract expiring, we had always had absolute control over the package of our product." However, once the recording agreement ended, "It was completely out of our hands, because we were naive in those days. We never made a contract where we would control the tapes after . . . the contract expired." (Harrison made his comment after Capitol released *The Best of George Harrison* in 1976 which Harrison "had absolutely nothing to do with" and was attacked by music critics as an unbalanced presentation of his Beatles and solo work.)

But Allen Klein emphasized that Apple Corps' royalty from the sale of preexisting Beatles product was gravy from which "every dollar that [Apple Corps] receives on royalties [from] Capitol or through the buy-sell is pure profit, other than the payment of mechanical royalties to music publishers" and ABKCO's commission of 20 percent from Apple's gross income. "Other than that, [the Beatles] have relatively no expenses at all," Klein said.

○ ○ ○ ○ ○ On September 20, 1969, the Beatles gathered at Apple's 3 Savile Row headquarters in London for the signing of the new Capitol contract.

"Each and every word in that agreement was read by their British solicitor to them," said Klein. He recalled Paul McCartney being the one who asked that the detailed contract be recited to the Beatles by Peter Howard, who was ABKCO's man at Apple. But it "was not because of the friction between McCartney and Lennon," Klein claimed. "I believe that McCartney was stalling for time so that his brother-in-law lawyer [John Eastman] could arrive from the United States to go over this agreement."

Although John Lennon is the Beatle who signed the Capitol contract on behalf of Apple and his band mates, he later couldn't remember the September 20 meeting. "I have no clue about it at all," he said.

But at the Savile Row summit, Klein described the recording contract to the four Beatles as simply giving Capitol the North American rights "to manufacture and distribute and sell when Apple delivered it in the form that Apple delivered it." John Eastman argued each Beatle should have his own US company, but then said he would support the new Capitol/Beatles contract. McCartney, who had rejected Klein's representation from the start, was now ready to agree to the signing of the Klein-negotiated Capitol contract.

Both Ringo Starr and George Harrison had previously walked out on the group, though briefly; Starr during the studio sessions for the so-called White album, *The Beatles*, and Harrison during the filmed *Get Back* project that became the *Let It Be* album. McCartney said that during the September 20 meeting, "[I]t got a little bit, 'Well, why are we doing this? Are we sure the group is going to continue?' 'Oh, sure, it'll all continue.'"

But as McCartney talked at the gathering about the Beatles getting back to musical basics, John Lennon announced, "Well, I wasn't gonna tell you till after we'd signed the Capitol contract. Klein asked me not to tell you. But, seeing as you asked me, I'm leaving the group." "So that was it," McCartney said. "We signed the new Capitol deal in a bit of a daze not quite knowing why we'd done it."

Allen Klein claimed the buy-sell deal would make it easier to determine the music-publishing royalties owed the Beatles. That is, with Apple Records Inc. deemed the "manufacturer" of Beatles product under the September 1969 agreement with Capitol, the Beatles would know "how many records Capitol had sold in the past, what the mechanical payments were to [Northern Songs' US affiliate] Maclen Music Inc., and we could trace it through to the royalty payments and say, 'Ah-ha you did not pay us correctly.'"

To butter up Lennon, Harrison, and Starr, Klein offered to sell them a total of 40,000 shares in ABKCO. Klein later claimed that, in January 1970, the three Beatles in return agreed to an increase in ABKCO's commission from the renegotiated Capitol Records contract, a decision that a lawyer for Paul McCartney later claimed "took place completely behind" McCartney's back. ABKCO also secured agreements signed by Harrison and Starr to serve as worldwide administrator for the band's Apple Publishing Ltd. songs and for Harrison and Starr's individual publishing companies, respectively Harrisongs Music Ltd. and Startling Music Ltd.

In spring 1970, Klein again improved the Beatles' financial picture by negotiating an agreement for Apple Films with United Artists Corp. to distribute the *Let It Be* movie. The deal gave Apple Films 50 percent of the adjusted gross receipts from the film's distribution. Morris Finer, an English lawyer for John Lennon, George Harrison, and Ringo Starr, claimed the deal "made an absolute fortune for all four Beatles," who until then had a 20 percent profit participation from United Artists for Beatles movies.

○ ○ ○ ○ ○ Neither the renegotiated Capitol Records agreement nor the *Let It Be* movie deal convinced Paul McCartney to seek peace with Allen Klein. A few months later, Paul would claim that ABKCO took commissions from the Beatles' full record-royalty rate, rather than from just the increase Klein had obtained. But McCartney wasn't the only Apple artist who locked horns with Klein. James Taylor, the first artist signed to Apple, also detested Klein.

"The day before I became the head of Apple's A&R, James Taylor came to see me, a friend in the States had given him my number," said talent scout Peter Asher. "The logical thing was for me to sign him to Apple."

In a June 1, 1968, memo, Asher wrote Apple Records chief Ron Kass, "We intend to start recording [James] about the 20th June, by which time he will have enough songs rehearsed and arranged with me. He is ready to discuss contracts and things as soon as you are."

McCartney and Lennon disagreed, however, over the quality of Taylor's music. "Paul liked James' tape, but John heard it once and didn't," Asher recalled. John Lennon said, "Who needs the Iveys (Badfinger) and James

Taylor, Yoko and my album's great." "I still have the [press] clipping," Asher recalled. "It was very strange to work under those circumstances."

Taylor's debut album *James Taylor* sold poorly when it was released early in 1969. Beatles insider Tony Bramwell said, "When the album didn't set the world alight, Klein acted aghast, shocked that James hadn't made a fortune immediately." But Taylor and Asher wanted out soon after Klein took over Apple's operations. "I decided that both my career and James' would be better served outside of Apple," Asher said, "and I think what has happened has proved me to be right. There were some legalities, but when we left they really didn't care."

Paul McCartney recalled Taylor and Asher saying, "'We like you, we like the guys, but we don't like this Klein guy and we don't like what's going to happen.' So I said, 'Why don't we just give [Taylor] his album back and say, 'There you go, man, you've made us some money, fabulous, thanks, peace.'" But Klein reacted, "You kidding? We've got his contract! We can hold this guy for ever."

James Taylor feared Klein was also "after my writing. I know he is. He's in charge of my money now. He's also responsible for my career. And it terrifies me." James's father Isaac cosigned the June 12, 1968, exclusive recording contract his twenty-year-old son entered into with Apple. But James turned twenty-one in March 1969 and in September sent a notice to Apple disaffirming his three-year recording agreement.

The label didn't respond to Taylor's letter for nearly a year. By then, James had signed to Warner Bros. Records. His 1970 Warner album *Sweet Baby James*, with the hit single "Fire and Rain," became the first megaseller of the new era of introspective singer-songwriters. In negotiating Taylor's Warner contract, Peter Asher made sure to obtain a contractual promise from label president Joe Smith that Warner would indemnify Asher and Taylor if Apple decided to sue over James's exit from the Beatles' record company.

With Taylor now a hot music property, Allen Klein began preparing legal assaults in England and the United States over Taylor's departure from Apple. On July 1, 1971, Larry Eno, a lawyer at ABKCO's New York law firm Rosenman Colin, wrote Harold Seider at ABKCO, "As I told you on the telephone today, we are anxious to know the English law involved in the action against Taylor in that country." Then on July 9, ABKCO executive (and Allen Klein nephew) Michael Kramer wrote Peter Howard at Apple Corps that the lawyers at Rosenman Colin were "still awaiting the English law governing the Taylor situation." But Kramer warned Howard that "our position has been severely prejudiced by our delay in responding" to James Taylor's September 1969 contract-disaffirmance notice.

The complaint that Rosenman Colin drafted for filing in New York state court didn't name Taylor as a defendant. It focused instead on Warner Bros. Records, Marylebone Productions and its principals Peter Asher, who managed and produced Taylor, and New York lawyer Nat Weiss. In the draft, Klein's Apple Records regime alleged the defendants had gained "unconscionable profits," and "knowingly interfered with the contractual relations between [Apple] Records S.A. and Taylor and intentionally and without justification induced and enticed Taylor to violate, repudiate and break" the Apple agreement.

The draft further asserted Apple's exclusive ownership of the Taylor track "Fire and Rain," on the grounds that James had made an earlier recording of it in Los Angeles in January 1969 while still under contract to Apple. But according to Paul McCartney, ultimately the Beatles agreed among themselves that Taylor should be released from his Apple contract.

8 "To Stop Klein"

Paul McCartney boycotted day-to-day involvement in Apple Corps as soon as Allen Klein gained control of the Beatles' companies. But McCartney came roaring back into Apple's affairs when on December 31, 1970, he filed the most famous intra-band lawsuit in music history: the "writ" in the High Court of Justice in London to formally end the Beatles' band partnership, though McCartney claimed he was "very anxious" for Apple Corps to continue as a company. (In England, a writ is a summons served on defendants that states the plaintiff's basic claims. A "statement of claim," which is filed later, explains the plaintiff's allegations in more depth.) In the suit, McCartney named Apple Corps, John Lennon, George Harrison, and Ringo Starr as defendants. Yoko Ono's constant presence at Beatles studio sessions was a highly publicized thorn in McCartney's side. EMI chairman Joseph Lockwood remembered of Yoko's aggressive approach, "She came into the Manchester Square offices with John for lunch one day and I put her down at the end of the table with my assistant. Then she put a tape recorder on the table and taped the whole lunch."

George Harrison said, however, that the goal of McCartney's court action was "to stop Klein from becoming our business manager." In a Q&A insert for his 1970 debut album *McCartney*, Paul had stated his relationship with Klein "isn't. I am not in contact with him and he does not represent me in *any* way." But London litigator Morris Finer, the trade union and commercial law expert who defended Lennon, Harrison, and Starr against McCartney's suit, taunted McCartney in court by saying he "seems to live in a world where everyone is either a seraphim or angel, or ape or viper, where there is precious little room for the intermediate atmosphere in which most people live."

Yet, it was Harrison who described McCartney's demeanor from a spring 1970 phone conversation as acting "like Atilla [*sic*] the Hun. I had to hold the receiver away from my ear." McCartney later acknowledged that suing his Beatles mates "was a terrible decision." "Imagine, seriously, having to front that one out," he said. But, McCartney explained: "I think really when Klein and the lawyers got in, then there wasn't even room for that good-natured tension. This was like playing Monopoly on a very large scale with lawyers. I never used to be very good at the game, anyway. I used to get very tense during Monopoly. And when it was real houses and real money and real Park Lanes and real Savile Rows, it got very fraught."

McCartney's statement of claim charged the other three Beatles with "willful and persistent breaches" of the band's 1967 partnership agreement. McCartney alleged that his bandmates had "taken it on themselves to exclude Plaintiff from his proper share in the conduct of the partnership business by purporting to appoint and by retaining ABKCO," an arrangement McCartney argued was invalid. McCartney claimed he "reasonably distrusts Mr. Klein," including because of the 1968 delisting of the Cameo-Parkway company from the New York Stock Exchange and the recent US government tax prosecution of Klein. McCartney also claimed he had been unable to obtain certified audits of Apple's finances.

In the lawsuit, McCartney accused his fellow Beatles of paying ABKCO a 10 percent commission on royalties going back to the pre-Klein January 25, 1967, contract with EMI Records. The suit also challenged Lennon, Harrison, and Starr's choice of Klein as the band's manager on the ground that Klein was improperly taking a management commission from the full 25 percent royalty rate under the Beatles' renegotiated 1969 Capitol-EMI contract, instead of, as Klein had promised in his May 1969 Beatles management agreement, only from the 7½ percent royalty increase that he obtained for the Beatles in that negotiation.

McCartney also attacked Apple's May 1970 release of the *Let It Be* album with what Paul viewed as heavy-handed production additions by Phil Spector. McCartney said he hadn't known in advance that Spector was adding drums, horns, voices, and strings to Paul's "The Long and Winding Road" and that other McCartney songs on the album were "changed considerably." Paul claimed this was an "intolerable interference with my work." (The Spector-produced version of the album nevertheless won both Grammy and Oscar awards for "Best Original Score" and "Original Song Score.")

As Klein remembered it, Phil "called me, he wanted to see me just out of the blue and he indicated that he really wanted to work with the Beatles." Klein and Spector then traveled from the United States to England to meet with them. "[I]t was up to John Lennon and Lennon wanted Spector," Klein claimed.

Klein negotiated Phil's producer agreement on behalf of Apple Corps. As a teenager in the 1950s, Spector wrote, sang, and played several instruments on the number one hit "To Know Him Is to Love Him" by his group the Teddy Bears. (George Harrison kidded that Phil would "fall over if you said . . . that he was a rock singer.") By the early 1960s, Spector introduced his over-the-top "Wall of Sound" production style on recordings like the Righteous Brothers' "You've Lost That Lovin' Feelin'" and Ike & Tina Turner's "River Deep–Mountain High." Spector later produced best-selling solo singles and albums for John Lennon and George Harrison, including John's "Imagine" single and album, and George's "My Sweet Lord" single and *All Things Must Pass* album.

But, "Don't ever do it again," McCartney had written Allen Klein on April 14, 1970, about Spector's involvement in the *Let It Be* album, though Morris Finer, trial lawyer for the other Beatles, claimed Spector's effort was "a perfectly honest and competent attempt by someone to get this record into shape."

Paul became additionally incensed when Allen Klein slotted the release of the debut solo album *McCartney* for after *Let It Be*. Klein blamed Lennon and Harrison for the decision, though they relented and *McCartney* was released in April 1970, prior to *Let It Be* but a month after Ringo Starr's debut solo album *Sentimental Journey*. Ringo said, "When I told Paul that the rest of us wanted to delay his solo album, he went completely out of control. He was shouting at me, prodding his fingers towards my face saying: 'I'll finish you now' and 'You'll pay.'" In his lawsuit, McCartney insisted "there is no possibility" the Beatles would ever record together again.

McCartney's suit wanted a receiver to be appointed to sort out Apple's chaotic finances while his Beatles partnership dissolution claim moved through court. At an ex parte High Court hearing before Justice Edward Stamp on January 19, 1971, only counsel for McCartney's side appeared. David Hirst, McCartney's lead lawyer, was a top libel litigator in England before expanding his practice into commercial law. He pleaded to Stamp that "there probably is not enough in the kitty to meet even the individual Beatles income and surtax liability." (As Hirst spoke, government commissioners were assessing huge back taxes on the Beatles that Hirst claimed were the result of Klein's failure to compile proper accountings.)

○ ○ ○ ○ ○ With his wife Linda at his side, a bearded Paul McCartney — but none of the other Beatles — attended an eleven-day High Court hearing with lawyers from both sides that began on February 19, 1971. "So insecure," McCartney said of his feelings about the case. "Half the reason I grew the beard. It's often a cover-up. And I had this big beard and I went to the High Court and actually managed to save the situation. But my whole life was on the line at that point. I felt this was the fire, this was the furnace. It had finally arrived. And we used to get shakes in our voices in court."

A reporter for the Newspaper Enterprise Association described the London courtroom as "full of lawyers, whose flapping black robes gave them the appearance of vultures circling over the kill." The *Evening News* in London published a cartoon of Justice Stamp at the courtroom door singing, "I don't care too much for money . . . money can't buy you love . . . !"

New Musical Express journalist Norm Smith, who covered the Beatles since their early days, noted that "one of the biggest ironies of the situation is that Lennon, prophet of peace, and Harrison, man of God, seem to have jumped into the fray with extraordinary relish." With Harrison's "My Sweet Lord," Lennon's "Power to the People," and McCartney's "Another Day" all vying on the UK singles charts at the same time, Smith observed, "I believe that on the charts now we see not a release of Beatle music out of coincidence, or for the sake of it, but a subtle yet open warfare between them which may have more than a little to do with the current court case."

In an affidavit read in court by his counsel, John Lennon emphasized that after Brian Epstein died, Apple was besieged by "spongers" and hindered by an undisciplined staff. Lennon said that Allen Klein "is certainly forceful to an extreme but he does get results." Ringo Starr expressed surprise and disappointment, in his affidavit, that Paul McCartney filed suit, rather than following through on a "promise" to convene a meeting of the four Beatles in January 1971 to try to resolve their differences. (Starr jokingly asked his lawyer when taping the comments for the affidavit whether the recording should be in mono or stereo.)

Allen Klein didn't testify at the hearings, but he did submit a lengthy forty-six-page affidavit that responded to McCartney's charges. Klein trumpeted accounting figures showing he doubled the Beatles' income in 1969 and increased it by several times in 1970. Apple defense litigator counsel Morris Finer added, "This naughty animal is defending himself to show that from the start he was acting properly and in the Beatles' interest." Finer claimed that Klein's 1969 renegotiation of the Beatles' Capitol Records contract was "the big agreement which has been so responsible for the increase in income." But David Hirst argued for McCartney that Klein entered the Beatles' lives "on the crest of a wave. He could claim no credit for the wave, let alone the ocean across which it moved."

As for Phil Spector, Klein contended that after a Beatles' private screening of the *Let It Be* movie on November 18, 1969, McCartney was "enthusiastic" about Klein's suggestion that Spector "should join Apple." But Klein also acknowledged that November 18 was the last time he and Paul McCartney saw each other, though back in New York in December he received an early morning phone call from McCartney. "He said something about me not giving interviews to newspapers and leaving his in-laws alone. I asked him what he meant but he hung up," Klein said.

In his court statement, Klein warned that appointing a financial receiver for Apple Corps "will make it impossible to recruit new artists, and it will create enormous confusion in the minds of companies and individuals having dealings with Apple as to whom they should account and with whom they should deal." But Justice Stamp, soon to be promoted to lord justice of the Court of Appeals, sided with Paul McCartney. On March 12, 1971, with none of the Beatles present in court, he approved London accountant J. D. Spooner as receiver and manager of the Beatles & Co. finances. Stamp was clearly skeptical of Klein, describing as "a rotten point" Klein's insistence that, after deducting product costs, he had taken a smaller management commission from the Beatles' record royalties than he was entitled to. It didn't help in Stamp's view that Klein had by now been convicted in us court of failing to file employee-withholding tax returns.

Paul McCartney's partnership dissolution claim could now proceed. Justice Stamp noted in his March 12 decision, "I reject what I think to be a fanciful notion that there is some sort of analogy between that idea of democracy, enabling a majority to overrule a minority, and the law of partnership."

John Lennon, George Harrison, and Ringo Starr appealed the receiver's appointment but withdrew the filing because, Lennon said in a public letter to McCartney, "[I]f we didn't do what you wanted, you'd sue us again." But McCartney commented about leaving the Beatles, "You just don't want to know about your ex-wife or ex-husband. After all the bitchiness, you feel the desire for a complete break."

° ° ° ° ° J. D. Spooner served as the court-appointed financial receiver of the Beatles partnership until January 1973, when he was succeeded by his accounting colleague Stephen Gray. Both Spooner and Gray found it difficult, however, to oversee the Beatles' finances. They naturally faced resistance from the Lennon-Harrison-Starr faction, which still had Allen Klein and ABKCO as their manager in New York. To John Lennon, "the receiver wasn't normal, I know that." The business-averse Lennon admitted, "I don't know what he's supposed to do in actuality."

Spooner's responsibilities included paying each of the Beatles £1,000 per month out of partnership profits (increased to £3,000 per month in 1973). In addition, the court mandated him to compile an accurate accounting of the Beatles wide-ranging business activities. But Spooner had to maneuver controversies that arose between him and EMI, and with Apple Corps. Apple had given United Artists the US distribution rights for the *Let It Be* album and the companion documentary film. EMI wanted its royalty of 22.5 cents for each copy of the *Let It Be* album sold in the United States, but United Artists was remitting those payments to Spooner, who placed them in the Beatles partnership account. EMI claimed its share should be kept out of the receivership.

Even as EMI battled Spooner, its in-house counsel Malcolm Brown wrote him that "we shall continue to avoid taking sides in the disputes which arise between you and Apple Corps Ltd." But, Brown continued, "As we see it, the point has been reached where these disputes are seriously damaging our commercial relationship with Apple," which "could grind to a halt if the present impasse persists."

EMI's lawyer cited several primary concerns. These included Spooner's refusal to approve payment to Apple of the royalties accruing from the Beatles' pre-1967 recordings, on the ground that the Beatles had yet to agree among themselves how to treat this pre–Beatles & Co. income. When EMI decided to hold on to these royalties pending a resolution of the issue, "Almost at once," according to Malcolm Brown, "Apple refused to agree to release" a live album of the Beatles 1964 and 1965 performances at the Hollywood Bowl in Los Angeles. Brown said EMI was "very anxious to issue it. Delay in doing so is causing us and everyone else concerned substantial loss." Spooner claimed, however, that the delay was due to infighting between Paul McCartney and the Lennon-Harrison-Starr block. In addition, though EMI claimed it owned the Hollywood Bowl recordings, Spooner noted that Apple had told him "that they laid absolute claim to it as their property." Capitol-EMI didn't release *The Beatles at The Hollywood Bowl* until May 1977. (The poor sound quality of the concert tapes also affected the timing of the album's release.)

Another issue Brown emphasized to Spooner involved Apple Corps' claim to its 50 percent share of profits from a *Let It Be* book, today a collectors' item, which was included in the record's initial UK release. Apple also wanted to be reimbursed for the costs it incurred in producing the book. J. D. Spooner contended the book fell within "merchandising activities" mentioned in the 1967 Beatles & Co. partnership agreement and should thus be allocated to the partnership's account. To convince Spooner to hand over the funds, Peter Howard at Apple insisted that Apple Corps entered into its December 1969 agreement with EMI for the *Let It Be* packaging not as a Beatles & Co. partner but on behalf of itself. "I cannot see that you can, with any justification, maintain that Apple's share of the profit on the book is accountable to the Partnership as partnership income," Howard told Spooner, urgently adding, "The printers are in fact making an additional claim of £12,337.36 and this is the subject of litigation between Apple and the printers at this point in time."

On November 25, J. D. Spooner submitted an affidavit to the High Court in London in which he stated that he had "received and satisfied myself as to details of" Apple's *Let It Be* book expenses and instructed EMI to at least reimburse Apple for those costs.

∘ ∘ ∘ ∘ ∘ When Stephen Gray took over as Beatles & Co. receiver in 1973, he protested to the English court that he initially "had been impeded by reason of my not being able to exercise such direct personal supervision of partnership activities as I considered to be necessary in Apple's offices."

But Gray didn't think this was "deliberately intentional." For one thing, the 3 Savile Row offices were being renovated and Apple's business was now administered out of an office at 54 St. James Street.

However, Gray further complained, he often didn't become aware of Beatles and Apple's activities until after "having seen a press announcement." He also said he hadn't been allowed full access to the financial records of Apple or of the individual Beatles, the latter "which I need to do with a view to satisfying myself that no partnership assets or liabilities are reflected therein of which I am unaware." This included for individual record production activities by any of the Beatles. Gray thus asked the English court to order Apple, Lennon, Harrison, and Starr "to permit me to carry out a full inspection" of all relevant financial records.

Apple Corps managing director Neil Aspinall blamed the Beatles' shaky financial condition on "the prolongation of the negotiations" since June 1971 to settle Paul McCartney's dissolution suit. Frank Caola, Apple counsel from Frere Cholmeley & Co. in London, noted that settlement discussions in New York in January 1974 had "resulted in a certain measure of agreement." But, Caola continued, "I am sorry to say that, because of last minute proposals put forth by Lee Eastman in relation to the pre-1966 recordings (which were covered by the Beatles' first recording agreement with EMI), it has not yet been possible to reach final agreement."

Caola wrote Stephen Gray on January 18 that, "to continue in business," it was "essential that Apple Corps should be provided with money to meet its immediate liabilities . . . as it has now practically exhausted the limits" of a £1,367,000 overdraft account the National Westminister Bank had approved for Apple. By January 1974, Apple Corps had drawn £1,353,024 from the overdraft account, which came with a hefty 16.5 percent annual interest rate. Caola asked Gray for £680,000 of which £300,000 was to cover corporate taxes. But Gray wrote back that Lee Eastman "made it clear to me that his client will not agree to any further advance of profits from partnership funds to Apple Corps," especially because John Lennon, George Harrison, and Ringo Starr now controlled Apple Corps with Paul McCartney largely an absentee.

○ ○ ○ ○ ○ Paul appeared to be using the High Court's appointment of an accounting receiver as financial leverage to pressure John, George, and

Ringo into reaching terms with him in his partnership suit against them. It would take another year until all four Beatles agreed on how Apple Corps should be funded. When they did they stipulated: all royalties earned from their pre-December 1966 recordings were to be paid to Apple; those from recordings made December 1966 forward would go 80 percent to Apple Corps and 5 percent to each Beatle; and all royalties earned since October 1, 1971, from solo works were to be remitted fully to each respective Beatle.

But it wouldn't be the seemingly ever-present Allen Klein who represented Lennon, Harrison, and Starr in this comprehensive agreement, because by then Klein's management relationship with his three Beatles clients had fallen apart.

9 · Remnants of the Relationship

espite his cost-cutting measures and staff reorganization, Allen Klein hadn't helped Apple Corps run smoothly. Sales of Apple non-Beatles artists in the early 1970s were limited mostly to hits by the Beatles-sounding Badfinger. Case in point: the last artists Apple signed were multi-instrumentalist brothers Derrek and Lon Van Eaton. Based in Trenton, New Jersey, they caught the attention of Nat Weiss, partner with the late Brian Epstein in the us-based Nemperor Artists that successfully managed The Cyrkle, a pop-rock band that had two major hits, "Turn Down Day" and Paul Simon's "Red Rubber Ball."

Weiss and Epstein had cruised the gay social scene together. Lon said that when he and Derrek went up to Weiss's Manhattan office, "The walls were decorated with those classic *Vanity Fair* magazine illustrations of British lawyers in wigs, with hard-ons subtly visible through their robes." "But Nat had a very different demeanor than Allen Klein," Lon noted, "Nat was a sweet man; smart, soft-spoken, a bit overweight. He had very understated facial expressions, almost a British-type reserve."

Weiss asked artist manager Robin Garb "if I was interested in representing" the Van Eatons, Garb said. Garb, who did become their manager, shopped a seven-song demo tape to several record companies. In June 1971, Apple A&R executive Tony King wrote Garb that George Harrison was interested in the Van Eaton demos. Harrison called two weeks later.

"Nat Weiss negotiated the Apple deal for us," Lon said. "We had better offers from two other labels but, of course, took the deal with the Beatles' company." When Derrek and Lon arrived at Apple's office in London, however, "It was in a bit of a shamble. No one really knew what was going on," Lon recalled. But the brothers hit it off well with Harrison, who produced their single release "Sweet Music" at Abbey Road Studios, with Ringo Starr and Jim Gordon on drums and Peter Frampton on an acoustic guitar. The backing track sounded similar to Harrison's solo recording "Isn't It a Pity."

Beatles associate Klaus Voormann produced the Van Eaton's 1972 Apple album *Brother* at Apple's new recording studio at 3 Savile Row. The album was well received by music critics, even called "staggeringly impressive" by *Rolling Stone* album reviewer Stephen Holden. But after "Sweet Music" failed to be a hit, George Harrison sent a telegram to ABKCO/Apple promotion director Pete Bennett and New York label manager Al Steckler that screeched, "What the 'fuck' is the matter out there? 'Sweet Music' is a No. 1 Hit!"

"We got a call to go to Allen Klein's office," Lon Van Eaton said. "Both Pete and Al were there. They were eager to please George. Klein said to us, 'What do you want us to do? We'll do whatever you want.' We didn't know what to say. We asked for more studio time." But as with other Apple artists, the Van Eatons' first album marked the end of their term at the Beatles' record label.

○ ○ ○ ○ ○ Though they had initially believed Allen Klein could save Apple Corps, over time John Lennon, George Harrison, and Ringo Starr became disenchanted with him. By 1973, Lennon took to calling Klein's company "grABKCO." The Beatle trio's unhappiness peaked in a series of meetings in Los Angeles that began in February 1973 with their English lawyers from the London firm Frere Cholmeley. The discussions covered the planned release by Capitol of two Klein-driven greatest-hits packages, *The Beatles – 1962-1966* and *The Beatles – 1967-1970*. These albums were aimed at combating pirated Beatles product hawked on TV. But Lennon — and McCartney — reportedly were uncomfortable with the album projects. A label executive confirmed, "There is a feeling that perhaps Klein exceeded his power with these albums."

While in Los Angeles, John and George played on sessions for the *Ringo* album, the post-Beatles breakup project that came closest to a Beatles reunion. John also contributed the song "I'm the Greatest," George the song "Sunshine Life for Me (Sail Away Raymond)" and compositions he cowrote with Ringo and Beatles confidant Mal Evans. Paul and Linda McCartney wrote and later recorded in England the backing vocals for the track "Six O' Clock."

Lennon, Harrison, and Starr announced on March 31, 1973, that they were terminating their relationship with Allen Klein, which already was one year beyond their original three-year written agreement with him. Lennon used the occasion to praise, rather than damn, McCartney's father-in-law by observing that "due to the presence of Lee Eastman looking over Paul's shoulder all the time — and therefore looking over Klein's shoulder — [Klein's] movements were hampered. We can now be thankful for that situation. We knew it was beneficial all the time playing one off against the other, and eventually we ended up here."

Klein responded to the contract termination by issuing an ABKCO press release that stated it was he who had "severed the remnants of his relationship with the singing group" after his management contract expired "without agreement to continue." The press release claimed "it was not in the best interest of ABKCO" to continue managing Apple Corps and acknowledged this ended Klein's plan for a "possible acquisition" of the Beatles' company, which he hoped might occur by ABKCO purchasing a majority of the Apple Corps' stock from Lennon, Harrison, and Starr.

On June 18, 1973, John Lennon sent his assistant May Pang to begin retrieving Beatles' possessions from Klein. Pang arrived at ABKCO's offices with a letter from John stating, "Enclosed is a copy of your inventory list that you sent to me of materials to be picked up. I am authorizing May Pang to pick up all the items." The list included Beatles and Apple artists' tapes, album and singles artwork, and movie prints such as *Magical Mystery Tour* that Klein had in his possession.

May Pang was already a familiar face at ABKCO when she arrived on her task for Lennon. She worked for Allen Klein's company in 1969 and 1970, and first met John Lennon there in December 1970. In June 1971, Apple Records Inc. hired her, though "I basically worked for John Lennon and Yoko Ono," Pang said.

But Lennon retained a soft spot for Klein. On July 6, 1973, John sent another associate to pick up additional tapes, as well as six of the Bag One lithographs that John had created as a wedding present to Yoko. He typed in the letter brought to ABKCO by this associate about an art item belonging to Klein, "We have been looking for your Glass Hammer piece but haven't found it yet." John cordially wrote by hand at the bottom of the note, "I think it got — will fix and send ya!" He closed the letter by crossing out "Sincerely," jotting in "Love" and, always one for word play, titled himself "President of Apple Records Inc*apacitated!*"

∘ ∘ ∘ ∘ ∘ The 1970 agreement that Allen Klein procured on behalf of Apple for United Artists to distribute the Beatles' *Let It Be* movie required UA to pay his 20 percent commission from Apple Films' receipts directly to ABKCO. But on April 10, 1973, Beatles lawyer Frank Caola from Frere Cholmeley wrote United Artists, "Abkco Industries Inc., no longer has authority to act in any way in relation to the affairs of our clients. . . . [Y]ou should withhold payments and information to Abkco." Klein attacked Caola's correspondence as "a form letter evidently addressed to all persons, firms and corporations with which the US Apple companies had contracts or relations." As proof, Klein cited an identical April 10, 1973, letter Caola sent to Essex Music International Ltd., which held the sub-publishing rights to Apple Music Inc.'s songs.

These letters were intended to cut Klein off from the in-perpetuity commissions Lennon, Harrison, and Starr had promised in their management agreement with him. The ferocious Klein lost no time in firing off a first round of lawsuits against his former Beatles clients. On June 16, 1973, ABKCO filed an action in Los Angeles Superior Court seeking repayment of a $270,350 loan Klein's company claimed to have made to George Harrison. In the trial-level New York Supreme Court in Manhattan, ABKCO sued Apple Films Ltd. and Apple Records Inc. on June 6 and John Lennon on July 6 — the same day that John had his "love" letter delivered to Allen Klein — in both cases also seeking repayments of loans.

John Lennon reacted to these litigations by seeking to delay Klein's attempt to depose him. In the fall of 1973, Lennon was recording a rock 'n' roll oldies project in Los Angeles with Phil Spector. Lennon's lawyer claimed the studio sessions involved "the usual and some unusual artistic pressures," and that "any interruption of [John's] professional work for an extended deposition would severely hamper his progress on the album." However, sitting for depositions soon became almost a second job for John Lennon. In January 1974, for example, he was deposed for four days in a row in the New York suit ABKCO filed against Apple Records.

Meanwhile, on November 1, 1973, Lennon, Harrison, and Starr sued ABKCO and Allen Klein in the London High Court of Justice. The English case charged Klein with financial mismanagement and breach of his fiduciary obligation to the Beatles and their companies. The suit even alleged that ABKCO ordered Capitol Records to manufacture excessive copies of the *Let It Be* album, then took commissions from the amount pressed, rather than copies sold.

Klein insisted the English suit was meant "to jump the gun" on yet another action he was about to file in New York state court. This one was a massive complaint that asked for tens of millions of dollars in damages. The suit was brought against all four Beatles, their affiliated English and American companies, Yoko Ono (in part over commissions allegedly owed ABKCO from the music-publishing management agreement she signed with Klein's company in January 1970), and Lennon, Harrison, and Starr's lawyers. The November 8, 1973, filing dug deep and contained a whopping forty-two causes of action. The complaint sought past and future management commissions as well as expense reimbursements. Klein even cited $20,000 he said George Harrison had promised to repay him for a loan ABKCO made to Al Aronowitz, the music journalist who first introduced the Beatles to Bob Dylan, during their 1964 US summer tour.

As a payback for being skewered in Paul McCartney's partnership dissolution proceeding, Klein's latest suit included the errant Beatle as a defendant on a $34-million count, when punitive damages were thrown in, that alleged McCartney conspired with the other defendants to "maliciously, wrongfully, fraudulently, intentionally" block payment of Klein's commissions.

In all, these lawsuits demonstrated the vast reach of Allen Klein's relationship with the Beatles. The litany of allegations set out in the suits that Klein filed seemed to be any he and his lawyers could come up with that might stick against his former management clients and their companies. But Klein said that, for him, such lawsuits were simply "tools of the trade."

○ ○ ○ ○ ○ Under the Beatles' 1967 intra-band agreement, 80 percent of the Beatles' income was supposed to go into Apple Corps. But a major responsibility of the court-appointed receiver in McCartney's dissolution action was to question and even refuse to pay the Beatles' personal expenses. "To tell the truth, there's a whole lot of money that's been held in receivership since Paul McCartney sued us," George Harrison said. "Actually, it's fortunate that he did sue us, because while the money is in receivership nobody can spend it." As a result, Klein claimed, Lennon, Harrison, and Starr approached him asking for interest-free loans. "And then they would not have to send their bills to the receiver and worry whether or not he would okay their payment," Klein said. "What was agreed was, after looking at what their monthly expenditures had been over the last two or three years, that ABKCO would put up one year's — you know, I think that is how we arrived at the £36,000: the amount of their living expenses."

The first loan amounts were the relatively modest £13,666 for each of the three artists. But the loan Klein made to Ringo came with a potentially large liability. In advancing the funds, Klein got Ringo to acknowledge in writing that the money could be treated "as a payment against the sale of any part" of Starr's interests in Apple to ABKCO. This was part of a plan Klein had to one day buy Apple Corps and merge it with his company.

Harrison and Starr later pleaded, however, that they lacked the business acumen to deal with Allen Klein on a level playing field. George said, "I have never had any business training. I am generally ignorant of accounting and business practice and have never considered myself a businessman." Ringo claimed he "never took part in negotiating" any Beatles companies' contracts. As for Starr's Startling Music publishing company, he noted Klein "states that I made all the 'major decisions.' I do not know what he means by 'major decisions.'"

John Lennon simply admitted Klein's lawsuits campaign had become so thick, "Which one of them is which is indistinguishable to me."

○ ○ ○ ○ ○ When the legal battle with Klein began, John Lennon was living in New York City, at the Dakota apartment building on Central Park West, and maintained an office at ATV Music's Manhattan business quarters. "They let me have a little corner," he said of the modest office digs. But Paul McCartney, George Harrison, and Ringo Starr argued the New York courts lacked personal jurisdiction over them, because they were UK residents.

In McCartney's motion to be dismissed from Klein's suit, John Eastman argued the case allegations "involve essentially the same parties and the same issues" as Paul's December 1970 and the Lennon plaintiffs' November 1973 suits in England. Eastman said McCartney was an "infrequent visitor to America. He recently made a three day Christmas visit to visit his wife's family during which period he was served in this action. Except for this visit McCartney has not been to America for the last two years." John

Eastman went so far as to describe his brother-in-law Paul as "a stranger to the entire situation between Lennon, Harrison and Starkey [i.e., Ringo Starr] and ABKCO and Klein."

For their part, both George and Ringo claimed they had been in New York only a few times while Klein was their manager. According to George, for example, "I was in New York three times in 1970, mainly to promote my album 'All Things Must Pass'; twice in 1971 and once in 1972 about the [Harrison charity] Concert for Bangla Desh and the film and album of the Concert; once in 1972 to visit John Lennon; and once in 1975 for a deposition in a copyright infringement suit [i.e., the case brought against George over the song 'My Sweet Lord']." George added about a 1969 drug conviction in England for his possessing hashish, "I might be unable to come to the United States to appear as a witness there, because the United States authorities require me to apply for a visa each time I wish to enter the United States and they have not always been willing to grant me a visa."

Apple, however, used New York accountants and entered into "mechanical licenses" there for uses of Apple songs on sound recordings. ABKCO emphasized that though Allen Klein's management arrangements with Apple had been negotiated in England, "the great majority of all Beatles companies revenues originated in [the United States], the management agreements were performed in this Country and specifically in New York where ABKCO maintained its principal place of business."

New York Supreme Court justice Jacob Markowitz agreed with Klein. In denying Harrison and Starr's motions to dismiss, the mild-mannered Markowitz (known, however, for expressive prose) wrote in a December 1975 decision that Starr for one, "pervasively, unmistakably, undeniably, continuously and substantially conducted business in New York." The state judge additionally denied McCartney's severance bid.

The Beatles appealed to the New York Appellate Division. In June 1976, that court affirmed Justice Markowitz's jurisdictional ruling as to George Harrison and Ringo Starr. In discussing Starr, the appellate court oddly cited the least-songwriting Beatle's "composing activities, which he has exploited in the United States through attorneys and accountants whom he has retained in New York on a continuing basis." But as to Klein's conspiracy claim against Paul McCartney, "Exactly what those acts are cannot be discerned," the appellate judges wrote in letting McCartney out of the case.

The appellate ruling in effect recognized the historic division that McCartney had drawn between himself and Klein in Paul's own lawsuit against the other Beatles. Now it was Paul who was free of the Klein's litigation clutches in the United States, while Allen's earlier Beatles allies Lennon, Harrison, and Starr were pulled deeper into the mushrooming legal quagmire that Klein was laying out for them in New York court.

10 · To "Bleed" ABKCO

As Allen Klein fought to secure his claims against the Beatles in New York, John Lennon, George Harrison, and Ringo Starr shifted their English suit against him into high gear. To force Klein to divide his legal and financial resources between two active fronts, in December 1973 the Lennon bloc retaliated against Klein's growing US litigation offensive by increasing the number of plaintiffs in their English writ to thirty-two. These now included Yoko Ono, a defendant in ABKCO's litigation offensive in New York, as well as a Who's Who of Beatles-related entities.

They also submitted a statement of claim to the court further detailing their allegations against Klein and ABKCO. In it the plaintiffs aired a long list of grievances. These included that he allegedly advised the Beatles to borrow funds from their companies "without regard to money available for this purpose," took excessive management commissions, incurred excessive expenses, failed to lower the Beatles' tax liability and blocked the artists' attempts at auditing ABKCO's financial books.

The court statement also alleged Klein should have made sure Lennon, Harrison, and Starr retained "adequate independent legal advice" before they signed the May 8, 1969, management contract with ABKCO that gave Klein's company a perpetual entitlement to commissions from the Beatles. The artists said the letter agreement was instead explained to them by attorney Peter Howard from Joynson-Hicks & Co., "solicitors who were then acting and had previously acted for" Klein and ABKCO in legal matters.

Klein's former management clients went on to claim Klein falsely misrepresented to them the economic value of the September 1, 1969, and October 1, 1969, recording agreements with Capitol and EMI. In any case, Lennon, Harrison, and Starr insisted they never ratified the Klein agreements at issue (an opposite position from the one they took in the receivership proceeding brought by McCartney).

ABKCO had in fact pressed for a more detailed management contract. After he joined Apple, Peter Howard wrote his former employer Joynson-Hicks & Co. in December 1969 that Allen Klein was "becoming most anxious that a comprehensive agreement be drawn up to cover the many things that are left uncovered" by the May 8, 1969, contract. Though Klein had derided Brian Epstein's managing of the Beatles, Howard wrote to ABKCO's English lawyers "that one might use as a base for the new agreement, the Brian Epstein agreement which everybody seems to think was very fair."

On January 28, 1970 — with Howard present — George Harrison and Ringo Starr had convened an Apple board-of-directors meeting at 3 Savile Row. The meeting minutes cited the two Beatles as constituting a voting quorum. (Absentee John Lennon was the third board member. Paul McCartney refused to participate on Apple's board during Klein's reign.) "After a thorough review," according to the Howard-drafted minutes, Harrison and Starr did approve the new 1969 recording agreements with Capitol and EMI. Then "after a full and complete discussion," the two board members approved a letter of direction authorizing Capitol and EMI to pay Klein's Apple management commissions directly to ABKCO. They also agreed to make ABKCO the exclusive representative for George's Harrisongs and Ringo's Startling music-publishing companies.

○ ○ ○ ○ ○ In the US litigations, Lennon, Harrison, and Starr now tried to separate Allen Klein from his chief counsel, Rosenman Colin, which had also represented members of the Beatles in several litigations. George Harrison said he was "afraid" that the Apple parties' close relationship with Rosenman Colin may have resulted in the law firm using "confidential information concerning the defendants in the present litigation brought by Abkco against us." Most importantly, a disqualification would require Klein to find new lawyers who wouldn't have the depth of legal experience that Rosenman Colin had with him.

Rosenman Colin was a top-line Madison Avenue law firm whose co-founder Sam Rosenman had counseled Presidents Franklin Roosevelt and Harry Truman. Ralph Colin represented CBS broadcasting chief William Paley. The firm had been the training ground for future CBS Records presidents Clive Davis and Walter Yetnikoff, and handled legal matters for Allen Klein's companies before he managed the Beatles.

Max Freund was Allen Klein's primary lawyer at the firm. Attorney L. Peter Parcher, who represented Northern Songs in songwriting suits against John Lennon and Yoko Ono, recalled Freund was "brilliant. He worked 14 hours a day. He was imperious, fiercely supportive of his clients. A difficult, dangerous adversary."

George Harrison claimed when Klein became the Beatles' manager, he "said that we had never had independent lawyers and that we should have them. I do not know how the firm of [Rosenman Colin] was selected for us but it was later that I learnt that the firm also represented Abkco and Klein."

But a few days after the Beatles fired Klein, Max Freund had sent a letter to John Lennon stating that, because ABKCO retained Rosenman Colin to litigate its disputes with the Beatles, the firm would no longer defend Apple Records, Inc., in a suit that alleged the Lennon song "Come Together" infringed on the copyright for a Chuck Berry song. According to John, "I received similar letters in April 1973 from Mr. Freund relating to his firm's representation of Apple Records and others in a so-called [Beatles albums and tapes] piracy case, in a copyright infringement action relating to George Harrison's song 'Something' [Lennon was probably referring to 'My Sweet Lord'] and in relation to the Concert for Bangla Desh and the related record album and film."

For their court fights with Klein, Lennon, Harrison, and Starr retained new US counsel, Cleary, Gottlieb, Steen & Hamilton, which was founded in New York and Washington, DC, in 1946 and maintained a notable international law practice. The three Beatles then moved to have Rosenman Colin disqualified from representing Klein in the New York litigations, on conflict-of-interest grounds. Law-firm clients may sometimes sign written waivers of attorney conflicts of interest, but John Lennon complained, "I don't recall ever being told, or receiving any correspondence informing me, that if any conflict developed between the Beatles and the Beatles/Apple companies and Abkco, Rosenman would withdraw from representing us and might continue representing Abkco."

But Max Freund argued the disqualification motion was meant "to make it as expensive as possible for ABKCO to litigate." Allen Klein claimed that John Lennon, who often made provocative statements that weren't in his best interests, had told Klein in May 1974 that his lawyers' strategy was to "'bleed' ABKCO."

But though Klein's lawsuits against Lennon, Harrison, and Starr grew out of his management of the Beatles business affairs, both trial court justice Jacob Markowitz and the New York Appellate Division denied the disqualification bid. "While plaintiff's counsel represented the Beatles in the past, such prior representation does not impinge on the Beatles' interests herein," the appellate court wrote. The court added that, despite the extensive legal services rendered by Rosenman Colin on the Beatles' behalf, "No confidential information was imparted to counsel during the prior representation of the Beatles and there is no substantial relationship between the prior representation and these lawsuits."

∘ ∘ ∘ ∘ ∘ Allen Klein had wasted no time while the Beatles' disqualification offensive played out. In the interim, ABKCO filed a fresh round of complaints in New York state court against Lennon, Harrison, Starr, and their companies. In one suit, seeking management commissions and loan repayments, Klein included Subafilms and Harrison and Starr's individual music-publishing companies as defendants. ABKCO also filed the fourth suit to name John Lennon as a defendant. This one, filed in March 1974, claimed Lennon owed Klein a 20 percent commission from the sale of Lennon's Northern Songs shares to ATV in 1969. Klein demanded at least $900,000, plus interest.

The ever-expanding Klein/Beatles court calendar came at a high cost to both sides. Lennon's Cleary Gottlieb counsel Richard Hulbert calculated that, in one nine-month period beginning in July 1974, there were fifty-four days of depositions, a two-day hearing on jurisdictional issues, an additional twenty-two-day hearing in which Lennon testified for a full day, two case appeals and a variety of motions proceedings. "Simply as a matter of arithmetic," Hulbert determined, "a deposition or a hearing has occurred on approximately every other business day for the past nine months in this avalanche of litigation." Hulbert blamed this on Allen Klein's "piecemeal litigation strategy" that was intended to cause the defendants "maximum harassment and expense."

Klein's legal costs were huge, too. In 1976, he said that, during the prior fiscal year, ABKCO, which claimed a net worth of $4.7 million, had spent more than $800,000 in litigating the Beatles suits. This prompted an Apple

Records attorney to taunt Klein, "[I]s it not true that $4,158,281 of the net worth of ABKCO is in claims to rights from the Beatles?"

∘ ∘ ∘ ∘ ∘ Serious talks to settle Paul McCartney's partnership-dissolution suit against the other Beatles had begun not long after Lennon, Harrison, and Starr fired Allen Klein in 1973. The final agreement, reached by them in December 1974, provided that from October 1, 1974, forward all solo recordings and related income belonged to the individual Beatles.

McCartney's action officially drew to a close on January 9, 1975, when the London High Court of Justice confirmed the Beatles & Co.'s dissolution settlement. This included a transfer of £3 million from the about-to-be-discharged receivership to Apple Corps. "It's very hard," Ringo said about Paul's partnership case. "You sign a piece of paper in two minutes and it takes you 7 years to get out of it."

It then took until January 1977 for Lennon, Harrison, and Starr's London trial against Allen Klein to be set to begin. "It's going to be awful . . . a fiasco and a nightmare, because it's going to be open to the public and the press," George Harrison said. "I've got to put my body there, and I'll be sitting [in the courtroom], but really I'll be somewhere else." But the trial George feared never took place. Just a few days before, the parties managed to reach a global settlement that voluntarily discontinued all their pending Klein-related litigations. (Both Lennon and Harrison had already settled, for $135,000 and $281,000, respectively, the loan suits Klein filed against them individually.)

The settlement-papers signing took place at the Plaza Hotel, which was the Beatles' headquarters during their manic February 1964 arrival in America. Photographer Bob Gruen said John Lennon phoned him in the middle of the night to hurry over to the Plaza to capture the Klein settlement on camera. "When I arrived, there was an entire floor of lawyers and secretaries," Gruen recalled. And despite the time-drain, costs, and tensions of battling Klein, "On one level, John was amused by the intensity of the negotiations," Gruen said. "He told me that the original agreement between Klein and the Beatles had been two or three paragraphs on a single piece of paper. Now it was going to take an eighty-seven-page document to dissolve."

Under settlement terms, Apple Corps paid Allen Klein $4.2 million. At a press conference later at ABKCO, it was Yoko Ono who Klein praised for "Kissinger-like negotiating brilliance" in getting the deal done. "[I]t would never, never have happened if Yoko had not been there to calm us all down and be a total diplomat when the going got hot and tough," Klein effused.

But Linda McCartney griped, "It wasn't her money, really." In fact, to the dismay of Paul McCartney, who wasn't involved in the settlement talks, he was now liable to Klein for a quarter of the $4.2 million, through Paul's 25 percent ownership interest in Apple Corps.

But the publicly bubbly Paul later boasted it was his December 1970 suit in England against the other three Beatles that was the real catalyst for ultimately ridding Apple Corps of Klein. "I single-handedly saved the Beatle empire!" Paul exclaimed. "Ha! Ha!"

PART THREE

NOWHERE MAN

11 "In a Secret Vault"

O n April 25, 1972, immigration lawyer Leon Wildes went to the US Immigration and Naturalization Service's district office in New York City to see the agency's files on his clients, John Lennon and Yoko Ono. The INS, overseen by the US Department of Justice, had begun deportation proceedings against the married couple for overstaying their US visas. Wildes responded by filing applications to defer the proceedings while the Lennons sought permanent residence in the United States.

Now Wildes wanted to see all the materials the INS had on the Lennons. But moments before an INS attorney handed Wildes the Lennon case documents, "I saw him removing substantial portions of the files," Wildes said.

An hour later, when the deferral applications the Lennons' attorney had sent the INS nearly two months before were handed back to Wildes, they were still in their original, sealed envelopes, untouched and unprocessed, "in exactly the same condition in which I had filed them."

Twice before, Wildes had gone to the INS unit responsible for processing such "third-preference" petitions, which, if granted, would allow the Lennons to stay in the United States temporarily as outstanding artists of "exceptional ability." But each time Wildes was told "no one was aware" the petitions existed. That may have been because, according to Wildes, the Lennons' applications were "kept in a secret vault."

In trying to deport the Lennons, the INS relied on a guilty plea John entered in a London court in 1968 for possessing a small amount of "cannabis resin." But from the outset, the Lennons believed there was another motive. The "fact that we may have expressed views which differ from those of some government officials, may have influenced" the INS district director's "haste in deporting us, and his complete failure to act as required by law in adjudicating our applications." John and Yoko publicly and virulently opposed the Vietnam War and the reelection of US president Richard Nixon.

But John insisted he wouldn't leave the United States until he and Yoko gained custody of her daughter Kyoko from a prior marriage.

This was just the start of a four-year battle John Lennon would wage, with Leon Wildes at his side, through a frustrating labyrinth of us administrative and court levels. The case became the most notable immigration fight of its era involving a musician — and the most famous involving an entertainer since filmmaker/comedian Charlie Chaplin had been barred from reentering the United States in 1952, during the Cold War "red scare" era, for voicing support for a German composer alleged to be a Communist. The Lennon case, which involved federal surveillance of the artist, may seem less shocking in today's terrorist-obsessed world where the federal government collects massive amounts of digital data on most individuals. But it still rings loudly as a cautionary tale of free speech versus political repression of artists, as well as one that had a significant impact on federal guidelines for immigrant entries.

⚬ ⚬ ⚬ ⚬ ⚬ In 1968, Detective-Sergeant Norman Pilcher, from Scotland Yard's Drug Enforcement Squad, was a notorious figure to rock music's elite. Pilcher had promised to rid England of musicians who he claimed were corrupting the country's youth. Most famously, he had led a 1967 drug bust (later overturned) of the Rolling Stones' Mick Jagger and Keith Richards at Redlands, Richards' country home in England. In other cases, Pilcher arrested folk-rock singer Donovan and Stones' cofounder Brian Jones.

On the morning of October 18, 1968, Sergeant Pilcher knocked on the door of John Lennon and Yoko Ono's ground-floor London flat, where John was resting from finishing the lengthy studio sessions for the double album *The Beatles*. John was also in the middle of a divorce from his first wife, Cynthia. After journalist Don Short told John that the Beatle was targeted for a drug bust, John tried to clear any illegal substances from the Montagu Square apartment that he and the pregnant Yoko were renting from Ringo Starr. But once inside the flat, Pilcher's team of officers and drug-sniffing canines claimed they found several grams of hashish in a binocular holder on the apartment's mantelpiece and some more in an envelope.

"If I say that it's mine, will you leave her alone?" John Lennon pleaded to Pilcher, who replied yes. The Scotland Yard officials then brought John and Yoko to the local police station where they both were nevertheless charged with unauthorized possession under the Dangerous Drugs Act, and with willful obstruction for at first refusing to let the officers enter the premises. John and Yoko were then released on bail.

John claimed the arrests were a setup, that Pilcher was nothing more than "a headhunter." By the day of their November 28 hearing before a judge at Marylebone Magistrate's Court, Yoko had lost the couple's unborn child. "The impact of the proceedings needless to say added to her burdens," defense lawyer Martin Polden said. But Polden claimed John had "a good defence" based on the way Pilcher and his officers conducted their search, though "it would be essential" to have Ono testify. Polden decided "the only course open that would obviate the need for her appearance as a witness would be for" John to plead guilty.

A pale John Lennon took the rap at the twenty-minute hearing in the magistrate's court by pleading guilty to possession of 14.20 grams of cannabis resin; the other charges were dropped, including those against Yoko Ono. John was fined £150.

The next day, he and Yoko released their first album together, the controversial *Unfinished Music No. 1 — Two Virgins*, which featured nude photos of the couple on the front and back covers. A lawyer they had consulted prior to the album release told them about the photos, "If you want to end up in prison, go ahead."

John Lennon wasn't the last Beatle that Sergeant Pilcher arrested. On March 12, 1969, the day that Paul McCartney married Linda Eastman, Pilcher and his team raided George and Pattie Harrison's house in Esher. "Look what Yogi, our dog, has found!" Pilcher said holding up a brick of hash.

"Are you mad? You brought that with you," swore Pattie, who said the Harrisons were framed, too.

"The police were obviously excited to meet" George, Pattie recalled. "They stood to attention and were almost elbowing each other out of the way to get closer to him while Sergeant Pilcher went into his, 'I am arresting you . . .' bit."

The Harrisons were charged with hashish possession. Martin Polden represented them, too, in this case in a court proceeding that resulted in a £500 fine and made it difficult for the Harrisons to enter the United States. Pattie said that each time she went to America, "I had to go through rigorous tests and examinations." She described these experiences as "most humiliating, I had to sit in the narcotics lounge with all the other drug offenders when I arrived in America."

○ ○ ○ ○ ○ John Lennon and Yoko Ono first met in 1966, in London, when the Beatles' music was entering its experimental phase. John had stopped by the Indica Bookstore and Gallery to see a Yoko Ono conceptual art exhibition the shop was hosting. Beatles manager Brian Epstein had already seen Yoko's work at an Edinburgh art show. "I'm not sure I understand someone who sits inside a bag onstage and does nothing at all for a long time, but then, I didn't stay long. Two or three minutes perhaps," Epstein said about Ono's performance. Epstein, however, asked her to appear at London's Saville Theatre, where he was producing shows. Paul McCartney also knew Yoko, from when she had approached him for art funding and for Beatles song manuscripts. "She's very pushy," Paul said. "She keeps making demands as if she has a right."

Yoko Ono was born in Tokyo, Japan, on February 18, 1933, and for thirteen years attended the local Gakushuin Peers School, which her official biography described as "the elite school attended by Japan's finest families including the children of the Imperial Emperor." During World War II, the Ono family fled Tokyo for the Japanese countryside. Yoko's father, a successful banker, moved his family to New York in the early 1950s to serve as president of the Bank of Tokyo.

Yoko began studying music composition at Sarah Lawrence College in 1954 but left in 1956 to pursue a career in avant-garde arts. She explained her first creative works — in music, painting, poetry, and "Object" — as "being based on 'Event,' an Art Form." The Chambers Street loft concerts she initiated in 1959 attracted such notable musical and visual artists as John Cage, Marcel Duchamp, Jasper Johns, Robert Rauschenberg, and Andy Warhol. Two of Ono's "operas" premiered at Carnegie Hall. She also compiled an anthology, *Grapefruit: A Book of Instructions and Drawings*, and made a series of short films screened at universities. Her concept performances included "Cut Piece," in which audience members participated by scissoring off Yoko's clothes bit by bit.

John Lennon and Yoko Ono's relationship got off to a slow start, but by 1968 they were inseparable. They married in Gibraltar on March 20, 1969, and moved to a seventy-two-acre Tittenhurst Park estate outside London. In April 1970, the Lennons traveled to Los Angeles to participate in sessions with primal therapy guru Arthur Janov. In June 1971, they performed on stage with Frank Zappa and the Mothers of Invention at the Fillmore East in New York City. John and Yoko also made trips to the United States to pursue custody of Yoko's daughter Kyoko from a prior marriage to filmmaker Tony Cox. For each US visit, the US immigration authorities granted John Lennon a waiver from his 1968 drug conviction.

On one trip, the Lennons arrived in New York City on August 13, 1971. John stated in his "B-2" visa application that the purpose of this visit was to "edit film and consult with business associates at ABKCO Industries" regarding the September 1971 release of John's *Imagine* album (which contained the anti–Vietnam War song "Gimme Some Truth") as well as "to attend custody hearing in St. Thomas, Virgin Islands on September 16, 1971." The INS subsequently gave John and Yoko several visa extensions for this trip, for the ongoing Kyoko custody matter and to let the couple co-host the *Mike Douglas Show* talk/variety TV program for a week in February 1972.

Upon their August 1971 US arrival, John and Yoko immediately launched into a flurry of public activities. In Syracuse, New York, for an Ono exhibit at Everson Museum of Art, the Lennons attended a protest by members of the Onondaga Native American tribe over government seizure of tribal land to build a highway. John and Yoko also struck up friendships with radical-left youth spokespersons Jerry Rubin and Abbie Hoffman, and Black Panther Party cofounders and leaders Huey Newton and Bobby Seale. The Lennons often hosted their activist friends at the apartment John and Yoko rented from former Lovin' Spoonful drummer Joe Butler, at 105 Bank Street in Greenwich Village.

On December 10, 1971, John played a benefit in Ann Arbor, Michigan, in support of White Panthers leader John Sinclair, who was in jail on a ten-year sentence for handing two marijuana cigarettes to an undercover officer. It was John Lennon's first concert performance in the United States since the Beatles' 1966 summer tour. Several days after the Ann Arbor rally, the Michigan Supreme Court ordered Sinclair's release.

The next weekend, John and Yoko appeared at a benefit at the Apollo Theater in Harlem, for families of inmates incarcerated upstate in the Attica Correctional Facility, where thirty-two prisoners and ten guards had been killed in a recent uprising. During the Apollo event, John sang an acoustic version of "Imagine." In January 1972, he and Yoko performed the songs "John Sinclair" and "Attica State" on the nationally televised *David Frost Show*, where they were accompanied by David Peel and the Lower East Side, for whom John produced the album *The Pope Smokes Dope*.

John Lennon and Yoko Ono Lennon were involved in political and social causes in the United Kingdom, too. Shortly before traveling to the United States in August 1971, they demonstrated against British actions in Northern Ireland and to support the London alternative press magazine *OZ* after a trial in which its editors were sentenced to jail for obscenity (but acquitted on appeal).

John Lennon earlier claimed to be politically apathetic. A 1965 profile in *Current Biography* quoted him as saying that when he was a student at the Liverpool College of Art in the 1950s, "I got myself voted into the students' union just to get rock played." He added about public officials, "I haven't got time for politicians. I've never even bothered to vote."

But when the Beatles arrived in San Francisco in August 1964 for the beginning of their first major North American tour, Larry Kane, the news director of WFUN radio in Miami, Florida, who was traveling with the band, "asked Lennon about the [then-]undeclared war in Vietnam. It was a strange question to ask, and it caught him by surprise. His face lit up, and he launched a scathing diatribe against the *Gulf of Tonkin Resolution* [in which the US Congress formally authorized the use of military force in Southeast Asia] and the escalating conflict. I was taken aback by the intensity of his anger and knowledge base, and also by the eloquence of his protest," said Kane.

○ ○ ○ ○ ○ John's political activism quickly drew the attention of federal officials. After the John Sinclair benefit concert, FBI director J. Edgar Hoover notified the bureau's Los Angeles, New York, San Diego, and Washington, DC, offices to follow and document John Lennon's activities. Meanwhile, in early 1972, US Senate Internal Security Subcommittee staff members prepared a memorandum that concluded Lennon would participate in and help finance a huge demonstration at the 1972 Republican National Convention. (Lennon later publicly announced in advance of the convention that he had no plans to be there.)

This wasn't the first time the US government documented Beatles-related events. The FBI had begun compiling files on the Beatles in early 1964. One consisted of a newspaper clipping from a nationally syndicated column on labor issues written by Victor Riesel. In his article, Riesel discussed American Federation of Musicians (AFM) concerns that Beatles shows in the United States would take work away from AFM members. Riesel quoted AFM president Herman Kenin as saying, "Of course, we have a cultural exchange with other countries, but this is not culture. If [the Beatles] do get back in the country, they're going to have to leave their instruments at home, because there are enough musicians in the US and too many of them are unemployed." Riesel and the AFM president couldn't imagine the enormous impact the Beatles and their British Invasion contemporaries like the Rolling Stones, the Who, the Kinks, the Animals, and the Yardbirds would have in inspiring large numbers of American youth to not only pick up guitars, but to flood clubs and concert halls to quench their newly found thirst for live music.

Near the start of the Beatles' 1964 North American summer tour, the FBI clipped and filed an August 9, 1964, *Los Angeles Times* article by Art Berman titled, "Beatles' Visit Posing Top Security Problem." With the band scheduled to play the Hollywood Bowl on August 23, Berman noted, "Only last month a lesser-known British rock-and-roll group, Peter and Gordon [who had hits with Paul McCartney compositions], set off near-riots with personal appearances in Riverside and San Diego. In San Diego one girl was hospitalized and 85 youths were arrested." The article reminded readers about the Beatles' pandemonium on arrival at JFK Airport in New York City in February 1964, that "the crush of 4,000 screaming fans cracked the ribs of three policemen in perhaps the wildest airport reception ever seen there. Los Angeles International Airport officials, anxious to avoid a repetition of the New York scene, insist that the jet carrying the Beatles will not land at 'LAX.'"

But the summer of 1964 was already a powder keg of social change in the United States. Congress's Gulf of Tonkin Resolution on Vietnam in August had been preceded in July by President Lyndon Johnson's signing of the Civil Rights Act of 1964, the pioneer landmark legislation that outlawed ethnic, racial, religious, and sexual discrimination. On August 4, the bodies of civil rights freedom riders James Chaney, Andrew Goodman, and Michael Schwerner — murdered by the Ku Klux Klan — were found in Mississippi. On August 27, the office of a newspaper run by Pulitzer Prize recipient and anti-segregation advocate Hazel Brennon Smith was bombed in Jackson, Mississippi.

This violent backdrop made the FBI concerned about the potential for race riots at the Beatles' concerts. The band's tour opened on August 19 at the Cow Palace in San Francisco. The Republican National Convention in July had been the last major event at the venue. An August 19 FBI memo generated in the agency's Washington, DC, headquarters noted both the San Francisco and Los Angeles divisions had been "alerted to the fact that the thousands of teenagers gathering for the appearances of 'The Beatles' . . . could be a perfect vehicle for riots if racial elements or organization, subversive or otherwise, . . . capitalize on the emotional pitch of crowds of teenagers."

The local *San Mateo Times* newspaper did report after the August 19 Cow Palace show, "Oldtimers around the Cow Palace called it the wildest night in the history of the huge arena. Nothing at the Republican convention, or even the winning of the hockey championship two seasons back, could remotely compare with the pandemonium which greeted last night's visit by the four boys from Liverpool." But only two criminal citations were issued, one for drunkenness and the other for possession of a switchblade. (Though the Beatles' audiences were primarily white, to promote racial integration and civil rights, the Beatles insisted on a contract clause for their 1965 Cow Palace performance and other shows that stated, "Artists will not be required to perform in front of a segregated audience.")

In Kansas City, the FBI monitored the Beatles' September 17 performance at Municipal Stadium. Charles O. Finley, the owner of the Kansas City Athletics baseball team (which he moved to Oakland, California at the end of the 1967 season), paid the Beatles $150,000, reportedly the highest artist fee ever for one concert, though only half of the 41,000 tickets sold. A September 3 FBI field office memo claimed that, because the stadium was "located in a Negro residential neighborhood, the possibility of Negro involvement in any spontaneous action is recognized and Police Department plans cover this possibility."

Local authorities assigned 350 officers to cover the Municipal Stadium grounds. But the police received no specific information prior to the event about racial violence and the concert was peaceful. According to a September 18 FBI field-office memo, the police had only heard rumors "suggesting that one or two Muslims or ex-Muslims, unidentified, were overheard to say 'some trouble might occur'" at the stadium but "that these rumors were disconnected, were untrue and no credence should be given to them."

⁰ ⁰ ⁰ ⁰ ⁰ During the Beatles' second US summer tour, they paid a historic visit to Elvis Presley, on August 27, 1965, at his home in Beverly Hills, California. "It was one of the great meetings of my life," Paul McCartney gushed. The band worshipped Presley's musical influence, but subsequently discovered he tried to have them thrown out of the United States. Ringo Starr recalled, "The saddest part is that, years and years later, we found out that he tried to have us banished from America, because he was very big with the FBI. That's very sad to me, that he felt so threatened that he thought, like a lot of people, that we were bad for American Youth." "I've seen those famous Nixon transcripts," said McCartney, in which Elvis told President Nixon "'Well, sir, these Beatles: they're very un-American and they take drugs.'"

Nixon deputy counsel Bud Krogh recalled about the December 21, 1970, White House meeting between Presley and Nixon, "The President then indicated that those who use drugs are also in the vanguard of the anti-American protest. Violence, drug usage, dissent, protest all seem to merge in generally the same group of young people."

Of course, the drug-addled Presley, who was often so stoned on a mixture of uppers and downers that he was barely coherent, was proof that drug use and social dissent didn't always go hand in hand. But the president appreciated Presley's support. The Nixon administration soon became knee-deep in an effort to weed out radical musicians — principally John Lennon — who might challenge the president's escalation of America's war in Vietnam.

12 · "Get the Hell Out of the Country"

The US government's campaign to formally force John Lennon out of the country began in earnest in February 1972. On February 4, US senator Strom Thurmond, a conservative Republican from South Carolina, wrote US attorney general John Mitchell that "many headaches might be avoided if appropriate action be taken in time." Thurmond's letter echoed the Senate Security Subcommittee memo that discussed a proposed tour by Lennon and his activist allies to motivate young people — including newly enfranchised eighteen- to twenty-one-year-old voters — to vote against reelecting President Nixon. The subcommittee memo stated, "If Lennon's visa is terminated it would be a strategic counter-measure."

The US government moved quickly against John Lennon. On February 14, US deputy attorney general Richard Kleindienst wrote Immigration and Naturalization Service commissioner Raymond Farrell wondering whether Lennon could indeed be kept out of the country. On March 1, INS New York District director Sol Marks sent a notice to the Lennons' Bank Street apartment in Greenwich Village stating that their visas had expired and that they should voluntarily leave the United States by March 15. "Failure to do so will result in the institution of deportation proceedings," Marks's letter warned.

John Lennon had been denied access to the United States before. In May 1969, immigration officials cited his London drug bust in canceling a visa they had granted him as he and Yoko sought to spread their idealistic campaign for world peace and nonviolence. This was especially irritating to Lennon because Sergeant Pilcher's other bustees Mick Jagger and Keith Richards had received US visas (though they were questioned and searched upon US entry) only a few months after their arrests. John and Yoko instead held a public bed-in at a hotel in Montreal, Canada, during which they re-corded John's "Give Peace a Chance" anthem in their hotel suite.

During the bed-in, John chided, "In the U.S., the Government is too busy talking about how to keep me out. If I'm a joke, as they say, and not important, why don't they just let me in?"

○ ○ ○ ○ ○ John and Yoko first met immigration lawyer Leon Wildes when he was brought over to the couple's Bank Street residence by Allen Klein and Klein's lawyer Alan Kahn. "He's not a radical lawyer, he's not a William Kunstler, nothing like that," John said about the tall, trim Wildes. "We went to an immigration lawyer who knew about immigration."

Leon Wildes already knew INS district director Sol Marks when the Lennons' case came up. Wildes, a past president of the American Immigration Lawyers Association, had given Marks a personal reference when Marks sought the district director position at the INS. Wildes recalled that when he contacted him about the Lennons, Marks said, "Because it's you, Leon, I'm going to give them extra time. Then I want them to get the hell out of the country."

Marks was a lifelong bureaucrat who served as INS deputy district director from 1956 until he was promoted to the district directorship by US attorney general John Mitchell in April 1971. Marks had recently overseen the deportation of notorious "Happy Hooker" Xaviera Hollander, but granted an indefinite stay of deportation to mob boss Carlo Gambino, who lay in critical condition in a city hospital after purportedly suffering a heart attack. (Gambino lived in the United States until October 1976, when he died peacefully at his Brooklyn home while watching a New York Yankees baseball game on TV.)

Leon Wildes filed "third-preference" petitions dated March 2, 1972, asking the INS to allow the Lennons to temporarily stay in the country as artists of "exceptional ability," who would "substantially benefit prospectively the national economy, cultural interests or welfare of the United States." Wildes wrote, by way of example, that revenues from the sale of Beatles records "had impressive economic implications for England, where they were thought to have made a major contribution to Britain's balance of payments." (Wildes submitted figures that calculated retail sales figures for the band's singles, albums and tapes, from the band's start through September 30, 1971, were $220 million and $4.5 million for John Lennon recordings.)

In their INS petitions, both John and Yoko checked boxes indicating they

were seeking permanent US residence. At the time, they had begun recording their *Some Time in New York City* album, which was released on June
12, 1972, and prominently featured the couple's political songs. "Perhaps
no other living artist has contributed in a greater degree, both qualitatively
and quantitatively, to the culture of his generation than has John Lennon,"
Leon Wildes wrote the immigration authorities. The Nixon administration
no doubt saw it differently: the cover of *Some Time in New York City* featured a mock-up photo of President Nixon and Chinese chairman Mao
Zedong dancing together naked.

○ ○ ○ ○ ○ Numerous major showbiz personalities, such as actors Jack Lem-
mon and Fred Astaire, wrote letters of support for the Lennons. The March
2, 1972, petitions that Leon Wildes filed with the INS were accompanied
by support letters from the film curator at the Whitney Museum, film director Elia Kazan and his wife, filmmaker Barbara Loden, and national TV
talk-show host Dick Cavett. Cavett compellingly wrote that forcing John
Lennon to leave the United States "would be a kind of artistic or cultural
crime."

These letters made no difference, however, to District Director Marks,
who had received a phone call from associate INS commissioner James
Greene on March 2. According to a memorandum in which Marks documented the call, Greene told him to "immediately revoke the voluntary
departure granted to John Lennon and his wife," that "under no circumstances" should Lennon be allowed to remain in the United States. Leon
Wildes "didn't find out until much later that James Greene had called Sol
Marks to tell him that the applications I filed for John and Yoko should be
rejected. Greene said this had come from the INS Commissioner himself."

Marks wrote the Lennons on March 6 that he was revoking the option
he had given them to voluntarily leave the country by March 15. He said
that their third-preference petitions demonstrated "you have no intention
of effecting your departure" on their own.

INS agents took Marks' deportation notice to John and Yoko's Bank
Street apartment. "One morning we woke up and there was a knock at the
door, the bell, whatever, and they were saying that, 'We're gonna give this
paper to you.' And we just said, 'Oh, no, we're not gonna open the door.'
And they said, 'Well, we'll just slip it in.' That was the deportation order.

And John and I looked at it. 'What are we going to do!,' you know, it was really frightening." This was especially so because John and Yoko had a long way to go in their frustrating search to find Yoko's daughter Kyoko.

○ ○ ○ ○ ○ Tony Cox was an aspiring filmmaker with an obsession for Yoko Ono's avant-garde work. In 1961, aged twenty-four, he traveled to Japan in a quest to meet her. Yoko was married to Toshi Ichiyanagi, a successful Japanese pianist and composer. But when Tony arrived in Japan, he found Yoko confined to a hospital, the victim of a nervous breakdown. After Tony helped Yoko get released, he and Yoko "married" in November 1962 despite her legal status as Toshi's wife. But Yoko divorced Toshi, and formally married Tony in June 1963. The newlyweds' daughter Kyoko was born in the same year.

Yoko and Tony's marriage didn't last. By 1966, the year Yoko met John Lennon in London, she "acted as if she despised" Tony, observed Beatles associate Tony Bramwell. Yet, "[a]lthough it seemed that they no longer shared a bed, Tony ran around after Yoko at her every whim." After Yoko moved in with John Lennon, Tony stepped aside. "If he's fallen in love with my wife, well, people fall in love all the time," Cox shrugged.

Tony filed for a divorce in January 1969 in federal court in the US Virgin Islands, where he was then living. Yoko didn't attend the court hearing that dissolved her marriage to Tony, but in her answer to the divorce action she described the failed relationship as an "incompatibility of temperament." Her only demand was that, though Tony had been responsible for much of Kyoko's upbringing, Yoko didn't want him to have sole custody of their child. But without Yoko present in court, the divorce judge declined to rule on the issue. John Lennon later explained the divorce decree included "no arrangement made for the child because at that time we were more amicable, the two ex-parties, but you know how things get. They got worse and worse and worse, until it came we couldn't see Kyoko any more."

Tony and Kyoko were living nomadic lives, sometimes on money from the Lennons. In Hawaii and California, Tony did allow Yoko to briefly see Kyoko. In January 1970, John and Yoko visited Tony, his future wife, Melinda, and Kyoko for several weeks in Denmark. Later, Cox filmed twenty-four videotapes' worth of footage of a four-day visit he and Kyoko had at John and Yoko's London-area home in February 1970. (Cox signed away his rights to the footage in 1996; in 2002, Yoko Ono paid $300,000 to acquire the tapes from the individuals who possessed them.)

John Lennon claimed Tony Cox "had not earned a living in the past ten years, you know, there was no sign of anything he's ever done. He is called a film producer, but the only films" he made were with Yoko. As for eight-year-old Kyoko, John said, "In the beginning days, we had her, and then he had her, and it was like that, but just one time he ran off and that was about two years ago and we have been chasing him ever since." Sometimes, John and Yoko were accompanied on their international hunt by Allen Klein, who had been with them for part of the visit to see Kyoko in Denmark. Klein said he also advanced travel funds to John and Yoko for the search, that between May 1971 and April 1973 he loaned the Lennons $34,629 to pursue custody of Kyoko.

In one instance, John said, he and Yoko were told, "Kyoko was seen in a car — going down so and so road with two men holding her" near Chicago. The Lennons eventually traveled to Majorca, Spain, where Tony was living in a Maharishi compound, as Kyoko resided separately nearby with Tony's wife. Tony allowed John and Yoko a one-day visit with the child, but when the Lennons tried to extend their time with Kyoko, Tony had them detained by police for allegedly abducting her from a school. The charges were later dropped.

Yoko asked a us federal court in the Virgin Islands, where Tony and Kyoko had moved, to intervene. Yoko filed a child custody motion there in June 1971. But us authorities made it difficult for her and John to attend the hearing. "At the last minute, immigration still hadn't given us a form to get in," John recalled, "and they told us, 'You can have just enough time to go for the court case.' And that was gonna be one day. And we said, 'That's fine.' But even as we got to the border, the thing still hadn't come through so we said to the man, 'Look, they're expecting us. Call Washington to let us in. We have a court case today!'"

As it turned out, the Virgin Islands federal judge awarded Yoko primary custody of Kyoko on September 24, 1971. Tony Cox initiated a proceeding of his own in a county court in Houston, Texas, where he had next relocated with Kyoko and his current wife, Melinda. As part of that proceeding, Tony and Yoko negotiated an agreement that gave Tony temporary custody of Kyoko, with what Tony's lawyer described as "elaborate" visitation rights for Yoko.

The Harris County Domestic Relations Court in Houston approved the arrangement in December 1971. But when Yoko arrived in Texas on December 18, Tony balked at allowing Yoko's lawyer to pick up Kyoko. At a December 20 hearing, the county judge asked Cox, "In your opinion at this time, it would upset your child to visit with her mother?" "Disastrous," replied Tony, who claimed he was "emotionally and psychologically unable to comply" with Yoko's visitation rights. The judge found Tony in contempt and sent him to jail for five days.

On March 7, 1972, the Texas court awarded Yoko temporary but sole custody of Kyoko. John Lennon said, though, "What we have now is a piece of paper. We have no idea at all where the child is." He added, "[W]e only got a third party's number on the order of the judge, which is the only phone call [Yoko] ever got from the child in two years, and the child was just talking like, programmed you know, like 'Turn your face to Jesus, Mother, he'll never forgive you for what you are doing to me,' and that's another fear we have of what the man is doing to the child's mind, you know."

On March 30, 1972, however, Yoko Ono scored another victory in the emotionally painful tug of war, when the us Court of Appeals for the Third Circuit upheld the Virgin Islands court's custody determination in Yoko's favor. But there was a catch. The Lennons could have custody of Kyoko only as long as they remained in the United States.

13 "National Security Risks"

The Immigration and Naturalization Service set John Lennon and Yoko Ono's deportation hearing for March 16, 1972. John's 1968 cannabis conviction in London remained the purported reason for forcing him out of the United States. But on March 14, 1972, Lennon's immigration lawyer Leon Wildes received potentially good news from English attorney Martin Polden, who had been John's British drug-bust defense counsel.

Polden wrote Wildes: "Certain members of the squad, who were involved in that arrest, have since come under scrutiny themselves" — particularly Detective-Sergeant Norman Pilcher, who, Polden wrote, "is now having his past activities enquired into and the nature of the enquiries are such as to lend support to the assertions" by John Lennon of being set up for the arrest. Polden said he was filing an application to have Lennon's drug conviction expunged. But "it could be some six to eight weeks before a decision is forthcoming or before the application is otherwise sufficiently advanced," Polden informed Wildes.

On March 15, Leon Wildes asked INS district director Sol Marks to cancel the March 16 deportation hearing. Wildes cited the Lennons' pending third-preference petitions to stay temporarily in the United States as prominent artists as well as the couple's ongoing effort to locate Kyoko.

Sol Marks wouldn't budge. The Lennon deportation proceeding convened on the morning of March 16 on the fourteenth floor of the INS district office at 20 West Broadway in lower Manhattan. The Statue of Liberty in New York Harbor could be seen from the hearing-room window. Leon Wildes directed John and Yoko to dress "in identical black suits, white shirts, black ties. They looked exactly alike. I told them to hold hands throughout the hearings and not let go. I wanted to show that they were a matched set and shouldn't be separated."

Ira Fieldsteel presided as special inquiry officer. (A special inquiry officer is in effect an immigration judge.) Leon Wildes described Fieldsteel as "distinguished, knowledgeable, highly cultured but following the party line."

District chief trial lawyer Vincent Schiano represented the INS in the deportation hearings. Schiano, known for his fashionable mod attire, made a name for himself by devising an expedited process known as MASH ("Multiple Accelerated Summary Hearing") that allowed for the negotiation of voluntary deportation pleas in illegal alien cases. "MASH prevents the alien from being ground down between the arrogance of government and the expense of an attorney," Schiano had said.

But Fieldsteel would require no INS officials to testify, at the Lennon hearings, about how the government agency typically decided to approve third-preference applications.

Leon Wildes told Ira Fieldsteel in the hearing room that the Lennons' efforts to find Kyoko had made it "practically impossible" for Wildes to have sufficient time to confer with them on the deportation defense. "[T]heir involvement in these very emotional type of [child custody] proceedings has just left very little time to do much else," Wildes claimed.

Wildes asked for a two-month extension to better prepare the Lennons. Fieldsteel gave him until April 18. Meanwhile, a staffer for US senator James Buckley, of the New York Conservative Party, informed Wildes that the Lennons were being hounded to leave the country because the Nixon administration considered them "national security risks." This made it essential that Wildes demand a meeting with INS national commissioner Raymond Farrell in Washington, DC, to give John and Yoko "the opportunity to be confronted with the allegations being made against them and to set the record straight."

Farrell directed INS general counsel Charles Gordon to respond to Wildes. Gordon, the son of eastern European immigrants and author of a multivolume treatise on immigration law, was "a liberal and someone in favor of a more open, fairer immigration policy," according to one INS official. But in his role as INS counsel, Gordon wrote Leon Wildes, "I don't see any point to such a meeting at the present time." It didn't make it any less stinging that Gordon signed his letter with "Warmest personal regards."

○ ○ ○ ○ ○ At the reconvened immigration hearing, in New York City on April 18, Wildes argued to Ira Fieldsteel that the Immigration and Nationality Act's definition of a "marijuana" conviction applied to drug trafficking, and not, as in the case of John Lennon, "possession presumably for one's own use." Wildes added about Kyoko, "Will it be then that the father [Tony Cox] simply intends to wait out his time until [John and Yoko] are removed from the United States in order that he can continue his illegal custody of the child?"

Wildes then dug into what he also saw as the real issue underlying the deportation case: the repression of the outspoken Lennons' First Amendment rights, "particularly with respect to our involvement in Vietnam. . . . These proceedings are deliberately an effort to silence the expression of serious dispassionate and sincerely held opinions that happen to differ with those of some of the officials of our government." Wildes insisted, "Nothing is more pernicious or destructive of our entire system of law than when the public has a feeling that the law is a tool whereby those in power can harass those who threaten or oppose them with otherwise lawful means."

But INS attorney Vincent Schiano claimed that "there is nothing in what" Wildes said that "would destroy the power of the government to institute the proceedings . . . because the problem of Mr. Lennon's conviction still stands."

∘ ∘ ∘ ∘ ∘ John Lennon nevertheless continued to speak out publicly against the Vietnam War. On April 22, Lennon spoke at the National Peace Rally in New York City. Several days later, he openly claimed that politics were behind the federal government's effort to deport him.

But on April 26, 1972, Wildes received a formal rejection from the INS district director of the immigration attorney's renewed request that the deportation case be dropped. The next deportation hearing was scheduled for May 2. On May 1, Leon Wildes raced to the Manhattan federal courthouse to file a lawsuit to stop the government's pursuit of John Lennon. The complaint charged Sol Marks "has willfully and oppressively delayed in, and refused to, adjudicate the third-preference petitions" regarding the Lennons' artistic value, something that Marks typically did within two weeks of submission.

Less than two hours after the court filing, Southern District judge Bernard J. Lasker, who was nominated for the bench in 1968 by liberal US senator Robert Kennedy, blocked the INS's May 2 hearing. The district judge ordered the INS to instead appear before *him* on the morning of the second, which would coincidentally be the same day J. Edgar Hoover died of a heart attack. "I carefully prepared affidavits about things I imagined were being done behind the scenes. I expected the government to oppose them with their own affidavits," Leon Wildes recalled, "but they never touched it" at the hearing. Instead, Sol Marks called Judge Lasker and said "'I'm ready to rule on the Lennons' preference petitions.'" Marks approved them the same day.

○ ○ ○ ○ ○ By May 1972, the Lennons were receiving broad public support, from liberal icons in the arts community and beyond. Honorary members listed on "National Committee for John and Yoko" official stationery included folk music icons Joan Baez and Bob Dylan, conductor Leonard Bernstein, New York Shakespeare Festival producer Joseph Papp, jazz singer Nina Simone, Motown superstar Stevie Wonder, singer-songwriter James Taylor, and United Auto Workers Union president Leonard Woodcock. New York mayor John Lindsay sent a letter of support to INS commissioner Raymond Farrell and a copy to US deputy attorney general Richard Kleindienst.

On May 11, national committee coordinator Jon Hendricks, a political activist and Yoko Ono arts associate, submitted over 100 letters of support to the INS. In his cover letter to Ira Fieldsteel, Hendricks claimed that deporting John and Yoko "might be viewed by the world as an indication of America's intolerance for interracial marriages."

Lord Harlech, a former British ambassador to the United States, wrote: "It may be that there is a theory that no danger arises for the United States of America if someone resides there for six months but that the danger does arise if he stays seven months or longer. This argument is so obviously ludicrous that I make no further comment on it."

Despite this support, *Rolling Stone* columnist Ralph J. Gleason wrote, "[T]o the shame of the whole world of rock, I do not see any indication that its leading figures give a shit about what happens to John and Yoko." Gleason said he so far had been contacted about the Lennon case only by Lennon record producer Phil Spector. Gleason asked his readers, "[I]f John Lindsay can make a gesture in this battle where are all the other heavies from Lennon's own people? There's no need to name names. I mean all of you." In 1975, though, middle-of-the-road pop singer and songwriter Neil Sedaka released "Immigrant Song," his hit-single tribute to John Lennon. (The record was marketed by Elton John's Rocket Records.)

And there were attacks from the political right. Syndicated conservative columnist Victor Lasky labeled the Lennons "political idiots." He wrote, "Their knowledge of global affairs is largely derived from hasty readings of semi-pornographic 'underground' publications." Lasky claimed John and Yoko's "services to the cause of furthering Communist aggression in Indochina and weakening this country's will to resist will undoubtedly win for them Hanoi's highest honors."

John Lennon "found it almost impossible to believe that so much effort was being expended against him," Dick Cavett said. "It's ironic that it would happen in the same year [comedian/film director Charlie] Chaplin was given an award 20 years after a similar kind of nonsense," Cavett also noted, referring to the honorary recognition of Chaplin at the 1972 Academy Awards.

∘ ∘ ∘ ∘ ∘ On the *Dick Cavett Show*'s May 11 broadcast, John Lennon tried to put the Nixon administration's fears about him to rest. He announced he wouldn't be participating in a protest performance at the Republican National Convention, which took place in Miami Beach that summer. "We've never said we're going; there'll be no big jam with Dylan because there's too much going on," Lennon said on Cavett's show.

Leon Wildes later noted that leftist activist Jerry Rubin had been "urging John and Yoko to go the convention, but I told them not to. There were these two guys in suits and ties who had been sitting in the front row during the deportation hearings, sometimes physically closer to John and Yoko in the hearing room than I was myself. John and Yoko's driver knew them from the drug squad at the New York City police department. I was afraid that at the Republican Convention it would be too easy for the government to drop something in John's pocket and arrest him."

John Lennon was certainly better off staying away from the Republicans' south Florida gathering. Wildes found out about the government's actual plans: "Sol Marks' office had a deal lined up with the FBI. If John went to the convention in Miami Beach, he was to be indicted for traveling interstate to provoke a riot."

As for Yoko's bid for permanent US residency, John said on Dick Cavett's program that, though she had lived in the United States for many years, she "never took out American citizenship because she never needed it. She was here half her life, she was educated here. And then she married an American. It never came up to change her citizenship. It was just always easy to come and go, she never thought of it."

But the same evening the May 11 *Dick Cavett Show* episode aired—which was the night before the Lennons' next scheduled deportation hearing—Leon Wildes learned by chance for the first time that Yoko Ono long ago had been granted permanent US residency. This occurred after she entered the country on September 13, 1964, as the wife of US citizen Tony Cox. "She had dropped off a whole pile of documents with me to see if there was anything in there we could use," Wildes recalled. "I opened the package and a 'green card' fell out with her picture on it."

At the May 12 hearing, Wildes handed Yoko's green card to Ira Fieldsteel. "I was even more shocked," Wildes said to the hearing officer, "when I considered that I inspected files of the Immigration Service and never had found a file under that number."

Ira Fieldsteel told Wildes that Yoko's permanent residency status meant "you apparently stand on two separate legal bases at this point." For John Lennon, it was whether he had intended to comply with Sol Marks' order to leave the United States by March 15. John said at the hearing, "I had no intention either way. We are looking for the child Kyoko."

INS attorney Vincent Schiano asked, "Do you intend to depart now?"

"[I]t's impossible to make up my mind," John replied, because "we don't know where [Kyoko] is. . . . Our whole life is built around that."

As he had at the April 18 hearing, Leon Wildes argued that John Lennon's drug conviction in England didn't fall within the purview of the term "marijuana" under the US Immigration and Nationality Act. On May 12, Wildes focused on what he claimed was a technical difference with "cannabis resin" that John had pleaded guilty to possessing in England.

Wildes procured an expert opinion from Dr. Lester Grinspoon, a psychiatry professor at Harvard Medical School and author of the book *Marijuana Reconsidered*. Grinspoon opined that the phrase "cannabis resin" in the English drug statute referred to a *Cannabis sativa* plant's flowers. The term "marijuana" in the US statute referred to a sativa plant's crushed leaves, Grinspoon had concluded. Ironically, cannabis resin (or hash) is stronger than a marijuana cigarette made from a sativa plant's leaves. But this was how Leon Wildes had to argue the technical point.

On May 12, Ira Fieldsteel told Wildes he would consider the issue later.

Now several character witnesses testified for the Lennons, including Dick Cavett, and the directors of New York City's Metropolitan Museum of Art and the Everson Museum of Art in Syracuse. As a constant presence in John's life since he became the Beatles' manager in 1969, Allen Klein was at the immigration hearing, too, testifying about the Lennons' economic interests, which Klein told Ira Fieldsteel "to a lot of hungry people . . . is kind of important." Klein said John and Yoko's "extensive" US business holdings "do an annual gross volume of 50 million dollars" (referring to Beatles revenues of which John owned one fourth) and that "100 to 150 families are dependent upon them for their livelihood."

Klein said about John's drug conviction, that Scotland Yard detectives "did the same thing" to Mick Jagger and Keith Richards, "who I also represented at the time and the court of appeals threw out that conviction." Klein didn't manage Lennon when he was busted, but insisted, "I would never have let him plead guilty at that particular time."

○ ○ ○ ○ ○ There was one more deportation hearing to go. It convened on May 17, 1972, amid rapidly growing public support for John Lennon. Pointing to a "monstrous pile of documents," Leon Wildes told Special Inquiry Officer Ira Fieldsteel, "I am in receipt of ten to fifteen thousand signatures on petitions which have been completely spontaneous action[s] on the part of a group in New York and on the part of a group in California." But Vincent Schiano countered that the government had its own "monstrous pile of documents," and he said, "I think it is in disagreement with this monstrous pile."

As for Yoko, Wildes told Ira Fieldsteel that she would be satisfied whether her 1964 permanent residency approval was reconfirmed or her recent application for permanent status was granted. "We'll take any kind of residence you've got," Wildes said.

John and Yoko were the only individuals to testify on May 17. John said he'd previously been to the United States on a number of occasions. "Mainly on tour with the Beatles, I guess, was the most times." (John's first

US entry after his 1968 cannabis conviction was in May 1970, when he traveled to Los Angeles with George and Pattie Harrison, and then on to New York for business matters. That summer, he also was allowed to reenter the United States with Yoko on a waiver for their primal therapy in Los Angeles.) "There were more [US visits], quite a few, actually," John continued. "Because we have been here for the [Kyoko] court case many times."

Leon Wildes asked, "Are you presently involved in any programs or activities for which your continued presence, or your joint continued presence with Mrs. Lennon, is required?"

"Well, there's many things," John replied, "from recordings, talent we discovered here to Yoko's own art work, which is — and both of us have been asked to do some work in Syracuse where Yoko previously had an exhibition. . . . And, of course, we have the main thing, apart from all our, you know, artistic endeavors, . . . looking for Kyoko, you know, we've got many people helping us look for her in this country. . . . And that's what we have planned for the next — forever — 'til we find her."

"I don't know if there is any mercy to plead for," John said for Fieldsteel's consideration, "but if there is any, I'd like it please for both of us and our child."

"And as far as you are concerned, is she a lost child, a kidnapped child, or what?" Vincent Schiano wanted to know.

"Well, it couldn't be a kidnap case because it's only a civil case," John answered, "and we can't get federal help in that way, so it's not legally a kidnapping." Instead, the Lennons used private detectives. "All we ask for is for it to be done quietly so the child not be made a public spectacle, that's all we're frightened of, is her becoming a famous child, we don't see why she should have to be."

Yoko also testified about the time she previously spent in the United States. "I think it is over half my life," she said. Yoko acknowledged about Kyoko, "It is true we have hired many detectives," but after Kyoko called complaining that she felt harassed, "I had to cancel several detectives that had been hired, and had to replace them with some people who are more personal friends of ours. I don't want this information to go out of this court because — "

"Well, you just can't ask everybody just to keep quiet," Ira Fieldsteel cut in. "You are in a room full of representatives of the press."

"Would you want to become a resident of the United States if your husband's application were denied?" Vincent Schiano asked Yoko.

"[Y]ou are asking me to choose between my child and my husband," she replied, clutching a handkerchief and holding back tears. "I don't think you can ask any human being to do such a thing."

But it would be nine long months until Yoko would know whether she would have to make that decision.

The Beatles' first dedicated manager Brian Epstein in October 1963, just as "Beatlemania" took off in the UK following his band's wildly successful appearance on the British TV program *Sunday Night at the London Palladium*. Dean/Mirrorpix/ Newscom

The triumphant Beatles and Brian Epstein arrive back in London from their 1964 US summer tour. By December, Epstein's management company, NEMS, would sue its authorized US merchandiser Seltaeb for alleged mishandling of the Beatles' merchandise revenues. Daily Mirror/Mirrorpix/Newscom

The 1964 "Ride the Landslide!" promotional flyer that Remco Industries, the authorized U.S. manufacturer and distributor of Beatles dolls, sent to its dealers. U.S. National Archives

The Beatles at Brian Epstein's London home in May 1967 for a party celebrating the premier of the band's epiphanic *Sgt. Pepper's* album. Epstein died at the residence in August 1967 of what the coroner ruled was an accidental overdose of drugs. Daily Mirror/Mirrorpix/Newscom

Allen Klein, the Beatles' last manager, in July 1969. At the time, Klein was intent on renegotiating the Beatles' recording agreement with Capitol Records. DM Eric Harlow/Mirrorpix/Newscom

R & B/pop singer Sam Cooke in the recording studio in 1964. Cooke was the first major artist whom Allen Klein managed. Everett Collection/Newscom

John Lennon (*left*) and George Harrison both enthusiastically supported Allen Klein as the Beatles' manager but later became entangled in a web of lawsuits with Klein after they fired him in April 1973. Keystone Pictures USA/ Zuma Press/Newscom

James Taylor with singer-songwriter Carole King in 1970. Unhappy at Apple Records, Taylor walked out of his recording contract with the Beatles' label in 1969 and signed with Warner Bros. Records, which released his breakthrough singer-songwriter album *Sweet Baby James* in 1970. Gysbert Hanekroot/Zuma Press/Newscom

John Lennon and Yoko Ono on the front steps of the Beatles' 3 Savile Row headquarters in London in December 1969, making the kind of political statement that caught the attention of US president Richard Nixon's administration—and prompted Nixon's team to launch a covert campaign that tried to bar John from moving to the United States in the 1970s. Keystone Pictures USA/Zuma Press/Newscom

opposite:
An Apple Corps business meeting circa 1969. At the table (*clockwise from center*), John Lennon and Yoko Ono—who were closely aligned with Allen Klein—Klein, Klein's man at Apple Peter Howard, Ringo Starr, Ringo's wife Maureen (*back to camera*), a teeth-gritting Paul McCartney, who from the start opposed Klein's involvement in the Beatles' business affairs, and Paul's brother-in-law, lawyer John Eastman. Christies Images Ltd./Zuma Press/Newscom

Morris Levy, the mobbed-up music-industry executive with the big hands who sued John Lennon claiming that Lennon's Beatles song "Come Together" infringed on the Chuck Berry song "You Can't Catch Me" that Levy owned. Deborah Feingold

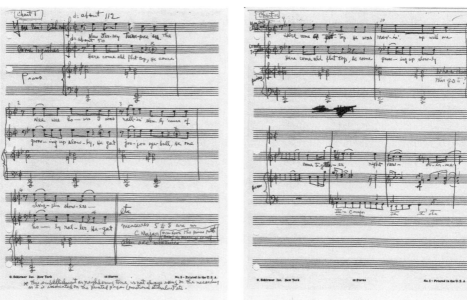

The original handwritten comparison prepared by Morris Levy's expert witness William Dawson in Levy's suit that alleged John Lennon's "Come Together" infringed on the Levy-owned Chuck Berry song "You Can't Catch Me." Dawson then concluded that "substantially all of the melody of 'Come Together' is similar to the basic melodic material of 'You Can't Catch Me.'" U.S. National Archives

John Lennon and Chuck Berry perform together on the *Mike Douglas* TV show in February 1972, ironically when Lennon was fighting Morris Levy's copyright infringement lawsuit over Berry's "You Can't Catch Me." ©Jeff Albertson/Corbis

Chiffons members Judy Craig, Patricia Bennett, Barbara Lee, and Sylvia Peterson. Bright Tunes Music, the song publisher of "He's So Fine," the vocal group's biggest hit record, claimed in a February 1971 lawsuit that George Harrison's "My Sweet Lord" infringed on Bright Tunes' composition. Courtesy: CSU Archives/Everett Collection/Newscom

George Harrison (*left*) with his music mentor Ravi Shankar. It was Shankar who inspired George to organize the Madison Square Garden charity concerts in August 1971 to raise money for starving Bangladesh refugees. Unfortunately, the US Internal Revenue Service hounded Harrison for years afterward over tax issues related to the shows' revenues. Starstock/Photoshot/Newscom

George Harrison performing in Memphis in November 1974, during the first US solo tour by a former Beatle. When the Harrison tour hit New York City in December, George was besieged by private investigators hired by his former manager Allen Klein, who wanted George served with a lawsuit summons in Klein's attempt to seize George's Harrisongs publishing company. Dave Darnell/ Zuma Press/Newscom

Record promoter Pete Bennett (*left*), Phil Spector (*center*), and George Harrison listening to a prerelease mix of George's chart-topping solo album *All Things Must Pass*. Bennett was a key witness against his former boss Allen Klein in the US government's tax evasion case against Klein. ©Bettmann/Corbis

14 "Skullduggery Was Afoot"

pecial Inquiry Officer Fieldsteel issued his written decision on March 23, 1973. District Director Sol Marks announced the ruling at a press conference at the INS's New York office. The Lennons were in Los Angeles that day. Leon Wildes attended the New York event, for dramatic effect holding a yellow rose Yoko sent.

The immigration judge did grant Yoko permanent US residency. But he ruled John Lennon should be deported because, in Fieldsteel's view, "cannabis resin" and "marijuana" possession *were* the same for purposes of violating the Immigration and Nationality Act. Because the criminal proceedings against Sgt. Norman Pilcher in England that Martin Polden had so hopefully written Leon Wildes about weren't related to John Lennon's drug conviction, they were no help to John's immigration case, Fieldsteel said.

He concluded by finding that Kyoko's case wasn't enough to keep John Lennon in the United States, because, Fieldsteel said, the child custody situation was "at an indefinite impasse."

When asked at the press conference about Fieldsteel's harsh deportation ruling, Sol Marks shrugged, "I'm a law enforcement officer." But he added about John and Yoko, if sarcastically, "I enjoy their music."

○ ○ ○ ○ ○ Even though Ira Fieldsteel ruled against John, there *was* a victory for the Lennons in the immigration judge's decision. He found them to be "persons of exceptional ability in the arts," as they had claimed in their third-preference petitions, which would allow John to stay in the United States while his quest for permanent residency proceeded.

John and Yoko held their own press conference in New York City on April 2 to announce John was appealing Ira Fieldsteel's deportation order. During their press conference, the conceptually playful Lennons also announced they were founding their own virtual country, Nutopia, and even had a constitution ready.

The press conference took place just three days after John had severed his business ties with Allen Klein, over unhappiness with Klein's handling of John's personal matters and the Beatles' business affairs. John told the reporters that he hoped Klein's firing would clear the way for gaining access to Yoko's daughter Kyoko. John admitted the aggressive Klein had been "one of the major factors" in the "fear" held by Yoko's ex-husband Tony Cox. ("That's all right. I didn't trust him either," Klein said about Cox.)

The Lennons continued to participate in antiwar activities even after Fieldsteel's ruling. One was a protest on June 28, 1973, at the South Vietnamese embassy in Washington. The next day, John and Yoko showed up at the US Senate to see firsthand the nationally televised Watergate hearings on the June 1972 break-in by Nixon operatives at Democratic National Committee headquarters.

It was only two months later, in August 1973, that Leon Wildes finally got hold of written confirmation that there *was* a government plot to oust John Lennon from the United States. John and Yoko's driver — the one who had been a New York City police officer — mysteriously handed Wildes a typo-ridden memo titled "The Supervision of the Activities of Both John and Yoko Lennon." The undated memo's author, a "Supervisor, Intelligence Division, Unit 2" wrote to a "Regional Director, Group 8" that granting permanent US residence to John Lennon, "formerly of the Beattles [*sic*]," and to Yoko Ono "has been judged to be inadvisable." Thus "it was recommended that all applications are to be denied."

The government correspondence noted the Lennons' "contriversal [*sic*] behaviour," their relationships with Jerry Rubin and John Sinclair, and other activities that were "highly political and unfavorable to the present administration."

Leon Wildes described the memo as "substantial evidence that some skullduggery was afoot in government agencies." But he said, "I had a difficult time finding out which agency it actually came from."

The memo directed the INS regional director to "maintain a constant servaillence [*sic*]" of John and Yoko's Bank Street apartment. "There were instances of people coming to John's apartment to check the phone and when he asked them for ID, they would just disappear," Wildes recalled. "Outside the apartment building, there were these two guys on the street always fixing their bike. When John came out, they would hop in their car and follow him. The government wanted him to know he was under surveillance."

Wildes was caught in the government's surveillance net, too. "Yoko advised me that if I heard a screeching sound on my telephone, it was a sign that my line was being tapped." Both his office and home phones had that noise.

The Lennons' lawyer asked Ira Fieldsteel to require the federal government to disclose the specifics of its Lennon surveillance activities, including any by the FBI, CIA, INS, so-called White House "plumbers" covert operatives, and local police. Fieldsteel claimed he didn't have the authority to do so. In any case, Fieldsteel said, there were "defects fatal" to Wildes' request, including that the attorney hadn't specified "the particular evidence which it is claimed is inadmissible" in the Lennon deportation case by being "the primary product of an unlawful act."

Wildes countered that *"all* of the evidence" had been unlawfully obtained.

° ° ° ° ° Wildes had already opened up an additional legal front, however, in John Lennon's fight to stay in the United States. As far back as May 1, 1972, Wildes wrote INS district director Sol Marks asking for the immigration service's statistics on how many deportation cases against otherwise deportable foreigners had been postponed — so-called "non-priority" matters — and on what grounds. These non-priority dispositions were otherwise "shrouded in secrecy," Wildes said. Sol Marks didn't respond. So Wildes phoned Vincent Schiano, who said the INS didn't intend to reply at all to Wildes' request.

Wildes persisted. As much as a year later, following further frustrating exchanges, he sent Washington, DC–based INS associate commissioner E. A. Loughran an ultimatum: Wildes gave the agency thirty days to produce the information on non-priority determinations or, he warned, he would have "no alternative other than to" sue the US government to get the deportation deferral statistics.

But Loughran didn't blink. He returned the information application that Wildes had sent on the ground that Wildes hadn't included a three-dollar processing fee.

Wildes soon found out, though, that "district directors are required by internal operating practice to file a written report on every non-priority case." As a result, Wildes charged, the INS's foot-dragging violated John Lennon's constitutional due process right to a "full and fair hearing."

A new lawsuit by John Lennon, against higher levels of the US government, was now inevitable. The Freedom of Information Act (FOIA) complaint that Leon Wildes filed for John Lennon on October 18, 1973, in the Southern District of New York named the US attorney general as the first defendant. (Then US attorney general Elliot Richardson, who replaced Watergate affair casualty Richard Kleindienst in May 1973, abruptly resigned on October 20, after refusing to follow President Nixon's command to fire Archibald Cox, the special prosecutor looking into the Watergate affair. Solicitor General Robert Bork then replaced Richardson.)

For good measure, Lennon's lawyer filed a companion complaint to prove his client was in fact the target of illegal surveillance and a government conspiracy.

The two cases were assigned to Southern District judge Richard Owen, who coincidentally was the assigned judge in another current Beatles-related legal dispute: the copyright infringement suit against George Harrison over the song "My Sweet Lord."

○ ○ ○ ○ ○ John and Yoko were no longer living together when Leon Wildes filed the two federal cases, though John said, "We have been apart more than people think, for odd periods over the years." Yoko, now a permanent US resident, stayed in their Dakota apartment in New York. John paired off, at Yoko's choosing, with his personal assistant May Pang and in September 1973 headed to Los Angeles for several months to begin his infamous, months-long "Lost Weekend" that clashed with Leon Wildes' carefully compiled portrait of John as an artist who would contribute to American culture in an exceptional way.

In October, John began recording an album of rock 'n' roll oldies with Phil Spector. The sessions became riotous before they fell apart a few weeks later. Then two widely reported incidents at the Troubadour music club on Santa Monica Boulevard made John out to be nothing more than an annoying drunk. In the first incident, he had sat in the raised VIP section of the club with a sanitary napkin fastened to his head. A few weeks later, John was ousted from the venue — and later sued by a Troubadour waitress who claimed he drunkenly assaulted her that night — for shouting disruptive remarks during a performance by the Smothers Brothers folk-comedy duo.

"I remember someone yelling about pigs. It was fairly disgusting," Tommy Smothers recalled about being heckled by John.

○ ○ ○ ○ ○ The criminal prosecution of John Lennon's drug bust antagonist in England came to a head while John's case was before the US immigration appeals board. Sgt. Norman Pilcher retired from Scotland Yard in July 1972. Three months later, he was among the Yard's Drug Squad members charged with conspiring to falsify surveillance records and giving perjured testimony in the 1971 trial of a Pakistani family accused of smuggling marijuana. After the Pakistanis' convictions were overturned, the Scotland Yard detectives were accused of a criminal "cover-up."

On November 14, 1973, after a thirty-seven-day trial, London jurors found Pilcher guilty on two counts of perjury. "You poisoned the wells of criminal justice and set about it deliberately," Criminal Court justice Melford Stevenson admonished the former tormentor of rock stars. "Pilcher guilty of perjury Sentence four years Letter follows," Martin Polden immediately telegrammed Leon Wildes.

Wildes informed the US Board of Immigration Appeals on November 16 of Pilcher's fate. Wildes emphasized that in England attorney Polden was looking into whether the Pilcher verdict was sufficient ground for reconsideration of John Lennon's drug plea. As a cautionary measure, Wildes and Lennon asked US district judge Owen to enjoin the BIA from ruling until Lennon obtained the information on non-priority deportation determinations that he sought in the FOIA suit.

Owen agreed that Lennon's claim of prejudged governmental action in the deportation proceeding was "provocative." But the district judge was yet another in the lengthening line of federal officials to rule against John Lennon. Even with the evidence Wildes was accumulating, Owen decided there was "no showing that any Immigration official involved in this proceeding has not exercised his independent judgment."

○ ○ ○ ○ ○ It took until June 13, 1974, for the US Attorney's Office to get to Leon Wildes the copies of the cases Wildes and Lennon wanted in which immigration applicants had been granted non-priority status. To Lennon's lawyer, the 1,863 INS decisions he received demonstrated the sweep of the immigration agency's discretion in such cases.

But the case materials that Assistant US Attorney Joseph P. Marro, the government counsel in the Lennon FOIA litigation, sent Wildes were in a mess. "They were not filed chronologically, nor were they filed according to the Section of the law under which an alien was deportable; they were not filed alphabetically nor according to any other logical classification or system which I could discern," Wildes said.

The US Attorney's Office did admit that exactly why an individual was deemed a non-priority "is not provided for either by statute or regulation and is merely an informal Service policy." But the INS's unpublished operations instructions, which Wildes had also obtained, revealed that the immigration agency did take "humanitarian factors," including "family situation," into account, when deciding whether to defer a deportation.

As far as the US government was concerned, though, the release of the non-priority dispositions made John Lennon's FOIA suit moot. But these were only some of documents Lennon sued over. His FOIA action also asked how many US deportation proceedings there had been and how many deportations actually ordered. As late as May 14, 1976, Leon Wildes complained to Judge Owen, "I have written for this information on a number of occasions without success."

15 "I'm a Doctrine Now"

The Board of Immigration Appeals issued its ruling in the Lennon case on July 10, 1974. Like Ira Fieldsteel, the BIA saw no distinction between the parts of a cannabis plant. The skeptical immigration board said of John's claim that he had been framed by Sergeant Pilcher, "[W]e do not believe that the [English] Dangerous Drugs Act of 1965 created an offense which permitted the conviction of persons whose possession was innocent and readily explainable." The BIA concluded that Lennon "chose instead to take a calculated risk by pleading guilty to the charge."

The BIA refused to delay the deportation case while Lennon pursued his federal lawsuits in New York. Sidestepping Lennon's concern about government surveillance, the BIA observed that "all" Leon Wildes "has presented is a photocopy of an undated memorandum indicating that some unknown party wished the respondent to be placed under surveillance. Counsel has refused to divulge how, when, and from whom that memorandum was obtained. We need more information than has been presented to warrant a remand for further hearing before the immigration judge."

Now it was the BIA that gave John Lennon sixty days to leave the United States. This time, music industry representatives spoke up about Lennon's plight. Record executive Clive Davis fretted, "This country was founded by free-thinking great minds, but the breed is a diminishing one." "If John Lennon is deported, I'm leaving too . . . with my musicians . . . and my marijuana," singer Art Garfunkel protested.

The BIA's ruling forced Leon Wildes to play yet another procedural card. On September 6, 1974, he appealed the decision to the US Court of Appeals for the Second Circuit. John could remain in the United States pending the outcome of the appeal.

By September 1974, some of John's key adversaries had left the Immigration and Naturalization Service. INS district director Sol Marks retired to

Florida. Despite John Lennon's lengthy immigration battle, when Marks stepped down the *New York Times* praised him for "speeding up hearings."

INS chief trial lawyer Vincent Schiano resigned from the Immigration and Naturalization Service in December 1973. He did so after being reassigned from full-time counsel to an advisor's position in a phoneless cubicle from where he continued to work on the Lennon case. In December 1972, the INS had hauled Schiano before a grand jury for allegedly taking bribes in exchange for helping individuals with active immigration applications. Schiano claimed he had been demoted, however, in retaliation for objecting to government interference in some of the INS cases he was pursuing. One case involved a suspected Nazi concentration camp chief who was now living comfortably in the United States. Files on such alleged war criminals, many who had become involved in scientific and military developments of high value to the US government, often mysteriously disappeared from the INS's New York office.

Schiano's criticism of the INS sounded like John Lennon's might. "[T]hey'd get me for spitting on the sidewalk," Schiano said. "It'd be cheaper for them to pay for a hit [murder]."

∘ ∘ ∘ ∘ ∘ Only a few days after the Board of Immigration Appeals ruled against him, it looked like the situation might be beginning to brighten for John Lennon. On July 31, 1974, the House of Parliament in England approved the Rehabilitation of Offenders Act, which essentially expunged from criminal records such minor convictions as John's 1968 guilty plea. The new law was set to take effect on July 1, 1975.

In August 1974, President Richard Nixon resigned from office under pressure from revelations about abuse of power in the Watergate scandal. The same month, syndicated investigative reporter Jack Anderson, himself the target of a foiled murder plot cooked up by Nixon operatives, wrote about the deportation disposition documents that Leon Wildes obtained from the INS. Anderson reported that "the United States harbors hundreds of ex-felons, many with more serious drug records [than Lennon] under the non-priority status that permits them to stay in the country. For that matter, murderers, rapists, robbers and even one bigamist are allowed to remain for 'humanitarian' reasons."

Wildes and Lennon approached federal legislators to see whether "private" legislation could be passed to protect Lennon from being deported. "We met with a number of congressmen and senators," Leon Wildes recalled. But Congressman (and future New York City mayor) Ed Koch "felt it wouldn't be a good idea to introduce a private bill, in case it wasn't successful." Koch did introduce public legislation to establish a deportation waiver for immigrants who had a simple marijuana possession conviction. But such legislation wasn't enacted by Congress until years later, allowing a waiver for immigrants convicted of possessing up to 30 grams of the federally controlled substance. Today, of course, many states have legalized the use of medical marijuana and some, like Colorado and Washington, permit the sale of marijuana for recreational purposes.

∘ ∘ ∘ ∘ ∘ The files that the FBI collected on John Lennon's political activities during the Nixon administration were startling for their ineptness and lack of revelations. This included recounting John's public comments as cohost with Yoko in February 1972 on the *Mike Douglas Show*, the popular talk and variety afternoon TV program on which John's invited guests included Jerry Rubin and Black Panther activist Bobby Seale. The FBI files also contained copies of press reviews of Lennon concerts and of publicly available news reports about him. In a report labeled "Confidential," an FBI informer wrote down the lyrics to the song "John Sinclair" that Lennon had sung at the public political rally in Ann Arbor, Michigan, in December 1971. Lennon published the lyrics on the cover of his 1972 *Some Time in New York City* album.

But on January 2, 1975, US district judge Richard Owen dismissed a motion by John Lennon to suppress any government evidence that may have been obtained through the illegal use of electronics. Owen believed the Justice Department's claim that it had "no information indicating that any conversations of plaintiff were overheard or that any premises known to have been owned or leased by plaintiff were covered by electronic surveillance."

Owen decided, however, that Lennon was entitled to contact government officials and see government files to determine whether he was being subjected to politically motivated "selective prosecution." The district judge acknowledged government officials couldn't "with impunity, immune from judicial review, institute a deportation proceeding solely as a penalty for the lawful exercise of constitutional rights" of political speech.

o o o o o Judge Owen's mixed ruling only reinforced John Lennon's determination to carry on his immigration fight for as long as it took. After reuniting with Yoko in early 1975, John said, "I can last out, without leaving here, another ten years, if that's the way they want to play it."

The US government was willing to oblige. A July 1, 1975, statement by US attorney Paul Curran adhered to the party position that "there was no illegal surveillance" of John Lennon. To further bolster the argument that Lennon should be deported, the government's appellate brief to the Second Circuit cited recent INS statistics that between 1973 and 1975, more than 700 foreigners were found deportable due to drug convictions, mostly for marijuana possession. The government's brief derisively added that "the record indicates that Lennon's conduct may not be as 'wholly innocent' as he would have the Court believe."

But media pressure against the government reached a crucial point when, on July 31, 1975, *Rolling Stone* published a full copy of the February 1972 letter that Sen. Strom Thurmond had sent to US attorney general John Mitchell urging high-level action against John Lennon. (Mitchell had resigned in June 1972 to run President Nixon's reelection campaign. He was convicted in February 1975 of several criminal counts related to the Watergate scandal and spent nineteen months in jail.) The Lennons, however, had already given the INS a face-saving "humanitarian" reason to announce that it would temporarily suspend the Lennon deportation proceeding: Yoko was several months pregnant with the Lennons' son, Sean.

o o o o o The Second Circuit issued its appellate ruling on October 7, 1975, just two days before Sean's birth and John Lennon's thirty-fifth birthday. Leon Wildes brought the court decision for the Lennons to read at the New York City hospital where Yoko was waiting to deliver her baby.

Irving R. Kaufman, chief judge for the Second Circuit, wrote the appeals court's majority opinion. Kaufman had established himself as a pro–civil rights, pro–First Amendment jurist. But he was controversial for handing down a death sentence in 1951 to US citizens Julius and Ethel Rosenberg for allegedly passing secrets about the country's nuclear bomb program to the Soviet Union. In a major music case for which he wrote the Second Circuit's opinion in 1964, Kaufman ruled that twenty-three song parodies published by *Mad* magazine — including "Louella Schwartz Describes Her Malady," a parody of Irving Berlin's "A Pretty Girl Is Like a Melody" — were copyright "fair uses" that didn't infringe on the rights of the owners of the underlying songs.

In the Lennon case, Judge Kaufman acknowledged that "the power of Congress to exclude or deport natives of other countries remains virtually unfettered." He claimed the harshness of ordering individuals to be deported "surpasses all but the most Draconian criminal penalties." But the chief judge brushed aside Lennon's arguments that "cannabis resin" and "marijuana" were different substances, or that Britain's new law expunging prior drug convictions made John Lennon eligible to stay in the United States.

Instead, Judge Kaufman focused on the fact that a conviction under the English Dangerous Drugs Act hadn't required a defendant to know the substance he possessed was illegal. As a result, an individual given a bottle of amphetamine pills could be found guilty even if he thought he had received aspirin tablets.

"[W]e cannot imagine that Congress would impose the harsh consequences of an excludable alien classification upon a person convicted under a foreign law that made guilty knowledge irrelevant," Kaufman wrote, ruling for John Lennon and vacating the INS's deportation order. The Second Circuit didn't directly decide John's claim that he was being selectively prosecuted by the US government, but Kaufman added, "The courts will not condone selective deportation based upon secret political grounds."

The chief judge closed by praising John Lennon's doggedness: "If, in our two hundred years of independence, we have in some measure realized our ideals, it is in large part because we have always found a place for those committed to the spirit of liberty and willing to help implement it. Lennon's four-year battle to remain in our country is testimony to his faith in this American dream."

○ ○ ○ ○ ○ It was a solemn-looking but triumphant John Lennon — accompanied by wife Yoko and lawyer Leon Wildes — who found himself once again before INS Special Inquiry Officer Ira Fieldsteel, this time at the INS hearing room in Manhattan on July 27, 1976, to receive his green card for permanent US residency. "Yesterday, all of John Lennon's troubles seemed so far away and now it looks as though he's here to stay," *New York Times* began its article on the hearing by paraphrasing the popular Paul McCartney song. Author Norman Mailer, Japanese sculptor Isamu Noguchi, news reporter Geraldo Rivera, and actress Gloria Swanson all testified in support of John at the July 27 hearing, though permanent residency was certain.

Once he had his green card in hand, John beamed to reporters, "It's great to be legal again. The Immigration Service ha[s] finally seen the light of day. It's been a long and slow road, but I am not bitter." He continued, "The main thing is that I can travel now. Until today my attorney wouldn't even let me go to Hawaii for a vacation in case I couldn't get back. Whenever I flew to Los Angeles I was paranoid in case the plane was diverted to Toronto on the way."

John said he wanted to live permanently in New York because, "If I had lived 2,000 years ago I would have wanted to live in Rome. New York is the Rome of today."

But there was one last detail to the immigration case for John Lennon and Leon Wildes. It had cost John $2,376 to have copies of his appeals court brief and attached materials printed up. The Second Circuit ordered the US government to reimburse him for these costs. Though the amount of money was small, on December 8, 1976, Leon Wildes complained to the special assistant US attorney, "I have on a number of occasions called to your attention the fact that the outstanding order requiring the payment of costs by the government . . . has not been complied with." Wildes asked, "Would you be kind enough to see to it that the payment is made?"

More significantly, after the Second Circuit ruled, George Harrison called John Lennon to say that John winning his case had made it easier, at least for a Beatles applicant like George who had his own English drug conviction, to get into the United States. George, who claimed he had also been set up by Scotland Yard detectives, told John, "I don't need to get one of those entry waivers anymore. They said it was based on the 'Lennon doctrine.'"

"John immediately called me up," Leon Wildes recalled, "and said, 'How do you like that? I'm a doctrine now.'"

16 ○ Say You Want a Revelation

John Lennon was no longer a high-profile political activist when his immigration battle came to an end. For the next several years, almost until his death in December 1980, he retreated to domestic life with Yoko and their son Sean at their Dakota home in New York City. John declined press interview requests, too. "I remember shaking his hand the day he won the battle for his green card," recalled Chris Charlesworth, the US correspondent for the British newspaper *Melody Maker* who previously interviewed Lennon several times. When Charlesworth asked for a new interview, John wrote back that "he was invisible now. I still have the postcard, but I never communicated with John again," Charlesworth said.

Jon Wiener, a history professor at University of California–Irvine, concluded Lennon's withdrawal from the political arena had a lot to do with the government's agenda in the immigration case. In Wiener's view, the "withdrawal from activist politics was forced on him by the Nixon administration's abuse of power." In February 1981, Wiener filed a Freedom of Information Act request to find out more. The Immigration and Naturalization Service sent him the documents it had. The CIA had little to offer but it was important because its investigative powers were supposed to be limited to foreign, rather than domestic, intelligence-gathering activities.

The FBI was a stick in the mud. The bureau withheld from Wiener more than two-thirds of the 281 pages it had compiled on Lennon and redacted large portions of the documents it did send.

With backing from the American Civil Liberties Union of Southern California, Wiener sued the US government in March 1983, under the Freedom of Information Act, seeking further disclosures from the FBI's Lennon files. Five years later, in February 1988, Central District of California judge Robert M. Takasugi, who had been appointed to the bench by Nixon's successor, President Gerald Ford, dismissed the complaint. In a cursory ruling, Judge Takasugi said he was satisfied that affidavits the FBI submitted to him from its agents adequately "carr[ied] the government's burden of proof to show that the FOIA exemptions [from disclosure of government documents] were properly applied in this case."

ACLU counsel Mark Rosenbaum scoffed, "If Peeping Tom surveillance of a dead rock musician constitutes national security, we might as well fold up and discard the F.O.I.A."

Wiener and the ACLU filed an appeal, and in July 1991 the US Court of Appeals for the Ninth Circuit reinstated the FOIA lawsuit. The Ninth Circuit's judges observed of the FBI's response to Wiener's documents request, that "'boilerplate' explanations were drawn from a 'master' response filed by the FBI for many FOIA requests. No effort is made to tailor the explanation to the specific document withheld." In fact, the FBI's response to Wiener was so vague that the indexes it sent with the agency's heavily redacted documents didn't even mention John Lennon.

In December 1993, the FBI decided to voluntarily release some more materials from its Lennon files. In February 1996, just prior to a scheduled trial before Judge Takasugi, the FBI proposed settling Wiener's suit. The September 1997 settlement agreement resulted in the release of 81 more pages on Lennon. The FBI also agreed to pay the ACLU's attorney fees and court costs for the FOIA litigation.

The newly obtained files contained some interesting revelations. Among them was the fact that on May 23, 1972, acting FBI director L. Patrick Gray had teletyped bureau agents in Houston and New York to look for Yoko's daughter. Gray wrongly claimed in the correspondence that the Lennons were "using delay tactics in deportation of attempting to locate Yoko Ono's child Kyoko Cox." Jon Wiener explained, "The FBI was investigating whether Lennon and Ono were participating in keeping Kyoko hidden to avoid deportation. They weren't."

(Yoko didn't speak to Kyoko until the mid-1990s. Until 1977, Kyoko and her father, Tony Cox, had been members of a religious sect known as the Walk, which Cox said practiced a combination of Eastern mysticism, Christianity, and the occult. But after Tony became disenchanted with the Walk, he once again hid with Kyoko and continued to remain out of touch from Yoko, though Tony did call John in November 1977 to discuss a possible reunion with both John and Yoko that never took place. "It was just like we were all in a big giant cosmic car accident and each of us were taken to separate hospitals, you know?" John said. But in 1997, Kyoko called her widowed mother from where the now-married daughter lived in Denver, Colorado, to tell Yoko that she had become a grandmother with the birth of Kyoko's daughter, Emi. Yoko said that in the interim years, "We were getting calls from people all the time claiming, 'I'm your daughter,' and there would be a photograph of some blonde, blue-eyed woman, but the first time I heard Kyoko's voice, I knew it was her.")

It wasn't until December 2006, however, that the federal government released the last ten documents from its Lennon archive — almost twenty-six years after Jon Wiener began his Freedom of Information Act quest and more than thirty-four years after the INS first ordered John Lennon to leave the country. Wiener acknowledged that "there is nothing in these latest documents that we didn't already know about" Lennon. "What this is really about is the FBI and the four presidents since Nixon who kept this secret. It's got to be an embarrassment to them that they fought so hard and for so long to keep something secret that is so public and so trivial."

Among the final documents, a February 1972 FBI memo stated: "Lennon has encouraged the belief that he holds revolutionary views . . . by the content of some of his songs and other publications." The FBI was especially concerned with the rally-cry recording "Power to the People," the March 1971 Lennon chart single that certainly was no secret.

The FBI had ended its file gathering on John Lennon's immigration case in December 1972, shortly after Richard Nixon was reelected president. (The agency opened a file later in the 1970s regarding an extortion threat aimed at Lennon.) Jon Wiener found no evidence of further government surveillance of John Lennon after 1972, and doesn't think he was under government surveillance either when he pursued the Lennon files.

But according to close Lennon friend Elliot Mintz, John was concerned from then on about government surveillance. "It had become almost like a paranoia with John," Mintz said. "And he remained very wary and secretive for the rest of his life."

In his later years, however, John Lennon was fascinated with the notion of electronic surveillance. According to Jack Douglas, who produced John and Yoko's last album *Double Fantasy* in 1980, John told him, "I wish somebody would bug me, because all the best things get said when there's no microphone around." Douglas said he then secretly recorded "[e]verything that was ever said in the control room or that came into the control room from the studio . . . right on through the very last day of mixing." When *Double Fantasy* was finished, the record producer reminded John, "Remember you said you always wanted somebody to bug you?" Douglas handed him about two hundred tapes. "He loved it, he absolutely loved it," Douglas said.

But the pop-sounding *Double Fantasy* release did lack the type of overt political statements that Lennon previously included in his works. Still, John's immigration saga had a larger lasting impact in several ways. "The use of the Freedom of Information Act as a litigative tool in the immigration field began with the litigation involving John Lennon," Leon Wildes said. "That case was a complete win," as the immigration agency for the first time made public its provisions for determining when deportations of otherwise excludable immigrants might be deferred.

John Lennon also obtained the precedential Second Circuit Court of Appeals ruling that gave greater consideration to an individual's due process rights when it came to how foreign laws should be interpreted by us authorities. Most importantly for musicians like Lennon, the Second Circuit had issued its warning that it wouldn't tolerate deportations of artists based on a secret political agenda by the federal government.

Jon Wiener recently noted he didn't know of any John Lennon–type deportation efforts by us presidents since the Lennon case. And Leon Wildes believed that, even as John and Yoko cited their pursuit of her daughter Kyoko as the primary reason for remaining in the United States, John "was 100 percent" concerned with the freedom of expression component of his immigration fight.

"The free speech aspect was part of his soul," Wildes said.

PART FOUR

GOT TO BE A JOKER, HE JUST DO WHAT HE PLEASE

17 : "I've Caught the Beatles!"

ctober 9, 1974, was a busy day for John Lennon. Not only was it his thirty-fourth birthday, but he was scheduled to be deposed in the lawsuit his former manager Allen Klein had brought against Lennon, George Harrison, and Ringo Starr alleging they owed Klein management commissions. Yet, Lennon spent much of Wednesday, October 9, at the Record Plant studio on West 44th Street in Manhattan, reviewing recordings he had made for *Rock 'n' Roll*, a tribute album to favorite songs from his youth. "It's something I've been wanting to do for years. In between takes on all sessions, Beatle days and since, we always messed around doing those sort of songs," Lennon said.

John had begun the *Rock 'n' Roll* project the year before in Los Angeles with producer Phil Spector. *Rock 'n' Roll* was delayed, however, after Spector seized and kept the tapes, purportedly to protect his financial investment in the studio costs for the album, then due to a car accident that Phil said had left him seriously injured. Lennon's calls to Spector went unanswered, but Lennon got the tapes back several months later after his label, Capitol Records, paid Spector $93,000.

"It was a weird day for a session," John Lennon said about October 9. "They had a big spread or something for my birthday, and birthdays are something I try to avoid. I try to work so they won't harass me about 'Happy Birthday.' But there was the spread and people coming and listening."

One unlikely guest stood out among the musicians and friends eating birthday cake and sipping champagne at the Record Plant: Morris Levy, a notorious music industry figure with reputedly extensive Mob ties. But Levy stood out in most crowds. He "had a helluva mug—big head, piercing eyes—and huge hands," recalled former CBS Records president Walter Yetnikoff, who knew Levy well. "When he stood, he towered . . . like a mountain. His rough-hewn face was covered in a scowl. Rather than talk, he barked. His accent was guttural New York street."

During a dinner with Levy the night before, John Lennon had asked Morris to stop in at the Record Plant to hear Lennon's versions of "Angel Baby" and "You Can't Catch Me," two early rock 'n' roll songs that Levy's Big Seven publishing company controlled. Lennon had agreed to record the Levy copyrights to settle a suit Levy filed alleging the Lennon song "Come Together," from the Beatles' 1969 *Abbey Road* album, infringed on the copyright for "You Can't Catch Me," written in the 1950s by Chuck Berry. John Lennon often acknowledged his musical influences, and Chuck Berry was near the top of the list. But Levy's complaint was the first serious infringement claim against one of the Beatles. KPM, the publisher of the Glenn Miller Band's copyrighted 1940s arrangement of the song "In the Mood," had protested Beatles producer George Martin's inclusion of a snippet of it in the Beatles' 1967 recording "All You Need Is Love," but that dispute was immediately settled with a payment to KMP that Martin said EMI ordered him to make. Morris Levy's infringement action over "Come Together," on the other hand, had serious implications for John's reputation as a songwriter.

Levy had arrived at the Record Plant midafternoon on October 9, 1974, with Phil Kahl, his music-publishing associate, and Lou Garlick, president of Ivy Hill Lithographers, which manufactured the album jackets for Levy's record releases. At the New York recording studio, Lennon played Levy "the tracks that belonged to him and a couple more, because I was not going to say, 'Well, now, get out, you heard your two songs.'" In fact, Levy liked what he heard so much that he believed he could gain an even greater opportunity for himself from Lennon's recording sessions beyond John just including some Levy-owned songs on the oldies album. So Levy made sure that, during the fall of 1974, he and John Lennon would become frequent companions. For his part, Lennon said, "I was intrigued by him as a character. That's one way of putting it."

∘ ∘ ∘ ∘ ∘ For many in the music business, Morris Levy was difficult to avoid; he cast a wide shadow over the industry long before his legal episode with John Lennon. Born in August 1927, Levy grew up in a rough section of New York City's Bronx borough and was sent to reform school after striking his sixth-grade teacher. As a teenager, Levy worked coat-check concessions in New York City nightclubs, where he linked up with an assortment of tough guys and mobsters, some of whom became his music-business partners later on.

"I used to book talent, run concert tours in Carnegie Hall for jazz shows," Levy said. "During the 1950s, I was involved with Alan Freed and rock 'n' roll packages." (Alan Freed was the pioneer rock 'n' roll disc jockey who Levy managed and whose career was torpedoed by a congressional investigation into radio airplay payola.) Levy was also the Mob's front man for the landmark Birdland jazz club he owned in Manhattan. In addition, he began operating music publishing firms and record labels, including Roulette Records, one of the industry's largest independents with an artist roster that included Pearl Bailey, Count Basie, Frankie Lymon, and Dinah Washington. David Chase, creator of the HBO series *The Sopranos*, has said the recurring character Hesh was based at least in part on Morris Levy.

Morris Levy first met John Lennon in February 1964, when the Beatles performed live on *The Ed Sullivan Show* from the Deauville Hotel in Miami Beach. Levy had arranged for the Beatles to use the swimming pool at his south Florida house, he said "because they couldn't swim in the hotel that they were staying at. They would have been mobbed."

It was during another crucial juncture in John Lennon's life that Morris Levy saw him again. When Morris attended John's birthday party in October 1974, John was not only in the middle of the complex legal battle with the Beatles' ex-manager Allen Klein, but he had also been separated since 1973 from his wife Yoko Ono. John was also awaiting the outcome of negotiations to resolve Paul McCartney's 1970 suit to dissolve the Beatles' partnership. And there was the fight against the politically driven efforts of President Richard Nixon's administration to deport Lennon from the United States. Nixon resigned his presidency in August 1974 over the Watergate scandal, but in July the Board of Immigration Appeals had ordered Lennon to leave the country.

"I had a hard year," John Lennon said about 1974. "I was tired, period." But Lennon would be soon be adding one more item to his list of woes: yet another lawsuit by Morris Levy.

○ ○ ○ ○ ○ Morris Levy originally sued over "Come Together" in Manhattan federal court on April 3, 1970. Levy's Big Seven Music filed a copyright infringement action against Beatles UK publisher Northern Songs, its US affiliate Maclen Music Inc. and the Beatles' New York-based Apple Records Inc. (Lennon wasn't named individually as a defendant.) Snapper Music, a publishing company Alan Freed formed to secure rights to songs in the movie *Rock, Rock, Rock*, had registered "You Can't Catch Me" with the US Copyright Office in 1956. Levy bought Snapper Music from Freed. "Freed got the rights to 'You Can't Catch Me' as a payola spinoff," said Levy counsel William Krasilovsky. "Then Freed needed money desperately, so he went to his friend Morris Levy, who said, 'I'll buy it.'"

In his song, Chuck Berry had sung, "Here come a flat-top." When John Lennon opened "Come Together" with "Here come old flat top," Morris Levy exclaimed, "It's wonderful! I've caught the Beatles!" Levy asked Krasilovsky, who coauthored *This Business of Music*, the first widely read book on the subject, to pursue Big Seven's "Come Together" infringement action. It was while working on the case that Krasilovsky first met rock 'n' roll pioneer Berry and became his lawyer for the next several decades.

In Big Seven's infringement action, Morris Levy sought the profits made from "Come Together," plus three times the then statutory licensing royalty of two cents per song for each record sold; destruction of the Beatles' master recording; and an injunction against continued exploitation of "Come Together." The "Come Together" defendants responded that John Lennon's "dynamic success with the public and with the overwhelming majority of music critics in this country should give rise to a presumption that underlying Mr. Lennon's creativity is not a secret ability to 'borrow' the material of other composers."

The primary method by which a copyright plaintiff establishes infringement is by showing that a defendant's work is "substantially similar" to the plaintiff's. Big Seven hired several musicologists to write its experts' reports. Harold Barlow, a songwriter, coauthor of the tomes *Dictionary of Musical Themes* and *Dictionary of Vocal Themes*, and a fixture on the expert witness circuit, prepared a note-by-note comparison of the first eight measures of Berry's song with the first four vocal measures of Lennon's song. Barlow found eighteen notes in common. In "Come Together," John Lennon had sung: "Here come old flat top / He come groovin' up slowly." Barlow lined this up with the section in "You Can't Catch Me" in which Chuck Berry sang: "Here come a flat-top / He was movin' up with me." Barlow concluded, "especially the similarities involving melody and text together, are sufficient in themselves alone . . . to make a worthy claim of infringement in this matter."

Big Seven also retained expert William Dawson, a graduate of the American Conservatory of Music in Chicago who organized the School of Music at the Tuskegee Institute of Alabama. Boasting his report was "a more accurate comparison" than Barlow's, Dawson spotted twenty-four notes in common in the first four measures of each tune. Dawson opined that "substantially all of the melody of 'Come Together' is similar to the basic melodic material of 'You Can't Catch Me.'" He also found strong similarities between the rhythms of the two songs and the patterns of the measures. In technical terms, Dawson explained, "under emotional influence, each artist sings at one time or another the third tone of the scale one half-step lower; at other times, one will sing the flatted third as an acciaccatura; i.e., sliding up from the flatted third of the major scale to the natural third of the major scale."

After the 1970 suit was filed, Big Seven wanted to depose John Lennon. But according to William Krasilovsky, to guard their privacy when they were in New York, "John and Yoko avoided daylight. They were living in the dark. I had private detectives looking for him." Lennon's manager Allen Klein offered Krasilovsky a deal: "Tell your detectives to stop looking for John. I will deliver him to you on my terms. You and your wife come to my place and stay overnight. We'll arrange for a private deposition."

"I was picked up by Klein's car at his residence around midnight," Krasilovsky continued, "and brought to meet with John and Yoko at the hotel they were staying at. Yoko was very militant about the situation and said that Chuck Berry should be thankful to John for putting him on the map. John Lennon's attitude was that Berry's music mentored him. Lennon was a compulsive fan. He had listened to the Chuck Berry record over and over again and said, 'It must have gotten into my subconscious with that "flat top" phrase.' We didn't have a court reporter present. Instead, we agreed on a handshake that Lennon would sign a stipulation of what his testimony would be. We manufactured a deposition for mutual convenience."

∘ ∘ ∘ ∘ ∘ In the brief deposition document, dated December 24, 1970, John Lennon claimed sole authorship of "Come Together," originally intended by him as a statement on counterculture politics. But he acknowledged that "ever since I was in my teens I was acquainted with the works of Chuck Berry, whom I consider one of the original rock and roll poets."

Chuck Berry recorded "You Can't Catch Me" in May 1955, at his first session for Chess Records in Chicago, along with three other original compositions, including his breakthrough national hit "Maybellene." In his autobiography, Berry recalled that prior to the session, "I had created many extra verses for other people's songs [that Berry performed in concert] and I was eager to do an entire creation of my own."

The lyrics in "You Can't Catch Me" were based on an experience Berry had while driving on the New Jersey Turnpike, when his Buick was "overtaken by some dudes with crew cuts (flat tops) who pulled up alongside us and passed us, waving." Berry revved up his car, which "smoking like a choo choo train" overtook the other vehicle, but he was pulled over by a state trooper and ticketed for speeding.

John Lennon wasn't sure whether Berry had "used the phrase 'flat top' to mean the second automobile, the driver of the second automobile or something else." But Lennon insisted "Come Together" had "nothing whatsoever to do with an automobile."

Lennon began developing "Come Together" as a campaign song for LSD guru Timothy Leary, who glommed on to the slogan for his proposed run for governorship of California. But Leary didn't follow through on the gubernatorial bid, so Lennon finished the song later. Lennon claimed he hadn't heard "You Can't Catch Me" for "approximately 10 to 11 years prior to the time I wrote my song" and not again until it was played for him at his deposition in the Big Seven case. (The Rolling Stones released a version of "You Can't Catch Me" in 1965. Though they were close friends of the Beatles, Lennon surprisingly claimed in his December 24, 1970, deposition, "I am not familiar with the recording.") As for Timothy Leary, Lennon said he "attacked me years later, saying I ripped him off." In his authorized biography *Many Years From Now*, Paul McCartney admitted to intentionally copying the bass line from Chuck Berry's recording "I'm Talking About You" for the Beatles' "I Saw Her Standing There." McCartney recalled that when John Lennon played his Beatles mate a draft of "Come Together," it was "a very perky little song, and I pointed out to him that it was very similar to Chuck Berry's 'You Can't Catch Me.'" But in a court affidavit,

Lennon emphasized that, unlike Berry's "You Can't Catch Me," the lyrics of "Come Together" were "a surrealistic stream of consciousness collection of words; to the extent they have meaning to anyone but me (and I've been [told] that many people don't understand them at all), the words are meant to describe the personality and characteristics of the 'old flat top.'"

Lennon added, "When I was a youth back in the 1950's," a teenager with a flattop haircut "was considered the coolest of the cool. When I used the popular 1950s phrase 'flat top' in the first line of 'Come Together,' I sought to describe the coolest of the cool in 1969, as he now appeared . . . i.e., a man with hair down to his knees, with unshined shoes, doing what he pleased, one holy roller who got to be free."

Prior common source is a defense to a copyright infringement claim. So, even if Big Seven could show the phrases "Here come" and "flat top" were copyright protectable, Lennon noted that the *Dick Tracy* comics villain "Flat Top" and the songs "Flattop Polka" by W. Schulz and "Flat Top Pickin'" by country artist Cowboy Copas were published uses prior to either the Berry or Lennon songs.

In any case, Lennon added about *Abbey Road* compositions, "in 1969 Paul McCartney and I wrote a song entitled 'Sun King' which begins 'Here come the Sun King. Here come the Sun King.'" And there was George Harrison's "Here Comes the Sun." "Neither Mr. Berry nor anyone else has ever claimed that the phrase 'Here come' or 'Here comes' in those songs infringed 'You Can't Catch Me,'" Lennon pointed out.

∘ ∘ ∘ ∘ ∘ Though Apple Records had been named a defendant in Big Seven's suit, Morris Levy's counsel William Krasilovsky recalled that Paul McCartney and McCartney's father-in-law, attorney Lee Eastman, "wanted no part of John Lennon's mistake and stayed on the sidelines. It wasn't a happy time for the Beatles, and Lee Eastman was nobody's fool. To the extent that Apple was sued, Lee got a warranty, so that any damages or cost would be borne by Lennon."

The "Come Together" litigation was overseen by New York federal district judge Thomas P. Griesa, described by *Rolling Stone* columnist Dave Marsh as "a small, middle-aged, but boyish-looking Kennedy type who seems unimposing until you sit next to him." Big Seven planned to call

Chuck Berry as a trial witness. But Morris Levy offered to drop the suit in return for 50 percent of the income from "Come Together." "I am calling the shots," Levy bragged.

William Krasilovsky's settlement talks with Apple Records' defense counsel Rosenman Colin were guided behind the scenes by ABKCO executive (and later John Lennon business advisor) Harold Seider. Seider had known Krasilovsky from when both worked early in their careers for well-known copyright lawyer John Schulman. Seider wasn't about to let Levy have a 50 percent stake in Lennon's song. Instead, he instructed Rosenman Colin "to tell the Big Seven attorney to 'stick it up his ass'; in other words no."

But on October 11, 1973, the night before the trial was to begin, the parties did agree to a settlement. "Judge Griesa had invited his wife to come to court that next morning to hear the case over the Beatles' song," Krasilovsky said. "I think he was angry we settled it 'behind his back.'"

Under the settlement terms, Big Seven agreed to withdraw its complaint in exchange for John Lennon's promise that "his next album" would contain renditions of "You Can't Catch Me" and two other Big Seven songs, which Lennon could choose. They would be "Angel Baby" by Rosie & the Originals and "Ya Ya" by Lee Dorsey, both Top 10 hits in 1961, though Lennon reserved the right to change his mind about the latter two compositions as long as he substituted two other Big Seven songs in their place.

The settlement further provided that Lennon would "use his best efforts" to convince the Beatles "to license to Big Seven three songs from the Apple non-Beatle catalog currently" in print on records by Apple artists, such as Badfinger, Mary Hopkin, and James Taylor, "excluding only those songs composed by John Lennon and Yoko Ono Lennon together and those songs composed by Paul McCartney and Linda McCartney together." If Lennon failed to get the Beatles' approval by December 31, 1974, he promised he would record two additional songs from Levy.

The Big Seven settlement made sense to Lennon because, in October 1973, he was recording his collection of rock 'n' roll oldies in Los Angeles with producer Phil Spector and already intended to record "Angel Baby," one of his all-time favorites. "Then I found out that [Levy] owned it. I thought, 'Great,'" Lennon said. Lennon's oldies project was part of an early 1970s trend, one in which artists and listeners turned back to rock 'n' roll's early years for reassurance following the turbulent 1960s. The Band, for example, had recorded the oldies album *Moondog Matinee* for Capitol Records.

Before the October 12, 1973, settlement hearing before Judge Griesa was over, Northern Songs defense attorney Peter Parcher wanted it included in the court record that John Lennon agreeing to record the Big Seven songs "in no way creates any inference so far as we are concerned that any infringement was proved or can be inferred from the settlement."

18 "I Am Always Worried"

With Morris Levy's infringement suit against him settled, John Lennon could better focus his music sights on his *Rock 'n' Roll* album project in Los Angeles. Unfortunately for John, however, the studio sessions were dominated by Phil Spector's legendary erratic behavior. Spector was signed to produce the entire oldies project with Lennon ceding control of the production to Spector, who had worked with the Beatles before, including on solo Harrison and Lennon projects, and on *Let It Be*, through the patronage of Allen Klein. During the oldies sessions, Spector's wild antics included showing up in the studio dressed as a surgeon with a stethoscope dangling from his neck, as a priest, and as a cowboy. The high-strung Spector was also fueled by uppers he was taking. Apple Records executive Tony King recalled that when he and Elton John stopped by the *Rock 'n' Roll* sessions, "Phil was running around, spieling like a madman. John was trying to keep the situation under control, because by this stage Phil was the mad one and John didn't want Elton thinking there were two madmen there."

"It got a little out of hand," admitted Spector, "because it was the first vacation either of us had taken since we'd started our careers. We partied and invited too many people to the party. . . . It wasn't healthy and it wasn't good."

The most frightening incident resulted from Phil's obsession with guns and security; in addition to his ever-present bodyguard, Spector usually had his own weapon on him in a holster. One night during an argument with Lennon aide Mal Evans, Phil fired a gun into the studio ceiling. It happened when Phil's mother was visiting, during the recording of "You Can't Catch Me." "I remember Phil's mother was in the control room," said May Pang, who was John's girlfriend at the time. "And suddenly there was a pop! Everybody went, 'What's that?' and crouched down — including his mother."

John Lennon told the gun-toting producer, "Listen, Phil, if you're gonna kill me, kill me. But don't fuck with my ears. I need 'em."

The sessions were living on borrowed time. Unbeknownst to Lennon, Spector, who had assumed responsibility for paying the album studio costs, was safeguarding his investment by taking the *Rock 'n' Roll* master tapes home after each session. "I didn't know that until one night they weren't available," Lennon said. Lennon tried contacting the unpredictable Spector, "but it is very hard to get through to him if he doesn't want to — doesn't answer phones."

"I asked everyone I knew" to help pry the tapes from Spector, Lennon claimed. "This was the first time I had never finished an album." Lennon decided to complete the production of the album himself. "[W]e wholeheartedly approved of it as an artistic matter," Capitol Records president/ CEO Bhaskar Menon said, considering that Spector "was for a fairly protracted period of time unavailable, unreachable." Al Coury, a Capitol senior vice president, said. "What happened was that Phil Spector got into a very bad car accident, and from what I heard, he had some facial lacerations from the car accident. Phil took off and disappeared, he wanted to go off and take care of his facial injuries."

While waiting for Spector to return the *Rock 'n' Roll* tapes, Lennon tried his hand at producing an album titled *Pussy Cats* for Harry Nilsson, his booze- and drug-infused "Lost Weekend" comrade during John's eighteenmonth separation from Yoko. While the album was made, John with May Pang lived "dormitory" style at a rented Santa Monica beach house in Los Angeles once owned by film mogul Louis B. Mayer, then actor Peter Lawford. The party crowd living at the house included Nilsson, Ringo Starr, Who drummer Keith Moon, and bassist Klaus Voormann, a Lennon friend since the Beatles' days in Hamburg, Germany.

But despite a studio and house visit from John's estranged Beatles partner Paul McCartney and Paul's wife, Linda, and impromptu jams with Paul, *Pussy Cats* was another strained project for Lennon. Just as the recording of the album began, Nilsson blew out his vocal chords. "Harry told me he'd woken up on a beach somewhere after a night out with John," *Pussy Cats* drummer Jim Keltner recalled. "They'd both been doing a lot of screaming the night before, which John was really good at, and the next morning Harry found his voice was completely shot."

"I [didn't] know whether it was psychological or what," Lennon said. "He was going to the doctors and having injections and he didn't tell me till later he was bleeding in his throat or I would have stopped the session."

In the summer of 1974, after returning to New York City, Lennon completed *Pussy Cats* and started recording *Walls and Bridges*, an album of new songs John had recently written in a creative burst. "[I]t seems to me three or four days before I went in to record *Walls and Bridges*, suddenly I had all these Spector tapes," Lennon recalled. "There were 30 boxes of Spector tapes."

To get the tapes back, Lennon business advisor Harold Seider had given in to Phil Spector's demand for a higher producer's royalty. Lennon explained that Capitol Records' parent company EMI "somehow had a deal in which every producer who produced a Beatle song got a negligible sum of money. Now when Spector grabbed the tapes or kept them, he had heard that [record producer] Richard Perry had got more money from Ringo." Tired of haggling with Spector's lawyer Marty Machat, Seider finally told Machat, "Look, whatever Richard Perry got on the *Ringo* album, I'd be satisfied on behalf of John with regard to Phil."

That gave Spector a contractual 3 percent royalty rate for US, Canadian, and UK retail sales, and 2 percent for the rest of the world. EMI also promised to reimburse Spector $93,000 in recording costs. (A record label usually advances funds to an artist or producer to pay for the cost of the album. The label then recoups the money from the sales of the artist's album. The Beatles' recording contract with Capitol-EMI didn't give the label the right to recoup advances it gave the band members. In Lennon's case, Capitol initially gave Lennon a modest $10,000, to record the oldies album, though as producer Spector apparently incurred the lion's share of the cost of the sessions.)

EMI had sent the producer's agreement to Spector in May 1974; Lennon signed off on it in a letter of direction to EMI's London office by assuming responsibility for half of Spector's royalty entitlement. (Curiously, both the EMI/Spector agreement and Lennon's letter listed the Big Seven Music songs "Angel Baby" and "You Can't Catch Me," but neither document mentioned the third Morris Levy–controlled song, "Ya Ya," that Lennon had promised to record in settling Levy's "Come Together" infringement case against him. These EMI agreements would later be used by Levy in trying to show that Lennon failed to fulfill the terms of the "Come Together" settlement.)

Capitol Records paid Phil Spector an initial $83,000 to return the tapes. Bob Mercer, EMI Records London-based managing director, sent Capitol A&R executive Chan Daniels, who had been a member of the Highway-men folk group, to pick up the tapes from Spector. But after ninety minutes of waiting at Spector's Sunset Boulevard office in Los Angeles, a "hyper-ventilating" Daniels placed a frantic call to Mercer. Apparently, Spector had finally appeared, but was brandishing an axe. "Chan ran down twelve flights of stairs. In the end I had to send in a US marshal to get the tapes," Mercer said.

∘ ∘ ∘ ∘ ∘ John Lennon was "naturally overjoyed" to get the *Rock 'n' Roll* tapes back, Bhaskar Menon recalled. However, Lennon thought that the public's interest in the oldies revival may have peaked. "I did fear that per-haps it was a little too late for an oldies package," Lennon admitted. But then, he said, "I am always worried." An immediate concern was that Spec-tor hadn't handed over all the session recordings. This led to additional talks with Marty Machat, but within a few days Spector sent the last two tape sets, after Capitol executive Al Coury offered him the additional $10,000 Capitol still owed him.

Lennon began reviewing the tape cache as soon as he finished *Walls and Bridges*. "I had to listen to all the boxes to find out the good versions of the songs. That's the first thing I did," though he now viewed the *Rock 'n' Roll* album project as "more time-consuming and complicated" than the making of the Beatles' *Sgt. Pepper's* album.

Meanwhile, a promise John made to Morris Levy in the "Come To-gether" suit settlement became part of the discussions for settling the complaint Paul McCartney filed against John Lennon, George Harrison, and Ringo Starr in December 1970 to dissolve the Beatles partnership. Ad-visors for all four Beatles met in New York City in July 1974 to outline the Beatles-partnership dissolution terms, including rights to income from solo Beatles recordings.

Harold Seider attended the New York meeting as John Lennon's rep-resentative. A lawyer since 1959, Seider worked in various roles at Allen Klein's ABKCO from July 1967 until he left the company in November 1971,

including as executive vice president and member of the board of directors. He helped with the momentous 1969 renegotiation of the Beatles'
contract with Capitol Records and had been involved in negotiations with
United Artists for the rights to the Beatles' *Let It Be* movie and soundtrack
album.

In his "Come Together" settlement with Morris Levy, Lennon had
promised he would try his best to get the Beatles to license to Levy three
tracks that Levy could choose from Apple's non-Beatles artist catalog. Lennon's promise came with the condition that if the Beatles didn't agree by
December 31, 1974, to the Levy license, John would record two more Levy-
owned compositions in addition to the three he already agreed to record
to end Levy's "Come Together" infringement suit. At the July 1974 Beatles
advisors' meeting Lennon's promise to Levy came up "very late at night, it
was one of the last points," Harold Seider recalled. "We had very heated
and extensive disputes, and I insisted that Apple agree to license to Levy's
firm the required non-Beatles masters." The advisors reached a consensus
to incorporate Lennon's commitment to Levy into the Beatles' partnership
settlement, though George Harrison had previously balked at licensing
solo recordings by his close friend, Beatles session-keyboardist Billy Preston, "so they were deleted" from consideration.

Morris Levy nevertheless grew impatient with John Lennon. On September 6, Levy's lawyer William Krasilovsky wrote Apple Records' New
York lawyers at Marshall, Bratter, Greene, Allison & Tucker for confirmation of when Lennon's "next" album — per the "Come Together" settlement, with three Lennon-recorded songs from Levy's Big Seven Music
— would be released. It was Harold Seider who called Krasilovsky to explain "there would be some difficulties in complying with the agreement."
Seider wanted the "Come Together" settlement agreement to be revised
to stipulate that *Walls and Bridges*, the collection of mostly new Lennon
material that Capitol Records was set to issue on October 26, would count
as Lennon's "next" album, though it contained only one cover recording
by Lennon of a Big Seven tune. It was *Walls and Bridges'* last track, on
which John sang a 55-second snippet of the Lee Dorsey New Orleans–style
R & B song "Ya Ya" while eleven-year-old son Julian Lennon banged away
on drums. "Okay, we're just sittin' in a 'La La'; I'll get rid of that," Lennon
announced as the track began.

Krasilovsky claimed this breached the "Come Together" settlement. Any change to the agreement "should be cleared with Mr. Morris Levy directly," he told Harold Seider. When Seider called Levy, Levy demanded a meeting with Lennon. So they arranged to get together for dinner on Tuesday, October 8, at Club Cavallero, a new private-membership venue Levy owned on Manhattan's East 58th Street that featured a backgammon room.

When Lennon walked in for what Levy later described as "that fateful evening," Levy and publishing associate Phil Kahl were waiting at a horseshoe-shaped booth in the club's dining room. With Lennon were his personal assistant/"Lost Weekend" lover May Pang, his UK aide Bernard Brown, and Harold Seider. Pang recalled, "After we sat down in the booth and had our drinks ordered, Levy leaned over to Lennon, said, 'What happened?'"

A nervous Lennon admitted he had recorded "Ya Ya" as a "gag," "a laugh" with his son Julian. John explained the problems he had with Phil Spector and in not completing the *Rock 'n' Roll* project before *Walls and Bridges*. "[I]t was not a plan or a plot," Lennon said. He had indeed recorded three Big Seven songs with Spector in Los Angeles — "Angel Baby," a full-length version of "Ya Ya," and "You Can't Catch Me," the Chuck Berry song that Levy had accused Lennon of infringing on with the Beatles' "Come Together." But, "Phil Spector was crazy," Lennon continued. "He came to the studio with bandages around his head pretending he was in an accident once, a revolver went off in the studio . . . and the entire recording sessions were a disaster area, there was no stability, it was absolutely a clean screw up." (Spector's serious car accident happened in March 1974, several months after he and Lennon had stopped working together on the *Rock 'n' Roll* album.)

"Well, that's spilt milk," the husky-voiced Levy responded.

"Morris, will a couple of hundred thousand straighten this out?" Harold Seider asked.

"No," Levy bluntly replied.

Lennon told Levy, "Out of the tapes, out of the nine songs, there is [*sic*] only about four or five that can be really salvaged, because the others weren't that good at all." Lennon was considering releasing a four-song EP (extended play) record of his better-sounding oldies tracks and selling it via TV to "avoid the critics," who he thought were "lying in wait for it," especially after *Rolling Stone* reviewed his 1973 *Mind Games* album as "unbearably pretentious" and Lennon's "worst writing yet."

Levy was all ears as Lennon spoke. Through his Adam VIII subsidiary, Levy was heavily involved in selling rock 'n' roll oldies over TV. He recently had great success selling a *Greatest Rock and Roll Hits* compilation via TV ads that featured "The Twist" singer Chubby Checker on more than 300 US and Canadian TV stations.

(Levy was mired in a royalty controversy over the TV package. In 1972, the Harry Fox Agency, which represented music publishers, conducted an audit to determine how many units of *Greatest Rock and Roll Hits* Levy's company had actually sold. Doc Pomus, a writer of many early rock 'n' roll hits, including the Drifters' "Save the Last Dance for Me" that was in a Levy TV album, complained he hadn't received any royalties at all. Levy, who kept the sales figures confidential, claimed his TV campaign was "just a small business that never gets records certified." However, Checker's manager Irv Machonic had been told by a manufacturing plant source that nearly 14,000 orders for *Greatest Rock and Roll Hits* were being placed daily.)

"There was a famous commercial for 7 Up where a guy comes on in a leather jacket and says, 'Hi, remember me,'" Lennon said, brainstorming about TV ad possibilities for *Rock 'n' Roll*. He wanted to do a parody of the 7 Up ad to burlesque the Chubby Checker commercial.

"If you want to do it, you know, I have the outlets," Levy boasted to Lennon. "Chubby had not had a hit in three years and his salary went from $300 a week to seven or eight thousand dollars a week, because these commercials go right to the heart of America through TV." Levy wrote some artist royalty figures and album sales projections on a cocktail napkin. He claimed he could sell six or seven million albums this way, but Harold Seider cautioned Lennon, "No, you are signed to an exclusive contract still to EMI at this point."

Turning to Seider, Levy asked, "When are you getting the next plane going to England" to talk to EMI? As Levy and Seider sparred, Lennon jotted down songs, such as Gene Vincent's 1956 rocker "Be-Bop-a-Lula," that might round out his oldies project. "My policy all the time is whenever they get into figures or talking about business, I just tune out," Lennon said. "Morris would look at me to make a conversation, and I would indicate, 'Don't talk to me; I am already in the studio.'"

∘ ∘ ∘ ∘ ∘ The meeting at Club Cavallero lasted two hours. Before it was over, Lennon asked Levy to come to the Record Plant the next day — John's thirty-fourth birthday — to confirm that the three Big Seven songs had indeed been recorded during the Phil Spector sessions. "How does he know I was not lying to him at the table?" Lennon said.

When Levy arrived at the Record Plant, he "was ushered into the studio control room and he sat down and we played him the songs," May Pang explained. Then Levy invited Lennon to return to Club Cavallero that night to continue celebrating Lennon's birthday. After attending a banquet honoring Atlantic Records chief Ahmet Ertegun, Lennon, Pang, Seider, and Bernard Brown headed over to Morris Levy's Club Cavallero reception for John. About two-dozen people showed up for the birthday festivities, including Lennon's former manager Allen Klein, though he was embroiled in a bitter court battle with John over management issues. (Levy called Klein the next day to ask for a discounted rate on the ABKCO-controlled Sam Cooke song "Bring It On Home to Me" that Lennon wanted to include on his oldies project.)

October 9 wasn't the last time Levy and Lennon met at Club Cavallero, as Levy continued to insert himself into Lennon's life. On Monday, October 14, they met at the club to discuss the additional oldies Lennon might record to complete the *Rock 'n' Roll* album. Levy claimed that Lennon grew to like the private club so much, "We got him a membership because he wanted to come in on his own."

During the October 14 meeting, Levy extended another invitation to Lennon. This one was for John to visit Morris's dairy farm in Ghent, New York, two hours north of New York City. Levy had already asked Lennon to come to the farm for the just-ended weekend, but John declined, citing a planned visit to the Long Island home of his Rolling Stones friend Mick Jagger. When Lennon arrived at Club Cavallero on October 14, he "was very excited," Levy recalled. "Probably the first thing that was said was, 'I got a title for the album,' *Old Hat*," which Jagger had suggested to Lennon.

According to May Pang, prior to the October 14 meeting John had told her that if Levy again invited him to the dairy farm, he "was going to try his very best not to go, you know, that he didn't want to go up to the farm because he was too busy" preparing for the *Rock 'n' Roll* recording sessions at the Record Plant. Sure enough, when Lennon sat down, Levy immediately asked, "You are going to come up to the farm this weekend?"

"I have too many musicians. I just can't go," Lennon demurred. "I have the studio time booked."

"Don't worry about it. Bring the musicians," Levy persisted.

"I got up from the table at that point and went to the ladies' room or something," Pang said. By the time she returned, Lennon told her, "We are going to the farm this weekend." "What happened?" she asked. The intimidating Levy "convinced me in going," Lennon confessed.

○ ○ ○ ○ ○ Levy litigator William Schurtman recalled his client's farm was "set up like a luxury resort. And the nearest neighbor was five miles away, so Lennon and his musicians could play to their hearts' content." On Thursday, October 17, Morris Levy drove John Lennon, May Pang, and Lennon guitarist Eddie Mottau up to the 1,200-acre dairy property in Ghent. "There was a lot of conversation in the car," Levy said. The technologically challenged Lennon, who hadn't obtained a driver's license until his late twenties, asked, "'What the heck are you doing with your foot off the gas pedal,' because I had it in cruise control and he had never seen that before. We discussed that for ten minutes, how it works."

Lennon's first view of Levy's upstate property was the large wheat silos that bore the name of Levy's son "Adam." When Lennon stepped into the main house, with its Italian tiles and marble floors, he joked to Levy, "In which wing do the cows sleep?"

On Friday and Saturday, John rehearsed his band in the living room of the guest residence at the farm. The musicians in attendance included drummer Jim Keltner, guitarist Jesse Ed Davis, and bass player Klaus Voormann, all veterans of the Phil Spector oldies sessions. "We had to send out — this is a farm community — to get a typewriter," Levy recalled, because the poor-sighted Lennon "wanted all the lyrics on a separate sheet of paper in all capitals."

In what became a contested issue, Levy claimed that, during the rehearsals, Lennon told the musicians that he was making the album for Morris. Lennon denied making such a statement, saying of the rehearsal sessions, "It's like being in a bath. You don't discuss it. You're having a bath." According to Jesse Ed Davis, Levy didn't attend any of the farmhouse rehearsals. "Nobody gets in John's sessions," the guitarist maintained.

○ ○ ○ ○ ○ Morris Levy and Allen Klein had known each other since the 1950s, when Klein pursued a royalty claim against Levy's Roulette Records on behalf of Jimmy Bowen, a member of the Rhythm Orchards, the Texas rock band that backed Buddy Knox on "Party Doll," a number two *Billboard* hit in 1957. In early 1973, when Klein was still representing the Beatles, he received a phone call from Levy proposing that Levy be given the right to release a two-album Beatles greatest-hits package for sale via TV mail order. Bootleg Beatles albums were being hawked on the tube, and Klein and the Beatles had been contemplating what to do.

The Beatles and Capitol Records did file suit in New York state court in February 1973 against Audiotape Inc., which was marketing a pirated sixty-song, four-album Beatles *Alpha Omega* set over TV. Print ads published in conjunction with Audiotape's TV campaign described the Beatles as: "Four raga-muffins with 'outrageous haircuts' that woke up the world." Audiotape had promised to indemnify participating TV stations against legal claims over the promotion and placed a million dollars in a New Jersey bank just in case. The Beatles and Capitol sought an injunction and $15 million in punitive damages, but the suit was quietly settled in May 1973.

Morris Levy and Allen Klein didn't strike up a deal, however, on Levy's proposal to distribute Beatles albums. Instead, in April 1973 Capitol released two greatest-hits packages, *The Beatles — 1962–1966* (known for its cover as the *Red* album) and *1967–1970* (known as the *Blue* album), through traditional retail outlets. However, in their phone conversation Klein did tell Levy that it was the Beatles, not Capitol, who had the right to determine who got the US mail-order rights to Beatles-related records.

○ ○ ○ ○ ○ On Monday, October 21, 1974, John Lennon returned to New York City from Morris Levy's farm to record the basic tracks for the additional songs needed to complete the *Rock 'n' Roll* project. These Record Plant sessions were completed on October 25. Levy now told Harold Seider what Klein had said to him the previous year about Beatles mail-order rights. Levy also saw an earlier interview with Klein in *Playboy* magazine in which Allen was quoted as saying that, under the Beatles renegotiated 1969 recording agreement with Capitol-EMI, "We got the boys increased royalties, but more important than that, we got them total control and ownership of their product in America."

Levy was convinced that he didn't need EMI's consent to release a TV package of Lennon's oldies recordings. When Levy informed Seider that he planned to market them as *John Lennon Sings the Great Rock & Roll Hits: Roots*, Seider exclaimed, "Shit! That's the record club rights" to Beatles' product, not TV mail order, that Klein must have been talking to Levy about. Seider told Levy, "It's a Mexican standoff, and Allen is wrong."

"Okay, Bubby," Levy replied. "And then he just — hung up," Seider said.

But Seider had cautioned Levy "that Klein and the Beatles and Lennon were in litigation" over the Beatles' March 1973 firing of Klein, "that Klein was, I believe, not terribly happy with me because I was now advising John and that Klein would be a spoiler and a troublemaker and please don't talk to Allen."

Levy had been calling Harold Seider every few days. He was determined to get a copy of the Lennon oldies recordings. On his own, Lennon agreed to meet Levy in late October 1974 at Club Cavallero to give him a 7½-inch, rough-mix copy of the oldies tracks. (Final studio mixes were done on higher-quality 15-inch recording tape.) When Lennon told Seider, a distressed Seider responded, "I am sorry you did that."

○ ○ ○ ○ ○ Despite Seider's concern about Klein, in November 1974 Lennon made a surprise visit to ABKCO's offices in Manhattan. He had been visiting the editorial headquarters of the trade magazine *Record World*, which was located in the same building as ABKCO. "On the way down from *Record World*, I popped in to say hello," John said.

"I hear you are doing an album with Morris Levy," Klein said to Lennon.

"Maybe," Lennon responded.

"Anyway," Klein continued, "you don't have to give anything to Morris or Capitol" because, as he had claimed to Levy, the Beatles retained the TV mail-order rights themselves.

"You must be crazy!" Lennon exploded. "We could have been putting these things out for years if there was such a big hole in the contract. How come we haven't been doing it? We could have been doing [exploiting these rights] for the last ten years!"

Meanwhile, Morris Levy kept dogging John Lennon. *Sgt. Pepper's Lonely Hearts Club Band on the Road*, a theatrical production by music impresario Robert Stigwood, premiered at the Beacon Theater in New York City on November 17, 1974. Both John Lennon and Paul McCartney attended. Morris Levy was there, too, after successfully pressing Lennon for complimentary tickets.

"I remember waving to [Morris] at the opening," recalled Harold Seider, who was back in New York from his California base as an executive at United Artists to review full drafts of the Beatles partnership-dissolution agreement on behalf of Lennon. In addition, Levy had persuaded Seider to meet with him yet again at Club Cavallero to discuss another plan Levy had for Beatles-related product. Levy was deeply involved in the "cut-out" business, through which unsold records returned to labels by retailers got redistributed for sale to consumers at rock-bottom prices. He had heard that Apple Records, which struggled to establish careers for many of its rostered artists, wanted to sell off records it was deleting from its non-Beatles catalog. Levy was also interested in unsold copies that United Artists had of the Beatles *Let It Be* album.

Before addressing Apple's record inventory, Levy wanted to know whether Seider had talked to EMI about the mail-order release of Lennon's oldies album. "Morris, what are you looking for?" Seider asked Levy. By now EMI had funded more than $200,000 in studio costs for Lennon's oldies project. Did Levy want a joint venture? "I would with John, but not with EMI," Levy answered. Levy thought TV sales of his Lennon *Roots* release would generate $1.23 in profit per album, of which he wanted a dollar. "If you take a dollar, there is certainly nothing left for John. It's cuckoo," Seider said.

○ ○ ○ ○ ○ "Whatever Gets You Thru the Night," John Lennon's vocal duet with Elton John from *Walls and Bridges*, had topped *Billboard* magazine's singles chart on November 16, 1974. It was the first Lennon solo release to reach that position. In one of rock's most famous stories, just before the track was issued, Lennon, who hadn't performed live since a TV appearance on the *Jerry Lewis Muscular Dystrophy Telethon* in September 1972, promised Elton that if the single reached number one on the charts, he would perform live on stage with Elton. To fulfill the promise, Lennon first traveled to Boston to see Elton in concert because "I had not been on stage for a long time. I wanted to know what the game was. I had forgotten." Thanksgiving night, John Lennon performed three songs with Elton John at Madison Square Garden, a performance that would be Lennon's last before a live audience. It was also the night when, after more than a year apart, he reignited his relationship with his wife Yoko Ono, who, unbeknownst to him, had been in the audience before greeting him backstage after the show.

Paul McCartney was also in New York City as the end of 1974 approached. Despite much prior public acrimony between them, Lennon said that the two former Beatles often got together when Paul was in New York. "We go to dinner and we talk." But in December 1974, McCartney was in New York to push through dissolution of the Beatles' band partnership.

George Harrison was in New York, too, in December. George had been on the road with his US solo *Dark Horse* tour. (He had recently started Dark Horse Records.) The final *Dark Horse* concerts were to take place at Madison Square Garden on December 19 and 20. "There was some speculation as to whether I was supposed to go on stage with him," John Lennon said. As with Elton John, Lennon first went to see George in concert, on December 15 at the Nassau Coliseum on Long Island. After that show, Lennon visited Harrison at the Plaza Hotel. But Lennon was a no-show on stage at the Garden. "I was a bit nervous about going on stage but I agreed to because it would have been mean of me not to go on with George after I'd gone on with Elton," Lennon said. "It got complicated," however, Lennon explained. "It had to do with the Beatles settlement coming to a head."

A who's who of Beatles' associates attended the Beatles-dissolution signing ceremony on December 19 at the Plaza Hotel, famous in Beatles history for being the music group's headquarters during their first US visit in February 1964. Paul McCartney's advisors — father-in-law Lee Eastman and brother-in-law John Eastman — were there to represent Paul, who had his wife Linda at his side. George Harrison had personal manager Denis O'Brien and attorney David Braun with him. Ringo Starr signed the settlement papers back in England to avoid being served with legal papers in New York by Allen Klein, but Starr's business manager Hilary Gerrard and attorney Bruce Grakal were at the Plaza summit. So was Harold Seider for John Lennon, along with the legal team of David Dolgenos and Michael Graham. Apple Corps manager-director and longtime Beatles confidant Neil Aspinall rounded out the momentous gathering, accompanied by several Apple lawyers.

John Lennon didn't show up. He instead had a balloon delivered to the Plaza with a note stating, "Listen to this balloon." Harold Seider called Lennon's apartment, which was just a few blocks away, but John wouldn't come to the phone. "I was home with John. It was up to me to tell Harold that John had decided to not go to the meeting at The Plaza," May Pang said.

According to Paul McCartney, "George blew his cool and rang him up: 'You fucking maniac!! You take your fucking dark glasses off and come and look at us, man!!' and gave him a whole load of that shit." Harrison was also sore at Lennon's reticence to appear on stage with him. Pang recalled that, when she answered George's phone call, he shouted as Lennon listened over her shoulder.

To quell tensions, Paul and Linda McCartney visited John the next day. Also on December 20, Lennon and Neil Aspinall met with Lee Eastman to discuss the complex terms of the dissolution agreement. That night, according to May Pang, Harrison, Lennon, and McCartney were all hugs at the tour-ending party George threw at the Hippopotamus Club in Manhattan. But Lennon still hadn't signed the Beatles dissolution deal; instead, he decided to leave for Florida, to visit Disney World with Morris Levy.

19 ○ Expedience on All Sides

orris Levy had played another card in his campaign to ingratiate himself with John Lennon by inviting John, May Pang (John didn't officially reunite with Yoko until January 1975), and John's eleven-year-old son, Julian, from his first marriage to Cynthia Lennon, to join Morris at Disney World in Orlando. Julian was visiting John from England for the Christmas holidays, and Levy's son Adam, who was in Orlando with Morris, was the same age as Julian.

John, May, and Julian flew to Florida on December 22, 1974. Lennon said he accepted Levy's Florida invitation "because I was so worn out anyway" from back-to-back studio projects "that I didn't know what to do with my son Julian." John figured that at Disney World, "I could sort of sit in a room or something and Julian could play with Morris's kid."

Levy saw the Disney World junket as an opportunity to pressure Lennon without other business distractions, about Levy releasing the Lennon oldies project through Levy's TV mail-order company, Adam VIII. But Lennon, Levy, their sons, and Pang spent only one day together at the massive Disney World amusement park. Because John had refused to attend the meeting the week before in New York at which the other Beatles completed their signing of the agreement that dissolved the band's partnership, on Thursday, December 26, Lennon's business advisor Harold Seider flew to Florida with a set of the dissolution documents for John to sign. When Seider walked into the living room of the adjoining rooms Lennon and Levy were staying at, in the Polynesian Village Hotel in Orlando, "one of the kids—somebody had one of those rubber masks that you put on your head, funny face," Seider recalled.

Levy soon "came in, he had just gotten up." Levy wondered whether Seider had flown to Florida to negotiate an agreement for Levy to distribute the Lennon oldies album. "What was happening in flying down like that?" Levy asked. "It's the breakup of the Beatles," Seider replied.

John Lennon spent Friday the 27th sequestered in Seider's room at the nearby Dutch Inn, going over the complex Beatles settlement documents "for the hundredth time," Lennon stated. The Lennon/Levy travel group then headed to Palm Beach, where Lennon and Seider continued their discussions on Saturday at Levy lithographer Lou Garlick's apartment, which Levy had procured for Lennon at the fashionable Sun & Surf. The Florida discussions between Lennon and Seider were so intensive, "We didn't see John Lennon for two days," Levy complained.

On Sunday, Lennon and Seider returned to New York. "We met John late that evening at John's studio and John signed the papers. I remember he had Polaroid pictures taken of him signing the papers." (As with many moments in Beatles history, recollections vary as to where Lennon actually signed the Beatles dissolution papers. May Pang recalled it was at the Polynesian Village Hotel at Disney World where she took the photos of John signing the dissolution documents. Harold Seider recalled the signing taking place in New York. Lennon alternatively said it was at his Manhattan apartment or "in Disneyworld in Florida with my son Julian. I thought it suited the occasion.") But Lennon still wasn't certain what the Beatles dissolution documents meant. Over a year later, he admitted, "It is beyond my ability of understanding it."

∘ ∘ ∘ ∘ ∘ Soon after returning to New York, John plowed back into his slow-moving *Rock 'n' Roll* project. On January 28, 1975, he met with Capitol Records senior vice president/promotion director Al Coury and art director Roy Kohara at the Sherry-Netherland Hotel in Manhattan to discuss the design and promotion of *Rock 'n' Roll*.

One album cover possibility was a mockup Lennon had prepared of different people's bodies, each with Lennon's face pasted on as the head. He also liked a mockup of the cover of Elvis Presley's *50,000,000 Elvis Fans Can't Be Wrong* album, on which Presley was dressed in a gold lamé suit and Lennon's head was pasted over Presley's. The *Rock 'n' Roll* cover that Lennon approved featured a photograph of him taken in the early 1960s by Jürgen Vollmer, one of the Beatles' friends from Hamburg, Germany. In the photo, Lennon stood, in black leather jacket and early rocker haircut, in a doorway beneath a neon sign. The Capitol promotion team called Vollmer from the Sherry-Netherland that night to negotiate use of the cover photo for $500.

Al Coury's position was that the album was strong enough to be sold through Capitol's regular distribution network, rather than TV mail order, and the decision was made to release *Rock 'n' Roll* through normal retail channels. For the advertising campaign, John wanted a 1950s-style ad featuring an actor combing back heavily greased hair. "I think we even discussed holding a dance party, like they used to hold the dance parties in the late '50s and the early '60s," Harold Seider recalled. "It would be a hell of a campaign."

According to Levy lawyer William Schurtman, Lennon had told Morris Levy that he wouldn't be ready to consider Levy releasing the oldies album until the Beatles settled their partnership dispute. "Otherwise," Lennon told Levy, "all my royalties from the album will go to the Beatles." "Levy reluctantly agreed to wait," Schurtman said. But when Lennon gave the album to Capitol, "Levy was furious and decided to go ahead on his own."

Morris Levy had called John Lennon several times following the Florida trip. "One of the telephone conversations was to let us know that he was back and 'How is John?,'" May Pang recalled. "The second one was to tell us Julian's toys were being sent up from Florida." Then Levy called again in late January, after Lennon's strategy session with Al Coury and Roy Kohara. The impatient Levy warned Pang to "just tell John that I am putting out" the oldies album, composed of the rough-mix tapes Lennon had given Levy back in October. "There is [sic] no hard feelings. If he wants to, he can re-mix just a couple of songs," Levy offered. "I respect his artistic ability."

"I was shocked," Lennon later said. "I thought he had a nerve asking me to edit the tapes while he is going to put them out anyway. But I was a bit stunned and scared because I thought I was in trouble." Lennon contacted Harold Seider that night, but Seider had already spoken to Levy since Florida. On December 31, David Dolgenos, a New York attorney for the Beatles, had sent Levy a list of seven non-Beatles masters that Levy could choose three from to distribute. The offer was part of the settlement of Levy's 1970 infringement suit against the Beatles' Apple Records and music publishers over Lennon's song "Come Together."

The seven choices in Dolgenos's letter included "Those Were the Days" by Mary Hopkin, "Carolina On My Mind" by James Taylor, and "Come and Get It" by Badfinger. Levy rejected all seven. Instead, Levy wrote Dolgenos that Lennon had "breeched [sic]" a different condition of the 1973 "Come Together" settlement agreement by not already releasing cover recordings of three Levy-controlled songs. But Levy added this had since been "resolved during meetings with John Lennon, Harold Sider [*sic*] . . . and myself" in fall 1974 at Club Cavallero in Manhattan. Under the purported resolution, Levy wrote, "John Lennon has recorded sixteen (16) sides which I will market throughout the world by use of television advertising. Please adjust your records to indicate that the original [settlement] is no longer of any effect."

Morris Levy had other, ongoing business with Capitol, including negotiations for his Adam VIII to get mail-order rights to some of Capitol's us catalog recordings. But Levy wanted to talk to Capitol Records president Bhaskar Menon about Adam VIII's TV marketing plan for the Lennon *Roots* release. Menon, the former head of EMI's India affiliate, had been president of Capitol Records since 1971. He was brought in to strengthen the label's prospects after its stock dropped from a high of $56 per share in November 1969 to a low of $6 per share in 1971, as a result of the record company's struggle to establish new artists in the post-Beatles era. Capitol in-house counsel Charles Tillinghast described Menon as having "a brilliant mind with great self-assurance combined with the ability to hobnob with the variety of talented artists, people of all levels of sophistication." But Menon balked at talking to Levy about the Lennon album; no meeting took place. Instead, Menon met with Harold Seider to discuss how to block Levy from releasing *Roots*.

Menon said he had recently heard from Lennon's former manager, Allen Klein. Klein, who Seider considered a spoiler in the Morris Levy controversy, had injected himself into the *Roots* dispute by placing several calls to Menon over a two-day period. Klein would first talk with Levy, then phone Menon. Klein conspiratorially told Menon: "I just think that this an awful thing to be happening to a fine fellow like you, and I just feel that I ought to keep you informed, more or less in the manner of a friend of the court."

Menon described his conversations with Klein as "strange and inexplicable." But it was from Klein that Menon had learned Levy claimed the right to release the Lennon tapes. Menon told Klein "that was bullshit," noting "the absence of any shortage of information on the subject even to outsiders" that the Beatles were signed to Capitol Records, that "unless someone were either, or, and, totally ignorant of the record business . . . no one would contemplate such a course of action."

Lennon "laughed it off" and denied having any conversation with Morris Levy that would have allowed Levy to think he had the right to release *Roots*. Menon, in any case, concluded that Klein should have "no particular role or status in this whole matter."

∘ ∘ ∘ ∘ ∘ Harold Seider went up to Morris Levy's Manhattan office on January 30, 1975, to confront the escalating *Roots* crisis. Seider bluntly informed Levy that "all bets are off," that Capitol wouldn't give Levy permission to release the Lennon oldies tapes and that "they were putting out the album themselves." Levy responded with "some profanity" and phoned his legal counsel William Schurtman to come right over.

While waiting for Schurtman, Levy defiantly played the rough-mix tape that Lennon had handed him at Club Cavallero of Lennon's version of "You Can't Catch Me." Suddenly, Levy's "Come Together" litigation lawyer William Krasilovsky walked into the office. "And I thought to myself, 'Morris didn't call Bill while I was there, so obviously Bill is there by pre-arrangement,'" Seider recalled. "So I got kind of nervous, 'what the hell is going on here.'"

Krasilovsky had ostensibly stopped in to discuss a case with Levy that involved the singer Sarah Vaughn, who recorded for Levy's Roulette Records. But Seider recalled Krasilovsky saying about Levy's planned *Roots* release "that the public will be served."

"I was a bit stunned by the kind of attitude that was going on there," Seider said, adding that within a few minutes William Schurtman appeared, too. Seider "got the feeling" that Levy "was trying to stampede me" and decided to leave. On his way out he bumped into Nate McCalla, a sometime Mob enforcer for Levy and owner of a successful independent label Levy distributed that charted national hits like "But It's Alright" by J. J. Jackson. McCalla was on his way in to talk to Morris about the band War, for which McCalla was artists' representative. "Oh, God. Irony of ironies," Harold Seider said of the match between the band's name and his just-ended meeting with Levy.

∘ ∘ ∘ ∘ ∘ Morris Levy continued to ready his *Roots* package by calling John Lennon photographer Bob Gruen for an album cover photo. "Don't worry," Levy said to Gruen, "I'll put the artwork together, and I'll make sure

John sees it." But Lennon warned Gruen, "Don't show him anything, and don't let him see anything." Levy instead used a fuzzy, soft-focus photo of Lennon, from another source, for the cover of *Roots*.

Lennon was back at work editing the *Rock 'n' Roll* tapes when, on February 7, Levy's Adam VIII started selling the *Roots* rough mix over TV. Adam VIII priced *Roots* — which contained two extra tracks of questionable quality, "Be My Baby" and Big Seven's "Angel Baby," that Lennon decided to leave off his official album release — at a low $4.98 per record and $5.98 per tape. Lennon heard about Levy's release from Jimmy Iovine, the assistant engineer at the Record Plant (and, in recent years, a chairman of Universal Music's Interscope Geffen A&M record label and cofounder of Beats Music). "Hey, what is going on? Your record is on TV," Iovine alerted Lennon.

Levy's move forced Capitol Records to rush-release *Rock 'n' Roll*, on February 15. To compete with *Roots*, Capitol lowered its customary suggested retail price from $6.98 to $5.98 per album. "Capitol wrote letters to everyone in the industry," William Schurtman said, "including the company printing Levy's album cover and the album's manufacturer, warning them to stay away from the project or face heavy damages." The label also sent cease-and-desist letters ordering TV stations to stop hawking the Levy package, which in the end sold only 1,270 copies and grossed less than $7,000, certainly not enough to cover Levy's manufacturing and advertising expenses. But Lennon feared being haunted by pirated copies of the unfinished-sounding *Roots*. Still, *Rock 'n' Roll* sold 342,000 copies in the United States in its first twelve months of release, a respectable number considering that Lennon's 1973 *Mind Games* sold 376,000 and 1974 *Walls and Bridges* sold 425,000 copies.

Bhaskar Menon blasted *Roots* as "inferior, inappropriate, frankly totally disgusting." He apocalyptically proclaimed it "a severe constriction, a severe eclipse of the whole image of Lennon and everything that he has stood for in the past, everything that he stands for today, the immense commercial importance, immense sociological importance, if you like, of this individual, yesterday, today and in the future."

○ ○ ○ ○ ○ Despite Menon's dire oratory, it was Morris Levy who first ran to the courthouse — to file a $42 million lawsuit through his Big Seven music-publishing and Adam VIII companies. The complaint in Manhattan federal court named John Lennon, Apple Records Inc. (Lennon was president), Capitol-EMI, and Harold Seider as defendants. Levy alleged not only breach of the 1973 "Come Together" settlement, but also claimed the defendants breached a purported 1974 Lennon/Levy oral agreement for *Roots*. "It is Lennon and not Big Seven who is seeking to have his cake and eat it too," Levy's lawyers argued.

Big Seven in part sought lost "mechanical" royalties due to Lennon having included only one of the three Big Seven compositions, "Ya Ya," on *Walls and Bridges*, which Levy contended constituted Lennon's "next album" under the 1973 settlement. Songs earn "mechanical" royalties from sales of recordings of those songs. In the early 1970s, the mechanical royalty rate, set by federal law, was 2 cents per composition, per record sold.

Levy also wanted to be compensated for additional song royalties he claimed he would have earned if Lennon had included a cover of Big Seven's "Angel Baby" on *Rock 'n' Roll* and thus attracted other artists to record cover versions of the song. "Any time we get an important artist to do a song, we feel that the basic value of the copyright has gone up," Levy claimed. But Lennon had decided not to release his cover of "Angel Baby" because of its poor performance quality. Levy nevertheless alleged he had lost an opportunity for substantial "catalogue enhancement." (Unsatisfied with his singing on "Angel Baby" in the Los Angeles sessions with Phil Spector, Lennon rerecorded his lead vocal in New York. But band and singer were out of tune, and Lennon said the track was too weak to be released. However, an authorized version of Lennon's "Angel Baby," in an extended reedit, was included in 1986's *Menlove Avenue*, a collection compiled by Capitol Records of previously unreleased Lennon recordings.)

Lennon responded to Levy's suit by claiming that the poor audio and packaging quality of *Roots* had violated his ability to control his public persona. (This "right of publicity," spelled out in New York Civil Rights Law §51, generally requires written consent of an individual for commercial use of his or her persona.) Capitol Records filed its own counterclaim against Levy, for injury to the worth of its Beatles catalog, which Bhaskar Menon claimed was "beyond any question the most valuable asset in the music business ever."

"They didn't think I'd show or that I'd fight it," a defiant Lennon said of Levy and his companies. "They thought I'd just settle, but I won't."

Levy had William Schurtman represent him in the Big Seven case. Schurtman's firm primarily handled international litigations and arbitrations, but in entertainment matters he had represented actor Cary Grant in a right of privacy suit against *Esquire* magazine, and Bang Records in a suit against its artist Neil Diamond. Schurtman first met Morris Levy when he was counsel on the other side of a real estate matter from Levy. Levy "said he liked the way I handled the real estate litigation and wanted me to be his lawyer in any litigation that might involve him or his companies," Schurtman explained, "and so I represented him in the Lennon cases as well as other cases."

Schurtman said that when he deposed John Lennon in the Levy litigation, "To show his disdain, [John] wore torn jeans, a t-shirt, and had long, stringy hair like on the Levy album cover. John refused to answer questions." But when the case went to trial in January 1976, "I came into courtroom early the first morning and the only other person there was a young man in a suit with a vest, nicely cut hair, wearing studious glasses, like an associate from a Wall Street firm. He said, 'Don't you recognize me, Bill? I'm John Lennon.'" Yoko Ono, with whom Lennon had reunited in early 1975, also attended the trial proceedings, sitting in the courtroom knitting a sweater for the Lennons' infant son, Sean. "It was reminiscent of the women in the French Revolution who knitted away while watching the guillotines," Schurtman said.

Schurtman claimed the presiding judge, Lloyd MacMahon, never liked Levy. "Levy had often been accused of joining the Mafia, though I never saw any evidence of it," Schurtman said. "Feds were constantly wiretapping his phone. He came up as a dangerous person." Schurtman recalled that when it came to presenting Levy's side of the case in the courtroom, "MacMahon rolled his eyes, shook his head. It got so bad, I had my associates make notes about MacMahon's behavior."

Because Lennon challenged Levy's use of the photo of a stringy-haired Lennon on the cover of *Roots*, Schurtman set out to attack the musician's packaging tastes by raising Capitol's refusal to release the 1968 Lennon/Ono *Two Virgins* album, which featured front-and-back nude photos of the couple. As Schurtman examined the album packaging in court for the name of the record company that did release the album, he recalled, "One of the defense lawyers jumped up and objected, 'He just showed a picture of a naked man and woman to the jury.' Judge MacMahon asked me to bring the album up to him. Though it had been pre-marked as an exhibit, MacMahon's face turned red, purple, every color of the rainbow. He took the album and threw it into a wastebasket in full view of jury."

The district judge quickly called a mistrial. "It was plainly prejudicial on its face," MacMahon furiously declared about the Lennon/Ono album cover. But the case promptly resumed with US district judge Thomas Griesa presiding over the second trial. Judge Griesa was already familiar with legal issues between Morris Levy and John Lennon because he had overseen Levy's "Come Together" infringement action. A former Justice Department lawyer appointed to the federal bench by President Richard Nixon, Griesa played flute in chamber ensembles.

Because Griesa's busy calendar would cause him to hear the case in starts and stops, the trial proceeded without a jury. Griesa dissected the proceedings into two parts: first, to hear Morris Levy's claims, then Lennon's and Capitol's counterclaims. The trial lasted through April 1976. "All this started because I got bored after *Mind Games* and just wanted to play some good old rock 'n' roll," Lennon groused.

○ ○ ○ ○ ○ Much of the case focused on what was said at the initial meeting between Lennon and Levy and their associates, on October 8, 1974, at Club Cavallero in New York City. Capitol Records' trial counsel Barrett Prettyman noted: "Half the table swore that John said, 'Fantastic idea. I'll send you the record and put it out and let's see how we do.' The other half at the table said [that John told Levy], 'Are you crazy. I'm under contract with Capitol Records. I can't do that. I'll send you a rough cut of the record just so you can see what I'm talkin' about, that it really isn't any good.'" Half of the people at the table, Prettyman concluded, "could not have been truthful."

Morris Levy was first to testify before Judge Griesa in the acoustically challenging federal courtroom in lower Manhattan. When Griesa asked Levy to speak up, the burly, husky-voiced Levy replied, "I haven't got my candies. I have polyps in my throat, your Honor."

Under direct examination by William Schurtman, Levy claimed that the terms of the "Come Together" settlement were worth "hundreds of thousands of dollars" to Big Seven. In addition to mechanical royalties from Lennon covers and attracting other artists to record Levy copyrights, "It would have enhanced the sheet music prospect of selling much more sheet music on the songs; [and earning radio airplay] performance monies around the world," Levy said.

Levy claimed that when he met with John Lennon and Harold Seider on October 8, 1974, an oral agreement began to gel for Levy to release Lennon's oldies recordings. "Lennon said as far as he was concerned, it was a dead package for Capitol," leaving Levy to believe the Lennon tapes were his for the asking.

20 ⦙ "Extraordinary Noise"

When John Lennon took the witness stand, on January 20, 1976, his trial lawyer James Bergen, from the Beatles' New York firm Marshall Bratter, asked him what rights Capitol's parent affiliate EMI had under its contract with the Beatles. "As far as I understand, they own everything I do, even if I speak," said Lennon, who by then had withdrawn from the music business and was spending his time at home raising his son Sean.

But Lennon described the development of the Beatles for Judge Griesa, from their early years ("when you are 22 and you get into your contract, you are so thrilled to be allowed in the studio and also you are ignorant, usually, that you have no idea what is going on") to "by about the third or fourth album [when] we virtually had taken complete control of the recording" including "the cover of the album, what was written on it, just everything to do with the production and even the selling and the ads in the papers — we controlled everything artistic about the albums."

John gave a detailed explanation of the production process for his solo works, from recording basic tracks to overdubbing, mixing the tracks down to stereo, and finally "mastering" them for overall, consistent sound quality. On the basic tracks, for example, he said, "I go around and say, 'Has anybody got any secrets I didn't hear?' Sometimes they will tell you when it is too late, 'Oh, yes, I played a wrong note here.'"

The *Rock 'n' Roll* sessions with Wall of Sound producer Phil Spector in 1973 involved "28 people playing live at once. I've have never done that before," Lennon said, calling it an "extraordinary noise." (For the final oldies sessions at the Record Plant in New York, Lennon employed a handful of players.)

It was during the sessions with Spector that the then pending copyright-infringement suit Morris Levy had filed in 1970 over "Come Together" popped up again. "I hadn't heard about it for four years or something," Lennon testified. But around the third or fourth day of the sessions, he got a phone call that "the 'Come Together' lawsuit is on in New York, you know and you are supposed to come.' I said 'Don't do that. You know, I am in the middle of working. . . . I can't think about something else that happened years ago. Just go and make a deal." The result was the 1973 settlement under which Lennon obligated himself to record the Levy-owned oldies "Angel Baby," "Ya Ya," and "You Can't Catch Me" on his "next album."

Attorney Bergen, who later became a sports lawyer representing major league baseball teams like the New York Yankees, asked about Lennon's October 8, 1974, meeting with Levy at the Club Cavallero. "Did you say anything to Mr. Levy that you considered that the Spector transaction was dead material."

"No," Lennon replied.

"Had the Beatles or you as artists ever had what you referred to as dead material?"

"One thing the Beatles and me never like," Lennon confessed, is "the idea of having a lot of material that is crummy left in the vaults, for when you die in an airplane crash, which is what a lot of rock and roll people do, then they release this material and they put strange people playing on it, which [happened] to such artists as Buddy Holly. The Beatles may have two tracks that were never released, and one of them is from 1962, and I have one, and there is the Spector tape [of a song Lennon cowrote with Spector but didn't include on *Rock 'n' Roll*], so now I have three that they could release if I died, which I would hate to have released." (On the 1995–1996 *Beatles Anthology* albums, the surviving Beatles added their performances to the Lennon solo demo recordings "Free as a Bird" and "Real Love.")

In choosing the songs for the oldies sessions with Spector, "Phil and I had many lists," Lennon explained. "[B]ut generally, we would decide the night before which one we were going to do the next day, although we must have gone through every rock and roll song we knew together."

Lennon cited the reasons for the songs he did record for *Rock 'n' Roll*: "'Be-Bop-a-Lula' was one of the first songs I ever learned, and I actually re-member singing it the day I met Paul McCartney. 'Ain't That a Shame' was the first rock and roll song I ever learned. My mother taught it to me on the banjo before I learned the guitar." Lennon included "Peggy Sue" because "I used to sing every song that Buddy Holly put out," Sam Cooke's "Bring It

On Home" because "I wish I had written it, I love it that much," and Larry Williams' "Bony Moronie" because "I remember singing it the only time my mother saw me perform before she died."

In finalizing which of his cover recordings to release on *Rock 'n' Roll*, Lennon had excluded his poor performance of "Be My Baby" (originally a 1963 hit for the Phil Spector-produced Ronettes) and the Morris Levy–owned "Angel Baby." Lennon felt his own version of the Levy song was "atrocious" and criticized *Roots* for using both of these cover cuts. "[T]his is like the rehearsal of a Broadway show. They have put the rehearsal out," Lennon complained to Judge Griesa. Then there was *Roots'* packaging featuring the "lousy picture" of Lennon that was "out of focus, and it's almost so ludicrous it's ridiculous. Even the bootlegs on the market look better than this."

Lennon said he "did lots of work on all the tracks" after he had given Levy the 7½-inch rough-mix tape that became Levy's *Roots*. For example, "on 'You Can't Catch Me,' the night we recorded it Phil Spector made a beautiful cut." Spector had pasted the intro section of Lennon's recording into the middle of the track, "a brilliant piece of editing." Lennon wanted to recreate the edit in New York but hadn't done so before giving the tape copy to Levy.

○ ○ ○ ○ ○ When John Lennon returned to the witness stand on January 29, Judge Griesa joked that he would award a prize, "some old tugboat models or something," to the most interesting witness he heard in the case. Then under cross-examination by Levy counsel William Schurtman, who was challenging Lennon's professed concern for well-thought-out album covers, Lennon testified he thought that the nude Lennon/Ono photos on the cover of the *Two Virgins* album had enhanced his reputation as an artist. "I have no shame about nakedness and I do not think it is bad taste to be naked," Lennon said, adding "otherwise every artist for the last 2,000 years would be on trial for nakedness or having to do with naked bodies. I am a trained art student and nakedness to me is beautiful."

"Did you run into any problems marketing that album?" Schurtman asked.

"Sir Joseph Lockwood, who was then head of EMI, decided that his company did not want to handle it. Only he did not have the guts to tell me to my face. He sent a letter to all his subsidiaries around the world. But he did ask me to autograph the album for him so he could take it home. And it did enhance my reputation, yes."

"Did you insist [to EMI] that you nevertheless be permitted to release [*Two Virgins*] through another company?" Schurtman probed. (After Capitol refused to release *Two Virgins*, Tetragrammaton Records, a US label owned in part by comedian Bill Cosby, released the album.)

"I don't remember the details, but they had the right of first refusal," Lennon answered. "If they don't think it is worth having, they are not going to stop me putting it out."

To bolster the argument that Morris Levy and John Lennon had made an oral agreement for Levy to release *Roots*, William Schurtman tried to establish a longtime link between Levy and Lennon. The lawyer handed Judge Griesa a Beatles photo that Lennon signed in 1974, "To Maurice with love, ten years later."

"What did the 'ten years later' refer to?" Schurtman asked Lennon.

"Morris had some vague connection with the pool in which the Beatles were swimming," Lennon explained about the band's February 1964 trip to Miami Beach for an *Ed Sullivan Show* TV appearance. "I don't know if it was true, [that Levy] either owned or knew the man that let the Beatles swim in the pool in 1964. To him it was a big event; to me it was a big nothing. . . . I'll give autographs to anybody that asks, provided I'm not eating."

"Remind me to get your autograph at the end of the trial," Schurtman quipped.

"You've had it. Your daughter had it," Lennon retorted. (Schurtman's fifteen-year-old daughter had obtained Lennon's autograph when she visited the courtroom.)

"I'm not responsible for my daughter's taste."

"No comment," Lennon replied.

○ ○ ○ ○ ○ Harold Seider, May Pang, Allen Klein, and musicians from the Lennon rehearsals at Morris Levy's dairy farm all testified at trial. Allen Klein complained he was "in an absolutely 'no win' situation. If Mr. Lennon is successful he will say he is successful in this venture despite my testimony; if Mr. Lennon loses, he will say it is because of my testimony."

After hearing the testimony from both sides, Judge Griesa admitted,

"We have confusion at the end of the story which is astounding to me. I don't know whether there was an agreement . . . or not." But on February 20, 1976, Judge Griesa ruled there had been no contract between Levy and Lennon. Griesa noted that when Lennon arrived at his October 8, 1974, meeting with Levy, "he did not do so as a free agent. Both Lennon and Apple were obligated to EMI and Capitol under a complex series of agreements. The agreements were not present for review or analysis at the October 8 meeting. No representative of EMI or Capitol was at the meeting."

Griesa acknowledged, "On a few occasions Lennon made statements to musicians and to friends of Levy that he was making an album for Levy." There may have been "a tentative agreement for Lennon to provide 15 or 16 rock and roll songs in the event that Lennon in fact made a record album for Levy," Griesa found, but their discussions failed to cement the crucial detail of how Lennon's record royalties would be calculated.

Now the Levy/Lennon case moved to John Lennon's right-of-publicity counterclaim that alleged *Roots* had damaged the commercial value of his public persona. A parallel clue to Judge Griesa's thinking on the issue was a trademark infringement trial he was also overseeing in 1976. It involved a lawsuit by Rolls-Royce against Custom Cloud Motors, which sold customizer kits to make Chevy Monte Carlo front grilles look like Rolls-Royce luxury cars. In March 1976, Griesa granted an injunction that barred Custom Cloud from continuing to manufacture its kits.

When phase two of the Levy/Lennon trial began in late March, John Lennon testified about how the ad campaigns for his albums were developed. For *Mind Games*, he had enlisted Apple Records general manager Tony King to dress up as the Queen of England and mimic her voice for TV and radio ads. For *Walls and Bridges*, Lennon asked award-winning director Chuck Braverman—known for *American Time Capsule*, a popular film short that condensed American history into three minutes—to make a commercial that simulated the turnable folds of Lennon's "face changing all the time" on the cover of *Walls and Bridges*. When Levy suddenly released *Roots* in February 1975, Lennon said there wasn't enough time "to make a decent commercial" for *Rock 'n' Roll*.

The *Roots* case had required Judge Griesa to become a student of John Lennon's music. Griesa listened to Lennon's music in court and outside of it at night. When music critic Dave Marsh was called to court by Lennon's lawyer to compare the sound quality of the *Roots* and *Rock 'n' Roll* albums, "As soon as the needle hit the grooves, Griesa said right away, 'There's no need to testify because I hear the difference,'" remembered Marsh, though he did spend an hour testifying about the two albums.

"I don't think there is any comparison," Judge Griesa agreed with Marsh. "*Rock 'n' Roll* is much better. The voice was very poor and indistinct on *Roots*. It was almost hidden there. I could not tell it was John Lennon singing, or anyone singing."

∘ ∘ ∘ ∘ ∘ Morris Levy spent much of the second part of the trial away from the courtroom, down in Florida. But his legal team now pushed his claim that if John Lennon had lived up to the 1973 "Come Together" settlement agreement, other artists would have recorded the Levy-controlled songs Lennon covered, resulting in significant monies for Big Seven Music. On April 15, 1976, Levy witness Fred Bienstock, a veteran music publisher, testified that when a well-known artist covers a song, royalties from subsequent covers of that composition by other artists can "go up dramatically."

Bienstock used "(They Long to Be) Close to You," a number one hit for the Carpenters in 1970, as an example. Bienstock said that the Burt Bacharach–Hal David composition, a minor 1963 chart release for *Dr. Kildare* TV star Richard Chamberlain, averaged about $1,500 in annual income until the Carpenters' version pumped the song's average revenues up to more than $50,000 per year. Bienstock opined that Levy could have earned more than $179,000 in additional income if John Lennon had released "Angel Baby" on *Rock 'n' Roll*.

Then Levy himself set out to prove how an artist would be attracted to recording Chuck Berry's "You Can't Catch Me" following the release of a Lennon cover version. To do so, Levy relied on *Stephen Stills Live*, a concert album that included a medley of "You Can't Catch Me" and Robert Johnson's blues classic "Crossroads" (though Stills's version of the Berry tune ran for one minute, six seconds, not much longer than John Lennon's fifty-five-second rendition of "Ya Ya" on *Walls and Bridges*).

But when James Bergen asked Levy on cross-examination if he had listened to Stills's take, Levy said he hadn't, because "since it came out I have been in court most of the time." Bergen handed the copy of *Stills Live* to Levy. It had been released in December 1975, after both *Roots* and *Rock 'n'*

Roll. "Doesn't it say recorded live March 8 and 9, 1974?" Bergen challenged Levy. "So Mr. Stills couldn't have recorded 'You Can't Catch Me'" after either of the Lennon oldies packages were released, Bergen suggested, diminishing Levy's lost revenues claim.

When the trial was over, Judge Griesa did decide that John Lennon breached the October 1973 "Come Together" settlement agreement. But Griesa found primarily against Levy's companies — by holding Lennon liable for only $6,795 for omitting "Angel Baby" from *Rock 'n' Roll*, then slapping Levy and Adam VIII with an injunction that barred them from continuing to market *Roots.* Griesa went on to award Lennon $35,000 for damage to his reputation from *Roots'* poor sound quality and packaging, as well as $100,300 in lost *Rock 'n' Roll* sales. Capitol-EMI received $290,000 in damages. In determining Lennon's lost income, Griesa calculated that *Rock 'n' Roll*, which sold 342,000 units in the United States, could have sold an additional 100,000 copies if not for *Roots* (though *Roots* sold only 1,270 copies). The 100,000 figure was based on averaging the sales of *Rock 'n' Roll*'s predecessor *Walls and Bridges* and successor release *Shaved Fish*, a 1975 Lennon greatest-hits collection. Both had exceeded 400,000 in sales.

Both Morris Levy and John Lennon appealed to the US Court of Appeals for the Second Circuit. The appeals court issued its ruling in April 1977. The decision opened with a quote from Lennon's *Walls and Bridges* song "Nobody Loves You (When You're Down and Out)": "Everybody's hustlin' for a buck and a dime / I'll scratch your back and you scratch mine." The Second Circuit agreed with Judge Griesa that Lennon had breached the "Come Together" settlement — "the parties have not been able to 'come together' at all," the appeals court punned — but refused to increase the $6,795 in lost song income that Griesa awarded Levy.

However, the Second Circuit said that, in coming up with a lost income award for Lennon, Griesa should have averaged in the artist's 1973 release *Mind Games*, which Capitol had used in projecting sales for *Rock 'n' Roll*. Averaging in *Mind Games*, which sold 376,000 copies, resulted in the appeals court reducing Lennon's award down to $49,913.

The appeals court added one more point to Levy's column by tossing out $10,000 in punitive damages that Judge Griesa had levied against Levy for relying on Allen Klein's statements that Apple Records, not Capitol, controlled the Beatles mail-order rights. "In fact, however, the Apple-Capitol contract did contain an exception for mail-order sales," the Second Circuit found, "so that Levy's reliance turned out to have been at least partially correct, even if simplistically misplaced."

○ ○ ○ ○ ○ After the *Roots* case, Morris Levy increased his influence in the music industry through his Strawberries record-store chain in New England that he later sold for $40.5 million. In 1988, however, Levy was convicted by a federal jury in New Jersey of conspiracy to extort in a "cut-out" (deleted catalog) records scheme and sentenced to ten years in prison. But before serving the time, Levy passed away in May 1990 of liver cancer, at his farm in upstate New York where he had once hosted John Lennon. William Krasilovsky, the lawyer Levy hired to pursue the underlying copyright-infringement suit over Lennon's "Come Together," recalled, "When Morris was dying, he said that was he how he was going to beat the government's rap."

Looking back, Dave Marsh said that Morris Levy's litigation against John Lennon had an overriding goal, to "send a message to the rest of the music industry about Levy's power and ruthlessness. He sued John Lennon to show that even a Beatle could not beat Levy's Mafioso ass. He put *Roots* out so he could say John Lennon was his punk."

For John Lennon, his fear that music critics would trash *Rock 'n' Roll* had quickly become a reality. *Rolling Stone* reviewer Jon Landau, who had also hated *Mind Games*, described Lennon's oldies effort as "self-conscious musical attitudinizing about rock roots, and poorly done at that." (Landau is now Bruce Springsteen's decades-long manager.) Lennon admitted the *Rock 'n' Roll* project, much of which was recorded in Los Angeles when he was drinking heavily during his separation from Yoko, "was such a mess that I can hardly remember what happened. . . . It was the worst time of my life, that record!" The album would be Lennon's last new-album release until *Double Fantasy* with Yoko Ono in 1980. When he withdrew from recording in the mid-1970s, John and Yoko did as Morris Levy had done: they invested in dairy cows in upstate New York.

But the Levy/Lennon saga had one more coda to play out. This occurred in January 1980, when Paul McCartney's father-in-law and legal advisor Lee Eastman invited William Krasilovsky and his wife to dine at Eastman's Manhattan residence. By this time, Chuck Berry had regained the copyrights to his key songs. "Lee wanted me to deliver Chuck Berry's song catalog to Paul McCartney; they wanted to buy it," revealed Krasilovsky, who through the "Come Together" case had met Berry and become his lawyer. "That's why Lee invited me over. Even Chuck didn't know about this."

That would have made Paul McCartney the owner of "You Can't Catch Me," the very song that Morris Levy brandished to chase John Lennon through the courts. But Eastman's discussion with Krasilovsky was interrupted by a ringing phone. "It was an emergency call from Paul McCartney, who was in Japan," Krasilovsky said. "He had just been arrested for possession of marijuana. Paul had used his right to call a lawyer to phone Lee Eastman, who went about finding counsel for Paul in Japan."

On tour with his post-Beatles band Wings, McCartney had been arrested after customs officials at Tokyo International Airport found a half-pound of pot in his luggage. Paul could have been sent to prison for seven years under Japan's strict laws but was deported instead after being jailed for nine days.

However, the discussions between Eastman and Krasilovsky went no further.

PART FIVE

ALL THINGS MUST PASS

21 · Here Comes the Summons

eorge Harrison stepped on stage at Madison Square Garden on the night of December 19, 1974, for the start of his final three shows of the first nationwide US solo tour by a former Beatle. A few days before, with tour-members sitarist Ravi Shankar and keyboardist Billy Preston at his side, Harrison told journalists during a White House visit with President Gerald Ford that he enjoyed working with these musicians more than he had being a Beatle.

In fact, on the afternoon of the December 19, George signed the historic agreement, at the Plaza Hotel in New York City, that settled Paul McCartney's lawsuit to break up the Beatles & Co. band partnership. But George had blown out his vocal chords during rehearsals for the solo tour, and his concerts were plagued by throat problems and poor press reviews.

As if that weren't enough, when the Madison Square Garden show began, another thorny problem lurked in the arena: a process server hovered near the stage eager to hand George a lawsuit summons from Allen Klein. George's former manager sought to seize George's Harrisongs Music Inc. Klein claimed he needed to do so to protect his company ABKCO, which managed George's music-publishing catalog, from Internal Revenue Service efforts to obtain back taxes that Harrisongs owed the government.

If Klein's lawsuit was successful, he would gain control of George's solo compositions from 1968 forward. These included the prized "While My Guitar Gently Weeps" from the Beatles' "White" album, "Something" and "Here Comes the Sun" from *Abbey Road*, and the bulk of the songs from George's massively successful first solo album *All Things Must Pass*.

Klein's suit, in New York state court, arose amidst the larger legal conflict that erupted after George Harrison, John Lennon, and Ringo Starr fired Allen Klein as their manager in March 1973. Klein claimed the Harrisongs suit was "a simple one unrelated to the total history of relations" between ABKCO and Harrison and his companies. But George's Los Angeles lawyer

David Braun said Klein had written him about the "enormity, complexity and sensitivity of" the Harrisongs matter. Braun believed Klein's complaint against Harrisongs was in retaliation for a management suit that George, John, and Ringo filed against Klein in England.

George had hoped that John and Ringo would perform with him at Madison Square Garden on the nineteenth, but they were no-shows — reportedly in part to avoid being confronted by Klein's process servers. Paul and Linda McCartney attended George's last Garden show on the night of December 20, but they sat in the audience wearing disguises.

○ ○ ○ ○ ○ George Harrison had been the target of summonses from Allen Klein at other inconvenient times, too. When opposing counsel was deposing George on June 26, 1973, in the infringement suit against him over his song "My Sweet Lord," a lawyer at Rosenman Colin — the Klein-affiliated firm that represented codefendant Harrisongs Music in the "My Sweet Lord" case — suddenly "left the room," George said, "and came back with a deputy sheriff who gave me copies of what I am told were an order of attachment and summonses and other documents in cases being brought by [Klein's] ABKCO against Apple Records and Apple Films Ltd." George claimed to be "very surprised" that Klein's counsel "should take this action especially as they had been involved in arranging the deposition." Or as George's copyright litigator Joseph Santora put it, "In walk two of Klein's thugs with legal papers they slapped on George."

Allen Klein's efforts to have George Harrison served with the suit to take over Harrisongs could have been the basis for a Monty Python comedy movie. George had traveled to New York City on Monday, December 16, 1974, after playing a concert in Philadelphia. At about 10:00 p.m. on the eighteenth, John Loiacono, a private investigator who worked for Klein's lawyers, went to George's New York City tour headquarters at the Plaza Hotel to serve George with the summons. Loiacono knocked at room 937, where Harrison concert promoter Barry Imhoff was staying. But when the imposing, three-hundred-pound Imhoff opened the door, he told Loiacono that George wasn't around and ordered the private investigator to leave.

Loiacono went to the hotel lobby to wait. There the Plaza's night manager told Loiacono that he couldn't serve a lawsuit summons at the hotel unless accompanied by police. As Loiacono later told it to ABKCO litigator Peter Nadel, at that moment "four policemen arrived in response to an earlier call from some other party about a disturbance." Loiacono convinced the officers to return with him to Imhoff's room. Imhoff allowed one of the officers to search the room, but there was still no sight of Harrison.

The next day, Loiacono went to Madison Square Garden, where preparations for George's show were underway. The persistent private investigator got backstage twice before being ejected each time by Garden security guards. So he obtained a ticket for that night's concert and walked down to the stage area while opening act Ravi Shankar and his group were playing. Loiacono's prospects appeared to be improving: his prey George Harrison sat on the side of the stage talking with current manager Denis O' Brien. Loiacono jumped into the moat that surrounded the stage platform, but he was once again repelled by a Garden security guard.

Loiacono went back to the Plaza at around 10:00 p.m. to wait for George, this time reinforced by three additional private investigators. Two of them took up watch outside the hotel, while the third stood near the elevators at the Plaza's 58th Street entrance. Loiacono positioned himself at the main elevator bank near the Plaza's 59th Street entrance.

Within an hour, George Harrison's entourage arrived from Madison Square Garden. Barry Imhoff immediately spotted Loiacono. To distract the process server, Imhoff began following him around the hotel lobby, asking questions while a cameraman and lighting assistant who happened to be with the Harrison group recorded the scene. This allowed George the opportunity to bolt from his car, and scurry through the hotel lobby into the safety of the hotel's kitchen elevator.

But Loiacono's process-serving adventure was far from over. Imhoff pointed him out to a Harrison bodyguard who Loiacono said was "about 25 years old, 6' 4" tall, 220 lbs., had blond hair and a blond beard, was extremely muscular and looked like a weightlifter." "Get that guy in the suede jacket," Imhoff commanded.

The escalating altercation quickly spilled out into the street as Imhoff and the bodyguard chased Loiacono to a car in which the other three private investigators were now waiting. When a New York City police car pulled up at the scene, "Imhoff and the bodyguard refused to identify themselves," Loiacono claimed. "Imhoff denied knowing Harrison, even though he was wearing the same black tee shirt with the emblem worn by the Harrison party."

Loiacono didn't leave. With the two New York police officers at his side, he returned to Barry Imhoff's Plaza hotel room, where a "large party was spilling out into the corridor." But Imhoff barred the warrantless officers from entering the hotel suite. When Loiacono insisted he still "would serve Harrison on stage if necessary," Imhoff and other entourage members broke into laughter.

On Friday, December 20, another of Allen Klein's investigators, William Ward, checked into a room on the Plaza's ninth floor, then went to Madison Square Garden for George's 4:00 p.m. concert. Like Loiacono, Ward gained access near the stage on which Harrison stood again watching Ravi Shankar's Indian musicians perform. Ward walked up to Harrison's thin, bearded and bespectacled manager Denis O'Brien, tapped him on the shoulder with Klein's legal papers and said, "I have summonses here for George Harrison; if I can't serve him I must serve you. May I serve him?"

"No, no, no," O'Brien said, backing away.

Ward dropped the papers at O'Brien's feet and announced, "You are served."

Ward did try to serve George personally later that night, at the Hippopotamus Club on East 62nd Street in Manhattan where Harrison's group was celebrating the end of the national tour. But as Ward later described the scene to Peter Nadel: "Eight men formed a circle around one of the car doors from which Harrison emerged. The whole group then made a fast dash into the club." Ward decided to leave because "it would be impossible to approach Harrison upon his exit from the club in light of the human wall of bodyguards surrounding him."

After all the cloak-and-dagger intrigue, Klein's process servers had to rely on more traditional means of getting the summons to Harrison, by leaving copies at the offices of George's New York lawyers and mailing another to George's Friar Park home in England. But as it turned out, the case wouldn't last long.

○ ○ ○ ○ ○ George Harrison had formed Harrisongs Music Inc. in the United States in March 1969. After the IRS audited Harrisongs' financial books in 1974, it sent a demand notice to the publishing company seeking $18,000 in back taxes. New York City issued a warrant against Harrisongs seeking at least $4,000 in corporate taxes and interest.

Allen Klein claimed that, since the IRS audits began, George "refused to deny or admit" he owned Harrisongs' corporate stock. ABKCO sent letters to David Braun seeking clarification, but Klein said, "No reply has been forthcoming." Even though ABKCO's lawsuit predicted, "Internal Revenue Service and other tax agencies will undoubtedly continue to make demands on" Harrisongs catalogue manager ABKCO, Klein was certainly willing to accept the responsibility in exchange for ownership of Harrisongs Music Inc. After all, he would get worldwide rights to George Harrison's musical compositions, outside the United Kingdom, for incurring relatively modest tax liabilities.

ABKCO had kept Harrisongs' financial books at ABKCO's offices since Harrisongs was founded. But David Braun charged that, after George terminated Allen Klein as his manager in March 1973, "ABKCO refused to turn over the HMI books and records and insisted upon continuing to manage the affairs of HMI." As proof, Braun noted that in June 1973 Klein wrote the Harry Fox Agency, the industry clearinghouse for publishers that collected song income from record sales, "to send all payments, checks, licenses, indeed 'anything having to do with Harrisongs Music, Inc.' to HMI, in care of ABKCO."

Klein argued, however, it was George Harrison who "had the sole power to sign checks on HMI's bank account." By June 1975, George admitted he owned Harrisongs Music Inc.'s stock and ABKCO agreed to hand over the Harrisongs legal and financial records it held. This allowed George to clear up his dispute with the taxing authorities. He said he had been disclaiming ownership of the publishing company because his English lawyers "told me I did not own it, although they seemed to have trouble making up their minds."

On June 17, the state court formally closed the ABKCO/Harrisongs case file. But Allen Klein would soon hatch an alternate plot for trying to turn George Harrison's music into a future revenue source for ABKCO. The original idea came to him in the middle of the copyright-infringement suit that was filed against George over his worldwide hit "My Sweet Lord," when Allen was still his manager. After the split from George, Klein would woo Harrison's foes in the infringement action.

22 "An Unmistakable Similarity"

A s potentially damaging as it may have been to George Harrison's songwriting legacy, Allen Klein's lawsuit to take over Harrisongs Music wasn't George's biggest music-publishing headache. The pending copyright infringement suit against him over "My Sweet Lord" challenged his originality as a songwriter and would span most of his post-Beatles career.

"My Sweet Lord," George Harrison's first major solo single, was released on November 23, 1970. It became a worldwide hit. But on February 10, 1971, a process server for the Brooklyn, New York–based Bright Tunes Music left a lawsuit summons for George at the 1700 Broadway offices of Allen Klein's "Afco [sic] Industries" in Manhattan. The Bright Tunes publishing company was formed by the Tokens — the vocal group that hit number one in the United States in 1961 with "The Lion Sleeps Tonight" — and their business manager, Seymour Barash.

Bright Tunes' complaint in New York federal court alleged that "My Sweet Lord" infringed on the publisher's copyright in "He's So Fine," a song that the Tokens produced on record for a "girl group" named the Chiffons. "He's So Fine" was written by Ronnie Mack, who assigned the copyright in his composition to Bright Tunes in August 1962. "When 'My Sweet Lord' came out, radio stations all over country would play half of that record and segue into 'He's So Fine.' The songs had practically the same melody," Tokens lead singer Jay Siegel recalled. "So we got a couple of law-yers who took our case on a contingency basis, because we knew George Harrison would have a much bigger budget than us to fight the suit."

The Chiffons' recording topped the *Billboard* US charts for four weeks during the spring of 1963 and made it to the Top 20 in Britain in June of that year. George Harrison claimed, however, that he never met Ronnie Mack and had rarely heard "He's So Fine" because English radio was "very limited" in 1963. "It was no event in my life," George said about the Chiffons' record.

But "He's So Fine" was on the *Music Week* charts in England during the seven-week run at number one of the Beatles' "From Me To You" in 1963. And the Chiffons were among the opening acts for the Beatles' first US concert on February 11, 1964, at the Coliseum in Washington, DC.

George Harrison had other Bright Tunes links, too. In 1969, he produced overdubs for a demo recording featuring Bright Tunes songwriter Stephen Friedland, who recorded as Brute Force and coincidentally wrote for the Chiffons. After the Tokens produced the initial version of Brute Force's "King of Fuh" (sung irreverently in the recording as the "Fuh King"), George heard the demo during a visit to attorney Nat Weiss's office in New York. George had a string section added to the recording and Apple Records pressed a limited run of 2,000 copies. He was probably in the mood to work on such a record, as he did his "King of Fuh" production work at London's Trident Studios on the night of January 10, 1969, the same day that he temporarily quit the Beatles and walked out of the filming of the *Let It Be* sessions at Twickenham Studios.

○ ○ ○ ○ ○ Bright Tunes' suit over "My Sweet Lord" was the first time that George Harrison was sued for copyright infringement. The complaint also named Apple Records Inc. and sheet music distributor Hansen Publications as codefendants with George Harrison and Harrisongs Music.

George Harrison wrote "My Sweet Lord" in 1969, while he, Eric Clapton, and Billy Preston were on a European tour backing the R & B-influenced rock group Delaney & Bonnie and Friends. Harrison had been listening a lot to the chart hit "Oh, Happy Day," a gospel recording by the Edwin Hawkins Singers. Between shows in Copenhagen, Denmark, George stepped away from a Delaney and Bonnie press conference, and took his guitar to a room upstairs where he was joined by Delaney and Bonnie's manager Alan Pariser and by Beatles confidant Mal Evans — credited on Harrison's *All Things Must Pass* solo album for "Tea, Sympathy and Tambourine."

"I was starting to try and come up with something, 'Hallelujah, Hallelujah,'" George said, "and at the same time I realized that as far as the rhythm, or the number of syllables, that hallelujah also happened to correspond with 'Hare Krishna,' which is also another source of my inspiration."

George went back downstairs to where the Delaney and Bonnie press conference was now over and asked members of the tour band — including drummer Jim Gordon, bassist Carl Radle, keyboard player Bobby Whitlock, backing vocalist Rita Coolidge, trumpet player Jim Price, and saxophonist Bobby Keyes — to sing along with him to the developing song. Alan Pariser recalled that "it was humorous to me because he was getting Delaney and Bonnie to sing the Hare Krishnas, because they were sort of into the gospel, Pentecostal thing at that time, and he was trying to point out to them that hallelujahs and Hare Krishnas all meant the same thing."

George continued to develop the composition over the next few days, including during a recording session he produced in London during which Billy Preston recorded "My Sweet Lord," featuring backing vocals from the Edwin Hawkins Singers, for Preston's second album for Apple Records. When Harrison recorded his own version of "My Sweet Lord" in 1970, he added a slide guitar intro, the extensive "Hare Krishna" chants, and a Sanskrit prayer near the end accompanied, he said, by "five acoustic guitars, two drummers, and a tambourine player and two pianos, maybe even a harmonium, a pedal harmonium, all paying live in the studio together."

After "My Sweet Lord" became a hit, Bright Tunes hired David Greitzer, a New York City School District supervisor of music and faculty member at the Manhattan School of Music, to compare the two songs. Greitzer found "an unmistakable similarity" between "He's So Fine" and "My Sweet Lord" "melodically, harmonically and structurally" as well as in "tempo and time values." But he admitted he couldn't "state unequivocally that the more recent song derives directly from the earlier song by intent of" George Harrison. A second Bright Tunes expert, Joseph Murrells of the Music Bureau Research in London, confidently concluded, however, that "the similarity is in my opinion indisputable."

○ ○ ○ ○ ○ While George Harrison fought Bright Tunes, John Lennon was involved in the case that alleged his Beatles song "Come Together" had infringed on Chuck Berry's "You Can't Catch Me," though Harrison's lawyer Joseph Santora said, "I had no contact with Lennon or his lawyers during those litigations."

For a while, Bright Tunes' lawsuit over "My Sweet Lord" moved slowly, because the publishing company was in dire financial straits and in the hands of a receiver by October 1971. "We lost a lot of money" through Seymour Barash, Jay Siegel said. "He had been a real estate lawyer who was a cousin of [Tokens member] Phil Margo, so we thought he'd be okay. But you could say he was our 'mismanager.'"

From George Harrison's perspective, Allen Klein "never gave me any indication" that the Bright Tunes case "was very important. It was never actually on a list of priorities." George said he didn't understand how serious Bright Tunes' copyright infringement claim against him was until a visit to Allen Klein's New York office in 1972. Klein had heard a cover recording of "He's So Fine" by country singer Jody Miller. Miller had previously scored a hit with "Queen of the House," her answer record to Roger Miller's "King of the Road." Miller's "He's So Fine" featured a country-styled rendering of George's slide guitar riff from "My Sweet Lord."

George recalled that Klein "was a bit excited and saying they stole the guitar parts. And then he played the [Miller] record and he said this and that, those bastards, they have, you know, really made it sound like 'My Sweet Lord.'" George asked Klein about Bright Tunes' suit, "Well, can't we do anything about it? Can't we just settle the thing?" George even raised the idea of buying the copyright to "He's So Fine."

Composer/pianist John Barham, who provided orchestral arrangements for Harrison's *All Things Must Pass* album on which "My Sweet Lord" appeared, recalled that keyboardist Tony Ashton, who with Barham had worked on Harrison's earlier *Wonderwall* album, "told George when he was developing 'My Sweet Lord' that it sounded like 'He's So Fine,' so George was aware of the resemblances." (Barham also provided the string arrangements that George Harrison added to Brute Force's "King of Fuh" and played on studio sessions for John Lennon.)

Barham added, "George usually was cautious as a songwriter, because he was competing with Lennon and McCartney and didn't want to be accused of taking from them. So it was ironic that his greatest composition might turn out not to be entirely his own."

Barham said the lawsuit affected Harrison's work on the 1973 album release *Living in the Material World*, the follow-up studio album to *All Things Must Pass*. "He was certainly in a strange mood during those sessions," Barham noted. "I hadn't seen him like this. He was also having problems in his marriage with Pattie and the added stress of trying to come up with an album to match *All Things Must Pass*."

Harold Barlow, the music expert Klein hired to help George, had already worked on an infringement litigation involving a Beatle. But that was for plaintiff Morris Levy in the suit Levy's Big Seven publishing company filed in 1970 against John Lennon over "Come Together." According to Klein, Barlow told him in the Bright Tunes case "that we could defend on the basis that the song 'He's So Fine' probably was predated by another song, and if he searched back far enough he would be able to threaten the composition or the copyright of 'He's So Fine.'"

But not much had developed in the "My Sweet Lord" case even by March 1973, when George Harrison, John Lennon, and Ringo Starr fired Klein. After the firing, Harrison received a letter, on April 9, 1973, from Rosenman Colin partner Max Freund informing him that the law firm, which was main counsel for Klein and ABKCO, would no longer be representing George in the "My Sweet Lord" case. (The firm continued, though, as case counsel to Harrisongs Music until April 1975.) Harrison protested, "No one had ever told me" that Rosenman Colin "might stop acting for me if there was a conflict between ABKCO and me."

George complained that by April 1973, the other Beatles "had some sort of management or some sort of legal representation and I was sort of left with nobody to take care of anything." But he soon retained music lawyer David Braun, whose clients included Neil Diamond, Bob Dylan, the Eagles, and Carly Simon. Harrison learned from Braun that from Los Angeles, "I had to come to New York on my way back to England to have a deposition about Bright Tunes." But after Harrison's June 26, 1973, deposition was done, the case seemed to recede. "I didn't hear anything more about it for quite a long time," George said.

Meanwhile, he was unhappy about another matter concerning "My Sweet Lord." Howard Kaylan and Mark Volman, the lead singers for 1960s folk-rock/pop band the Turtles, had reinvented themselves as the rock comedy team Flo & Eddie. On their 1975 album *Illegal, Immoral and Fattening*, they poked fun at "My Sweet Lord" and George's vocal problems on his 1974 tour. Flo & Eddie did agree to pay to use "My Sweet Lord," but Kaylan recalled that "we narrowly avoided being taken to court for libel and Harrison's office actually threatened to stop the album from being released."

David Braun had turned the Bright Tunes matter over to his litigating partner Joseph Santora in New York. On September 30, 1975, Santora wrote Harrison counsel at Frere Cholmeley in London, where George was also sued for infringing "He's So Fine," that Santora had met with Bright Tunes trial counsel Gideon Cashman.

Joseph Santora explained about the settlement conference with Cashman, "Assuming for purposes of the discussion a total of $300,000 in US [and Canadian] earnings [through March 1973] for 'My Sweet Lord,' we offered to compromise the US action for $50,000. Plaintiff's counsel has now responded with a counter-offer of $150,000," which Santora determined was "not outrageous" considering that he feared "the facts at bar suggest a real danger that a finding of infringement could be the outcome of an adjudication on the merits."

"The backdrop to this was that some people in Harrisongs' camp wanted to settle and some did not," Gideon Cashman recalled. "That I indicated [a $150,000 counter-offer] would be acceptable, that as such never happened. No doubt I had passed that number on to my clients, but no one was interested in biting. Santora's letter suggested a firmness that was never there. Perhaps he was doing a bit of politicking with his client to move the settlement along."

Ultimately, no settlement deal was reached and the case headed to the New York federal courtroom.

23 : The Rhythm of the Water Pump

The three-day, nonjury liability trial over "My Sweet Lord" began on February 23, 1976, at the New York federal courthouse at 40 Centre Street in lower Manhattan. District Judge Richard Owen was a former US Department of Justice antitrust litigator appointed to the federal bench by President Richard Nixon in 1973. The judge was also a trained pianist who composed publicly performed operas, sometimes sung by his soprano wife, Lynn.

"He's So Fine" songwriter Ronald Mack died in November 1963, only months after the Chiffons' recording of his song topped the *Billboard* charts. But his mother sat in the courtroom watching the infringement trial.

"Owen was a bright, no-nonsense judge," Gideon Cashman said, "but you didn't have to be a composer of opera to determine the music was strikingly similar." In its "striking similarity" claim, Bright Tunes alleged the songs were so much the same that Harrison could have only written his by copying "He's So Fine." Setting up Bright Tunes' case, Gideon Cashman had the Chiffons' and Jody Miller's recordings of "He's So Fine" played for Judge Owen, as well as recorded versions of "My Sweet Lord" by George Harrison, Billy Preston, and crooner Andy Williams. (The Chiffons also released a version of "My Sweet Lord," in 1975.) The plaintiffs' presentation also included an a cappella recording by the Belmonts, doo-wop singers who gained fame backing Dion DiMucci. The Belmonts' recording segued back and forth between the Mack and Harrison compositions.

Music experts David Greitzer and Thomas Shepard, the latter a vice president of RCA Records classical-music division, testified for Bright Tunes. When Greitzer came to the witness stand, Judge Owen disclosed that he was a trustee of the Manhattan School of Music, where Greitzer taught music education. "That doesn't affect anybody's thinking as to this witness, does it?" the judge queried.

"It's all right with the defendant," Harrison lawyer Joseph Santora replied.

"Very happy to meet one of the trustees, sir," David Greitzer said to the judge.

Under direct examination from plaintiff's cocounsel James Janowitz, Greitzer testified that fourteen of the first sixteen measures of "He's So Fine" and "My Sweet Lord" were the same. He discussed two musical sections common to each song: motif A, the repeated "sol-mi-re" segment that included the title of each composition, followed by the repeated "sol-la-do-la-do" of motif B (e.g., the "Hare Krishna" refrain in "My Sweet Lord"). During his testimony, Thomas Shepard emphasized the "unusual repetition of those motifs" in "He's So Fine" and their parallel sequencing in "My Sweet Lord." Shepard played key portions of the songs on a piano in the courtroom.

Bright Tunes' co-owner Jay Siegel observed that George Harrison's courtroom demeanor was "the same as his stage persona, quiet and calm." George's lengthy testimony started off the defendants' courtroom presentation by offering a detailed look into Beatles history. George started playing guitar when he was thirteen years old. "I mean actually the first year or so I wouldn't call it playing the guitar . . . in fact it was about six months to a year after I got my first guitar that I actually got it working, because I found a screw in the back of the neck and took it off to see what happened, and it all came in two pieces, so it took me about nine months before I could get someone to fix it back again."

"Skiffle" music was popular in England in the mid-1950s, Harrison explained, "a sort of country-western folk type mixture, but very simple, with the tea-chest bass and a washboard and acoustic guitar." He "played with lots of different groups." First, with his brother and a few friends, "and even the time like before the Beatles were sort of Beatles, John Lennon Paul McCartney and I were at least six different groups . . . and we'd change the name of the group depending on what color shirts we arrived in."

Under the direct examination by Santora, George noted that "Don't Bother Me," released in the United States on *Meet the Beatles!*, was the first song he wrote, in 1963, and that his 1968 composition "Something" had been recorded by about 150 artists.

"Until this lawsuit came about," Santora asked, "have you ever been sued before for copyright infringement with respect to one of your songs?"

"No," said Harrison, who had no formal musical training, and didn't write or read music. He explained that he used unorthodox methods to compose his songs. "I mean, for example, the police car [outside the court-house] was just going [Harrison makes the sound]. And that is a rhythm, straightaway." He added, "I was on a holiday in Sardinia, and the house I was staying in had a water pump that I think was for the circulation of the swimming pool. It was in a shed, and the rhythm that the water pump was making, I composed a song just starting with that rhythm."

"[C]an you tell us in your composing 'My Sweet Lord' which came first to you, the lyrics or the music?" Santora asked Harrison.

"Yes, the lyrics," George answered.

○ ○ ○ ○ ○ It was on the second day of the trial, with guitar in hand, that George Harrison demonstrated how the pieces of "My Sweet Lord" developed into a complete song. He also strummed portions of "He's So Fine," and contrasted the Chiffons and Jody Miller recordings of that song by noting about the latter that "the basic change is they added chords similar as 'My Sweet Lord' and they added slide guitar parts which have the same sort of sound."

On cross-examination, Gideon Cashman sought to establish that George Harrison had a history of relying heavily on preexisting music sources. Cashman pointed out that through 1963 "a substantial portion" of the Beatles' live performance repertoire was composed of songs by US writers. "Well, we'd absorbed hundreds and thousands of songs or musical ideas in order to perform," acknowledged Harrison.

"Indeed, even in the first Beatles album issued by Parlophone of England, the album entitled *Please Please Me* . . . [t]here were a number of American songs," Cashman observed. These included the Beatles' recording of the Burt Bacharach/Hal David composition "Baby, It's You," a 1961 hit for the Shirelles. "Were they similar in their style, if you know, to the Chiffons?" Cashman asked.

"I don't know," Harrison said.

"Did you ever perform the song 'He's So Fine'?"

"No."

According to Gideon Cashman, what happened next was a critical moment in the liability trial. First, Cashman asked Bright Tunes' expert Thomas Shepard to play from the written "lead" sheets of both "He's So

Fine" and "My Sweet Lord." Then Cashman asked Harrison, "Can you tell us whether the songs are strikingly similar to one another as played?"

Joseph Santora leapt to his feet from the defense table. "I am going to object to that," he exclaimed, "unless he wants to qualify Mr. Harrison as his own expert, because he is now dealing with the terminology that is a legal concept."

The words "strikingly similar" "also have common meaning," Judge Owen said to Santora in allowing the question. "Harrison looked like he was thinking rapidly," Cashman recalled. "After what seemed like a long pause, he answered, 'Yes.'"

With this, Cashman moved to the issue of Harrison's intent. Rather than trying to establish the alleged infringement was "willful," Cashman decided to "articulate the concept of 'subconscious infringement' because, even though there wasn't a jury, I was afraid of the Beatles' reputation, that they were so beloved and highly regarded."

Cashman continued cross-examining George Harrison: "When would you say was the last time, if ever, that you performed a song called 'You Really Got a Hold on Me'?" The song was a Smokey Robinson original that Robinson recorded with the Miracles, and the Beatles included as a cover recording on their US release *The Beatles' Second Album* and UK album *With the Beatles*.

"Performed it last time probably — you mean performed in front of an audience?"

"Or a recording or whatever."

"Is it called a performance if you just sing it in your bedroom?"

"I will take that, too. When did you sing it in your bedroom?"

"A lot. A lot. It's always been, you know, a favorite."

"Do you remember on direct [examination]," Cashman asked, "saying something in substance to this effect, that there would be times when a tune would come to you, but before you could get it down in any tangible form or record it, it would slip out of your mind and you would remember it years later?"

"I mean one example was, just last week I found a piece of paper," Harrison said. "I've got it in the seat of the Hammond organ I have at home, it opens up, and in there I just tend to push a lot of papers and stuff in order to keep it all together. I mean it's a tatty way of having a filing system."

"Are you claiming any originality in terms of the phrase 'Hare Krishna'?" Cashman continued.

"Oh, no, no. It goes back 5000 B.C.," George replied.

∘ ∘ ∘ ∘ ∘ After the second day of trial was over, Judge Owen listened to a tape of the music demonstration George had given in court. He also listened to the Harrison and Billy Preston versions of "My Sweet Lord." While listening closely to Preston's recording, the district judge made what he believed was a crucial discovery, which he raised in the courtroom the next day.

Judge Owen began the last day of the trial by calling George Harrison back to the witness stand, to question him directly about the development and structure of "My Sweet Lord." During the lengthy exchange, Harrison, who again played his guitar, and Owen sang song excerpts back and forth to each other. "You have got a chord pattern going that is as old as the hills," an unimpressed Owen said about "My Sweet Lord." "That E minor or A chord change has been used for years and years and years."

Judge Owen then told George that, while listening to Billy Preston's "My Sweet Lord" the night before, he had heard "a very fateful thing." It was a "grace" note—a stylistic embellishment that performers sometimes add to songs. This extra note, which Preston sang three times on his recording in motif B of "My Sweet Lord," didn't appear on Harrison's recording.

"Is that Billy Preston's? Is that his frolic, so to speak?" Judge Owen asked.

"I don't know," George answered.

"Billy Preston puts it in at the very place that the Chiffons put it in their recording," Owen observed. "You look at the Chiffons' score and their record, the second repeat of this thing. The first time when they do, [singing 'He's So Fine' lyrics] 'I don't know how I'm going to do it,' they don't have it in the second phrase; but, 'I'm going to make him mine,' they have that little extra note in that place, which is the second use of this, and Billy Preston does exactly the same thing."

"[U]nder a microscope, that one note may have amazing inference," Harrison admitted. But he insisted "the difference between one note or the other in my mind has no significance at all."

"I am just trying to ascertain whether any significance should attach to it in the course of this lawsuit," Judge Owen explained.

But George Harrison claimed it was "Oh, Happy Day" that had a greater influence on "My Sweet Lord." Strumming his guitar, he explained that the former was "just exactly the same, but the other way around, where Motif A is just the second half of 'Oh, Happy Day,' and here it goes after Motif B is the opening of 'Oh, Happy Day.' It's just a twist-around." Anyways, George said, "[W]hat people don't understand about music these days, is that it's not songs particularly or singers particularly," but the overall impact of the studio production of a recording. He claimed if the musical notes at issue in the court case "are owned by anybody," he "could have made ten variations, and I object to the idea of ripping off."

○ ○ ○ ○ ○ As his expert witnesses, George Harrison retained David Simpson Butler, a gospel musicologist, and Harold Barlow, who wrote books on music theory and said he had done more than 1,000 song-to-song comparisons for his clients. Butler testified that any similarities between "He's So Fine" and "My Sweet Lord" were due to traditional gospel-music composing techniques, though in contrast to Harrison he admitted he didn't see either of the two musical motifs being debated at trial in "Oh, Happy Day."

To support Harrison's "prior common source" defense, Harold Barlow gave examples of earlier songs with similar elements to both "He's So Fine" and "My Sweet Lord." These compositions included "Tara's Theme" from the 1939 movie *Gone With the Wind* and the Buckinghams' 1967 brass-rock chart-topper "Kind of a Drag." But Barlow admitted he hadn't previously seen the particular sequencing of motifs A and B that were in both the Mack and Harrison compositions.

24 "Fun Knocking Him over the Head"

Judge Richard Owen handed down his liability ruling on September 8, 1976, several months after the trial ended. Owen concluded that "My Sweet Lord" did infringe "He's So Fine" — but that George Harrison hadn't done so intentionally. The district judge emphasized George's courtroom admission that there was a strong similarity between the two works. Owen additionally noted about Bright Tunes' evidence, "This same conclusion was obviously reached by a recording group called the 'Belmonts' who recorded My Sweet Lord at a later time. With 'tongue in cheek' they used the words from both He's So Fine and My Sweet Lord interchangeably at certain points."

Judge Owen concluded that Harrison, "in seeking musical materials to clothe his thoughts, was working with various possibilities. As he tried this possibility and that, there came to the surface of his mind a particular combination that pleased him as being one he felt would be appealing to a prospective listener; in other words, that this combination of sounds would work. Why? Because his subconscious knew it already had worked in a song his conscious mind did not remember."

Owen then surmised, "Nevertheless, it is clear that 'My Sweet Lord' is the very same song as 'He's So Fine' with different words, and Harrison had access to 'He's So Fine.' This is, under the law, infringement of copyright, and is no less so even though subconsciously accomplished."

John Barham, George Harrison's recording-sessions colleague, later contended, however, that Judge Owen "avoided the central issue by picking up on the [Preston] embellishment the way he did, which wasn't really about the song's structure. The way the music was presented in 'My Sweet Lord' is more powerful than the song itself. It's like a painter; it's about the technique."

Harrison did acknowledge in his 1980 autobiography/lyrics book *I Me Mine* that for him songwriting "helps get rid of some subconscious burden."

But according to his first wife, Pattie, Judge Owen's ruling made George highly paranoid about listening to other artists' music. "After that we never had a radio playing in the house in case he was unconsciously [*sic*] influenced by a song he had heard."

○ ○ ○ ○ ○ Unfortunately for George Harrison, the infringement liability ruling, which took five years from when the suit was filed, signaled the start of a much longer phase of the "My Sweet Lord" litigation, the one in which the court would determine just how much George owed Bright Tunes for infringing on "He's So Fine." This second phase provided Allen Klein with an opportunity to begin a new legal attack against George. "We probably owed over $400,000 to our lawyers," Bright Tunes co-principal Jay Siegel said. "So Allen Klein bought the lawsuit from us."

Klein had begun negotiating with the Bright Tunes plaintiffs as far back as the pre-liability-trial settlement talks. He purchased "He's So Fine" from the publisher in April 1978 for $587,000 (Ronnie Mack's mother received $165,000 of the $587,000), then proceeded to litigate the damages issues against Harrison by seeking an increase to $1,599,987 in infringement damages. "It's a joke; having settled all the Beatle lawsuits [Klein settled his management litigation with Harrison, John Lennon, and Ringo Starr in 1977] he must have felt lonely not having somebody to sue," George said.

George learned about Klein's deal with Bright Tunes in the spring of 1978. "I had messages that Allen Klein had been in London on his way to the Cannes Film Festival," George recalled, "and I had a number of messages from different people saying that 'Allen Klein is trying to get hold of you.'" When George reached Allen in Cannes, France, he remembered the latter telling him, "'I have bought "He's So Fine." I thought I would do you a favor.' That's what he said, which I was a bit amazed to find out."

"I would prefer to talk to you when I come back to London on my way back to New York," Klein continued over the phone, though, according to George, "I didn't actually hear from him again after that."

Klein claimed, on the other hand, that after returning to New York from France, he left several messages on Harrison's home answering machine but didn't hear back from George, whose lawyers had advised him not to respond.

○ ○ ○ ○ ○ A nonjury trial on the infringement damages took place over eight days, from August to October 1979, in what was now captioned "ABKCO *Music Inc. v. Harrisongs Music Ltd.*" George once again faced Judge Richard Owen, whom he had parodied as a gum-chewing, gavel-banging-the-head jurist in the 1976 "This Song" video parody of the liability trial. ("This tune has nothing Bright about it," George sings in "This Song.") Joseph Santora recalled that when the "This Song" video was to be broadcast on *Saturday Night Live* on November 20, 1976, "George called to tell me to watch the show. When I saw the video, I thought, 'I hope Judge Owen doesn't see this.'"

Santora continued to serve as George Harrison's lead counsel. Allen Klein brought in Bright Tunes' litigator Gideon Cashman as his trial lawyer. "Klein had terminated our services when he took over," Cashman recalled. "I had never spoken to Allen Klein before in my life. Then one day, he calls up and says, 'I'm on the eve of the damages trial.' His counsel had been disqualified from the case, and he said he would like us to step in."

Central to the damages determination was how much of the success of "My Sweet Lord" could be attributed to the music of "He's So Fine." George Harrison testified that the popularity of his song was due to "a lot of different attributes, and the melody was, you know, part of it. I don't think it was a big part." He first cited his and Phil Spector's overall production of the album, "which I think was the success of *All Things Must Pass*" (though in the liability trial, George had said, "There were days when Phil Spector never even turned up.")

As for "My Sweet Lord" itself, Harrison claimed that "the sound of the guitars, the acoustic guitars, like five acoustic guitars and like they were recorded crystal clear and slide guitars put on top of that, I think right from the opening of 'My Sweet Lord,' I think that is a selling point of the song, is just the sound of the guitars and the way it moved."

George continued, "[A]s the record progresses, as the various instrumentation comes in and it builds and builds and builds, is a part of the appeal of the record. And the slide guitar intro and solo which is — I mean at the time I didn't realize but now today's people would term it as my trademark." And, George said, "[I]t took me quite a while to decide whether I should actually sing [the 'My Sweet Lord' lyrics], because let's face it, the pop music industry is not concerned about anything to do with spirituality."

Allen Klein testified in the damages proceeding about how, in 1971, he had met with Bright Tunes' Seymour Barash, who asserted "My Sweet Lord" was "a total infringement." Klein said they discussed the possibility of Harrisongs buying Bright Tunes' song catalog, that "that way there would be no question of whether or not there was an infringement and no embarrassment to anyone." But it "was shortly after that time that I believe Bright Tunes went into receivership," Klein said, "or there were disputes between the shareholders and Mr. Barash just disappeared from the scene." (However, Klein admitted later meeting with Barash.)

Joseph Santora asked, "Is it also safe to say, Mr. Klein, that whatever contacts you had with Bright Tunes after March 31, 1973 [the date Harrison, Lennon, and Starr ended Klein's management relationship with them], concerned the purchase of the 'He's So Fine' copyright for yourself or ABKCO?"

"Oh, yes."

"Do you recall ever telling Mr. Barash or suggesting to him in any way that you were still connected with Mr. Harrison in 1975?"

"Hardly," Klein replied.

When he issued the damages judgment, Judge Owen had calculated the US net earnings of "My Sweet Lord" at $2,133,316, of which he found that three-fourths, or $1,599,987, was "reasonably attributable" to George Harrison's use of the music from "He's So Fine." In a musical putdown of Harrison, Owen discounted the lead guitar part from "My Sweet Lord." "I conclude that the much-touted 'hook,' an introductory musical motive used by Harrison, was a minimal factor," Owen wrote.

Gideon Cashman recalled that in cross-examining George's valuation expert about how he had prorated the impact of such factors as the lyrics, the underlying music, and Harrison's popularity in contributing to the success of "My Sweet Lord": "I said, 'It only adds up to 90 percent. Where do you want to put the other 10 percent.' The expert said, 'Also into the lyrics.' I said, 'Why don't you recite them.' He started out singing, 'My Sweet Lord,' then hesitated and sang 'My Sweet Lord' again, then hesitated again. You could see him grimacing, trying to remember the rest of the lyrics, but he couldn't."

Judge Owen ended up deciding that the value of the music from "He's So Fine" attributed more to the success of "My Sweet Lord" than did

Harrison's lyrics. But Owen slammed Allen Klein's attempt to parlay the $587,000 purchase of the "He's So Fine" rights from Bright Tunes into a $1,599,987 payment from George Harrison. The district judge chastised Klein for "covert intrusion into the settlement negotiation picture in late 1975 and early 1976, immediately preceding the trial on the merits. At this crucial time Harrison made a settlement proposal which, at the time, Bright Tunes' lawyer regarded as 'a good one.' Unknown to Harrison, Klein, at that point involved in bitter post-firing [management] litigation with Harrison, made a substantially higher offer [i.e., $260,000] to purchase Bright Tunes' claim on behalf of ABKCO, thereby causing Bright Tunes to conclude that the level at which it had been negotiating with Harrison was far too low."

"I had no idea that Klein was negotiating with Bright Tunes behind the scenes," Gideon Cashman said.

"I couldn't believe Klein was such an asshole that he came in and bought the infringement claim against his former management client, George Harrison," Joseph Santora said. "We had fun knocking him over the head for it for the next several years."

Judge Owen concluded that Klein's conduct "irreparably destroyed" George's chances to settle the infringement suit before the liability trial. By doing so, Owen ruled, Klein breached his fiduciary obligation of special trust from when he was Harrison's manager. Owen limited ABKCO's recovery from Harrison to the $587,000 Klein paid Bright Tunes. Once Harrison remitted the $587,000 to ABKCO, the "He's So Fine" copyright would be his. "This is one of the few cases where a defendant found guilty of infringement ended up owning [the plaintiff's] song," Joseph Santora said.

(George already settled the companion infringement case that was brought against him by Peter Maurice Music in England. Under that agreement, the "He's So Fine" foreign sub-publisher got 40 percent of the UK income from "My Sweet Lord.")

But accounting disputes remained between Harrison and Klein, including that, in April 1980, Klein negotiated what Santora alleged was a secret agreement with Harrison's music-publishing agent, Essex Music International, that gave ABKCO a share of revenues from "My Sweet Lord" outside the United Kingdom and North America. The intractable Harrison and Klein thus continued to battle each other through a series of complex district court and federal appeals court rulings.

Klein's lawyers charged in 1986, "Harrison astonishingly creates a completely new set of 'facts' which he finds more to his liking." Joseph Santora countered about the "Dracula-like" litigation: "Whenever defendants feel that they have finally driven home the stake, up pops Klein with contradictory testimony, a post-trial motion or a hitherto concealed agreement in either hand."

Judge Owen issued a ruling in November 1990 that ordered Harrison to pay a share of "My Sweet Lord" royalties to Klein. But Klein attacked a reduced amount Harrison was required to pay ABKCO for Canadian, US, and UK rights to "He's So Fine." In October 1991, the Second Circuit appeals court ruled in favor of Harrison.

The Harrison/Klein accounting disputes were finally resolved in March 1998. Fittingly, the Second Circuit remarked along the way that the protracted court fight gave "true-meaning for those involved to the title of the Beatles' 'It's Been a Hard Day's Night.'"

25 · "The Largest Refugee Flight in History"

The country of Bangladesh achieved its independence — out of a civil war between East Pakistan, which became Bangladesh, and West Pakistan — in 1971, the same year that George Harrison was first served with the Bright Tunes' suit over "My Sweet Lord." With one of the highest population densities in the world, per capita income for the country's 75 million residents was less than $100 per year. Making matters worse, C. Lloyd Bailey, executive director of the US Committee for the United Nations Children's Fund (UNICEF), noted, "The civil war created the largest refugee flight in history. Nearly 10 million people were displaced — one in every seven of the population."

To ease the suffering, George Harrison's Indian music mentor Ravi Shankar proposed raising money for the Bangladesh refugees. George remembered, "I was in Los Angeles doing the 'Raga' soundtrack album [for a documentary about Shankar]. Ravi was talking to me and telling me how he wanted to do a concert, but bigger than he normally did, so that he could raise maybe 25,000 dollars for the starving in Bangla Desh."

The Beatles had performed at some benefit events — including a tour-closing one in New York City in September 1964 at which the Tokens, George Harrison's "My Sweet Lord" copyright-infringement adversaries, were an opening act. But Harrison was wary of affiliating with charities. His wife Pattie noted that, "they say a lot of these charities are just keeping the officials in money. I've been conditioned by George to feel this."

But George had played a UNICEF benefit concert in December 1969, backing John Lennon and Yoko Ono. Now, in 1971, just months after an English court approved Paul McCartney's request for a receiver to take Allen Klein's place in overseeing the Beatles' partnership assets, Harrison went to Klein, who still managed George, about the Bangladesh project. Klein responded that his ABKCO Industries "would pay the expenses for the hire and use of Madison Square Garden for the concert, and donate its

services for organization of the venture." The resulting benefit was scheduled for Madison Square Garden on August 1, 1971. There would be both
afternoon and evening concerts. In addition to Harrison and Shankar, the
shows featured an A-list of George's musical friends who agreed to waive
their performers' fees, including Eric Clapton, Bob Dylan, Billy Preston,
Leon Russell, and Ringo Starr.

John Lennon had hinted he might be there, too. "[W]e have to go to the
Virgin Islands to go to court about [the custody battle over Yoko's daughter]
Kyoko, and then I have to go to Texas about it, too," he told the *New Musical Express* in England. "If we got the kid back we might do it," John said,
though the Lennons didn't arrive in the United States until August 13.

Allen Klein appointed ABKCO's stocky promotion director Pete Bennett
to serve as security chief at Madison Square Garden, "to make sure that the
artists arrived and departed without any interference from fans or anyone,
. . . and also that the backstage area was completely free of anyone, press
included," Klein said.

George Harrison's set featured "My Sweet Lord," "Beware of Dark-
ness," and "While My Guitar Gently Weeps," among other original compositions. When he performed his new song "Bangla Desh," "Pattie and
I leaped to our feet with the rest of the audience, our hands raised above
our heads, clapping as hard as we could," Harrison friend and former Apple
Corps employee Chris O'Dell recalled. "We were so proud of George. . . .
That concert would be the model for all the big-name benefit concerts to
follow."

○ ○ ○ ○ ○ Ticket sales for the Bangladesh shows exceeded $280,000. Allen
Klein later declared, "100 per cent of the proceeds were written from Madison Square Garden to the US Committee for UNICEF." There would be an
album, too. "The question of recording was discussed between the artists
and myself," Klein said, "and it was decided that if [the concerts] came
out real well they would forego [*sic*] their artists' royalties and we would try
to make an arrangement with a record company to distribute it so that the
maximum proceeds would go to the charity."

Columbia Records and Warner Bros. were both interested in releasing
the album, but the benefit's organizers decided Capitol Records should get
the US vinyl distribution rights. The September 1971 distribution agreement

that Allen Klein and his ABKCO team negotiated for Apple Records with Capitol mirrored the two 1969 buy-sell agreements Klein had negotiated for the Beatles between the two labels. EMI managing director Len Wood noted that, in determining George Harrison and Ringo Starr's recording-artist royalties, which Harrison and Starr wanted to donate, from the US release of the multidisc *Concert for Bangladesh*, "one album will be deemed to be 'Beatle' product and the remainder of the package will be treated as 'non-Beatle' product," the latter thus paying a lower rate.

According to Klein, under the terms of the deal Capitol purchased the right to release the *Concert for Bangladesh* album from Apple at $8.60 per multidisc set, then charged its customers $10.00 wholesale per album, with a suggested consumer list price of $12.98. Apple was responsible for the album's recording and editing expenses. In addition, Klein said, "We estimated what the actual direct costs would be: the cost of physically making the box, the book, the [music] publisher royalty, the American Federation of Musicians' royalty, and then George Harrison decided on top of that he wanted to add five dollars, and he wanted that to go to the charity, and that is how the price was arrived at."

Capitol's vice president of marketing, Brown Meggs, claimed his label was "literally just covering our costs and overhead." Columbia Records president Clive Davis did obtain, for his parent label CBS Records, the right to distribute the vinyl album outside North America, as well as for Columbia and CBS to distribute the tape configurations of the *Bangladesh* performances worldwide. CBS, however, reportedly required a 25-cent "use" fee from each album for allowing Bob Dylan's performance to be included on the *Bangladesh* release — though Clive Davis insisted the fee wasn't related to Dylan but instead was to help Columbia meet the costs of distributing the *Bangladesh* tapes.

George Harrison wanted the benefit album to be released as soon as possible after the Madison Square Garden shows. But he became enraged by what he viewed as slow progress in getting the charity recording to consumers. In a November 23, 1971, appearance on the nationally televised *Dick Cavett Show* George blamed Capitol Records and its president, Bhaskar Menon. "It's just been hell," Harrison told Cavett. "This record should have been out a month ago, really." George threatened to release the album through CBS and, shaking his fist at the TV camera, invited Menon to sue him. "We're gonna play the 'sue me, sue you blues,'" George said, quoting what became a song on his 1973 *Living in the Material World* album.

The day after his tirade on *Cavett*, however, George phoned Capitol Records to apologize. Behind the scenes, EMI's Len Wood had written Apple Records Inc. on September 30 to say, "It is important that you let us have an edited tape at the earliest possible moment so that maximum effect can be given to the issue of the record by making the record available in as many parts of the world at the same time as is reasonably practicable."

Capitol Records released the three-disc set on December 20, 1971. By March 1972, the *Concert for Bangladesh* sold over two million albums in the United States. On March 9, Allen Klein gave UNICEF a $1.2 million check, the first from the revenues the concert album generated. Klein promised an additional $1.3 million would soon be headed UNICEF's way. In addition, US Committee for UNICEF president Guido Pantaleoni Jr. praised the $243,418.50 in Madison Square Garden ticket monies that Klein had forwarded to UNICEF's Children's Fund as being "the largest contribution from a single event of this nature," though George Harrison declined an invitation to participate in a ceremony awarding him with a UNICEF statuette for his charitable work.

In the midst of these triumphs, journalists began raising serious questions about Allen Klein's handling of the Bangladesh benefit monies. In a *New York* magazine article published on February 23, 1972, Peter McCabe, working on the book *Apple to the Core*, accused Klein of siphoning off the charity's funds. "There is no reason to think Allen Klein cares less about the plight of Bangladesh's wretched refugees than any other mortal," McCabe wrote, "but there is considerable reason to think that for Klein the concert in their behalf was also an occasion for business as usual."

McCabe had crunched finances for the *Concert for Bangladesh* album and concluded that $1.14 per of each album sold, adding up to several million dollars, was "unaccounted for." McCabe also thought that Klein was using George Harrison's *Bangladesh* album as leverage to negotiate contracts for other artists with Capitol.

The day after the *New York* article appeared, Phil Spector, who coproduced the *Bangladesh* recording, called the magazine's editorial offices to complain about McCabe's accusations. On February 28, 1972, ABKCO Industries filed a $150 million libel suit in state court in Manhattan. The suit alleged that McCabe's article was "false and defamatory," and denied ABKCO was earning income from the record project. ABKCO's complaint further charged that the *New York* piece "seriously impaired" sales of the *Concert for Bangladesh* album.

Klein bought trade publication ads to detail differences between Mc-Cabe's and Klein's revenue calculations. In difficult-to-decipher terms, the ads showed that, based on costs, Apple would lose money, whether album sales were 600,000 copies or as high as three million copies.

Klein continued to attack the McCabe exposé by holding what became a raucous press conference at ABKCO's Manhattan offices on February 29. Klein announced he had sued McCabe and *New York* magazine, then proceeded to explain his trade-ad figures. But according to *Rolling Stone* reporter Ben Fong-Torres, who was at the press conference, "Klein's figures not only slide; they seem to change, disappear or re-appear at will."

A shouting match soon erupted between Phil Spector and Bob Dylan pursuer/critic A. J. Weberman. Fong-Torres reported that when Weberman called Klein a "rip-off," Spector yelled back that Weberman should "go sell hot dogs in front of Dylan's house!" The Spector/Weberman confrontation spilled into the street after the press conference was over. But Klein and *New York* ended up settling the libel suit, with some observers claiming Klein feared revealing ABKCO's accounting books in open court.

o o o o o But Klein had other watchful eyes to worry about. The Internal Revenue Service intended to tax the *Bangladesh* album, concert, and film monies because Klein had failed to file for tax-exempt charity status prior to the Madison Square Garden shows. As George Harrison, author of the Beatles' invective "Taxman," saw it, the IRS's position was that "we think you might have been putting it on for your own profit."

Though George had often questioned Allen about the flow of revenues to UNICEF, he said Klein "did not give me a definite answer, but finally told me that it was necessary to get a tax problem sorted out first. I was surprised at this because I thought Klein would have made the necessary arrangements before the concert."

It wasn't until January 17, 1972, nearly six months after the August 1971 concerts, that ABKCO in-house lawyer Alan Kahn sent outside counsel at Rosenman Colin the documents necessary to qualify as a charitable foundation. These included the Madison Square Garden rental agreement, the official press releases for the concerts and album, and ABKCO's financial records related to the Bangladesh project.

On April 21, 1972, two months after the *New York* magazine article was published, ABKCO treasurer Henry Newfeld wrote Peter Howard at Apple Corps in London asking that George Harrison and Ringo Starr give Rosenman Colin the authority to act on their behalf in seeking an IRS determination "that there will be no adverse tax consequences" related to the *Concert for Bangladesh* monies. "In this case," Newfeld wrote, "since George and Ringo performed at the concert without pay, they might be considered to have contributed their normal pay to UNICEF. This would mean income to be reported and a limited deduction for the charitable contribution. That is the problem we are attempting to overcome."

° ° ° ° ° Tax status and Allen Klein's alleged misappropriation of a portion of the album revenues weren't the only financial hullabaloos hindering George Harrison's charitable goal. Paul McCartney's suit to dissolve the Beatles partnership became another complicating factor — less than a week before the Madison Square Garden shows were held.

On July 27, 1971, accountant James Spooner, the receiver appointed by the London court in McCartney's suit to break up the Beatles band partnership, wrote letters to George and to ABKCO/Apple Corps' Peter Howard about George's new solo single "Bangla-Desh." The record was to be released by Apple Records in the United States on July 28, 1971, and in the United Kingdom on July 30. Spooner's correspondence concerned the record royalties, which George planned to donate to the Bangla Desh Relief Fund. Spooner wanted Harrison to contact him "before any such arrangement is finalized." The receiver warned, however, "This does place me in some difficulty as, you may recall, the Court Order [appointing Spooner as Beatles receiver] imposed upon me the obligation to hold for the Court royalties not only on Beatles Group recordings, but on any individual recordings made by any of the individual partners."

Peter Howard wrote Spooner on July 29 that Harrison, John Lennon, and Ringo Starr all supported donating the royalties from George's "Bangla-Desh" single. Howard pushed Spooner to find out Paul McCartney's position on the issue. On August 20, Howard informed Spooner that

Harrison, Lennon, and Starr also agreed that George and Ringo's performers' royalties from the planned *Concert for Bangladesh* monies would be
donated, too. "Would you also please refer this to Mr. McCartney's advisors and press them for an answer," Howard entreated. "It seems to us that
this matter as with a number of other matters, is being delayed as a result of
Mr. McCartney's advisors not replying to your letters."

On September 9, Paul's London lawyer M. R. Lampard wrote Spooner
that McCartney "would have no objection whatsoever to the artist royalty
element of the recording of Bangla Desh being donated to the relief fund
but it does seem to me to be in contradiction to the Court Order." Lampard fretted, "I am particularly anxious that there should be no suggestion
whatsoever" that McCartney wasn't abiding by the court's receivership
instructions.

Spooner informed EMI's in-house counsel Malcolm Brown on October 1 that all four Beatles wanted the artist royalties paid to the Bangla Desh
Relief Fund and that he, the receiver, would agreed to it, too, if the court
overseeing his receivership did so. But on October 4, 1971, Howard wrote
Spooner, "I have still not heard from you with regard to your attitude concerning the donation." Howard blamed Spooner for getting in the way of
the concert recording's release: "Until this point has been cleared you will
appreciate that you are holding up the progress of this album."

On November 25, Spooner did let the High Court in London know
that Apple and the Beatles all backed giving the *Concert for Bangladesh*
revenues to the relief fund, though he worried "a taxation liability on the
partnership might arise," one that he had described to Peter Howard in
September as potentially "onerous."

o o o o o The British Treasury did demand a purchase tax from the *Concert
for Bangladesh* album income in Britain. In the United States, Rosenman
Colin filed the request on July 19, 1972, for the IRS to rule on the tax status
of the benefit concerts. Apple also retained tax specialists from the law firm
Weil, Gotshal & Manges, including Martin Ginsburg, husband of future
US Supreme Court justice Ruth Bader Ginsberg. A year and a half later, the
federal bureau had yet to decide the issue.

Now the executive director for UNICEF's US Committee joined the fray.
On January 29, 1974, the US Committee's C. Lloyd Bailey pleaded in a let-

ter to the chief counsel at the IRS for the release of the *Concert for Bangladesh* funds. Bailey claimed UNICEF had exceeded its $30 million budget for Bangladesh relief, which he said already was "the largest of all programs" in UNICEF's history. Bailey wrote the IRS that the United Nations humanitarian organization desperately needed the $3 million in "estimated income to what had already been received from the Concert, in order to cover the $30 million."

"I am convinced that it would be a mischanneling of funds if they were diverted into the tax revenues of the US government, rather than where they were initially intended to go," Bailey warned.

But the tax matter remained up in the air. After another three years passed, the United Nations relief agency became so frustrated that on July 29, 1977, it served Apple Corps, Apple Records, Apple Films, and ABKCO with a lawsuit it was filing in the New York County court. In the complaint, UNICEF charged the defendants with breach of contract. The suit also sought an accounting of the Bangladesh benefit monies. But the complaint was quickly withdrawn, before it permanently poisoned any future George Harrison/UNICEF relationship.

Still, the waiting continued. As late as 1979, George Harrison's current manager Denis O'Brien revealed that a "large percentage" of the benefit fund was still being "blocked" by the IRS, which had yet to decide whether the Bangladesh charity should be given tax-exempt status or be subject to federal taxation. "I certainly know in George Harrison's mind that if those funds ended up in the hands of the US government, that would be a catastrophe for him," O'Brien acknowledged. O'Brien calculated the blocked funds to be about $6 million. He estimated that $4.5 million of this would be paid to the IRS.

George Harrison optimistically wrote, however, in his 1980 autobiography *I Me Mine* that, after the years of discussions between Apple's lawyers and the IRS, "they have now almost got it covered" — though the IRS ultimately decided that income generated from George's Bangladesh project was taxable. Apple Corps' production director Jonathan Clyde noted in 2011, "I'm afraid that the IRS still take their cut even now." (The current US corporate tax rate is up to 35 percent of gross earnings, minus business deductions.)

At a minimum, the Bangladesh benefit brought much-needed attention to the plight of the starving refugees and established George Harrison's charitable legacy. Allen Klein boasted in 1972 that the Bangladesh project resulted in UNICEF receiving "more calls from concerned human beings, concerned young people, who became involved in helping other young people."

The *Bangladesh* album received the 1973 Grammy for Album of the Year. The same year, George founded the Material World Charitable Foundation, independent of the *Concert for Bangladesh* project. In 2005, his widow, Olivia Harrison, partnered with UNICEF for the George Harrison Fund. The same year, the rerelease of the *Concert for Bangladesh* album and film generated substantial additional monies for UNICEF — and the IRS. Perhaps most importantly, since the groundbreaking 1971 *Bangladesh* show, benefit concerts have become a common mission for musicians.

For Allen Klein, though, the Bangladesh tax mess was a prelude to a much greater personal entanglement with the IRS. By 1979, he faced the possibility of serving jail time — for evading taxes on Beatles-related income.

26 ∘ In the Bag

Harold Seider worked as an executive at ABKCO Industries for several years when, one day in the early 1970s, he walked into president/CEO Allen Klein's office, on the top floor of the forty-one-story office tower at 1700 Broadway in New York City's theater district, and saw something he hadn't seen before: Klein in his oversized leather chair counting what appeared to be a "pile" of cash on his desk, "a lot of money," Seider recalled.

ABKCO promotion director Pete Bennett was in Klein's office when Seider entered. "I stood there like a couple of minutes," remembered Bennett, who quickly left. "Then I saw Harold in the hallway." Bennett told Seider the money on Klein's desk had come from free, promotional records that Bennett sold. But these weren't just any records. When Klein renegotiated the Beatles' contracts with Capitol Records in 1969, he had demanded that the music group's Apple label, which Klein managed, receive 5,000 free promotional copies of each Apple album and single released through Capitol. Klein obtained the same generous provision when he gave United Artists the right to distribute the Beatles' *Let It Be* album, and for up to 10,000 promotional copies from Capitol for George Harrison's 1971 charity album *Concert for Bangladesh.*

In the music industry, record labels, like Apple, typically gave free promotional copies to radio stations and music critics. To get distributors to stock record-company releases, the labels often gave them free promotional copies as bonus records. But the money that Harold Seider had seen Allen Klein counting came from Bennett's sale to a local record distributor of the 5,000 promotional copies of *Let It Be.*

Bennett said Seider "says to me I am nuts and crazy. . . . 'Give him the money, you don't take a receipt? I am telling you, you are out of your mind going through these things of selling albums and giving him the money,'" which without proof of payment Klein could deny.

But this was business as usual at ABKCO. Bennett had been selling so-called "clean" copies of Beatles promotional records (i.e., without holes manufacturers drilled in such copies to prevent unreported sales) beginning with *Abbey Road* in 1969. He also sold "clean" copies of Apple releases by artists like Badfinger, Mary Hopkin, and James Taylor. Bennett was able to do so because Capitol customarily sent ABKCO undrilled copies of each release designated in the shipments as, "Free, no holes stated on order." This had been a trademark negotiating technique of Allen Klein's at least since 1966, when he obtained a similar provision in renegotiating record producer Mickie Most's deal with MGM.

In the early 1970s, Capitol charged its wholesale customers around $3.30 per copy for albums like the Beatles' that had a suggested retail list price of $6.98. Bennett sold Apple Records' promotional copies to distributors for $1.75 to $3.00 per copy.

Pete Bennett's customers paid him in cash, and sometimes in checks made out to front companies like Peter Music. Pete typically handed the money from each sale over to Allen Klein, after he took a cut of almost one-third for himself.

In June 1971, for example, after selling 5,000 undrilled promotional copies of Paul and Linda McCartney's *Ram* album to a record distributor, "I brought the money home because I got paid over the weekend on it and I left it in the kitchen cabinet in a bag," Pete said. That Sunday, June 13, Pete brought the bag full of money to Allen Klein's home on Palisades Avenue near the Hudson River Parkway, in New York City's ritzy Riverdale section. Allen had conveniently invited Pete to a party he was throwing to celebrate the birthday of his wife Betty, and in honor of special guests John Lennon and Yoko Ono. But Klein later denied that Pete gave him any money that day.

◦ ◦ ◦ ◦ ◦ Allen Klein and Pete Bennett first met in the mid-1960s, on a drive to Philadelphia with the president of the New York–based Cambridge Distributors, for whom Bennett worked, to have dinner with influential disc jockey Jocko Henderson. Allen was impressed enough with Pete to ask him to stop by a few days later at ABKCO's offices, which were then located in the Time Life Building on Sixth Avenue in midtown Manhattan. Allen was managing soul artist Sam Cooke. According to Pete, who promoted hit records for Nat King Cole, Allen told him that "he would like me to promote Sam Cooke because Sam Cooke would like to have the same promotion man that Nat King Cole had."

In March 1964, Allen offered Pete $200 a week plus expenses, and in 1965 hired him as a regular employee—though Allen said he didn't see Pete much, "unless, of course, he had performed a miracle and gotten our records on the charts." (In an attempt to turn Sam Cooke's 1964 version of "Tennessee Waltz" into a hit, Klein himself purchased 5,000 copies of the single from a distributor for RCA Records.)

In addition to Cooke, Pete promoted records by other Klein-affiliated acts such as the Animals, Donovan, Herman's Hermits, the Rolling Stones, and Pete's friend Bobby Vinton. Radio stations received up to 700 new releases each week, so record promoters faced intense competition. Pete explained, "When a manufacturer delivers DJ copies [of a release], which is probably about 100, 150 for the New York area, the promotion man will . . . bring them to the local radio stations in the area and will talk to the program director, and necessarily will talk to the DJ and tell him it is a good record: 'I would appreciate it very much if you could look at it,' and hope to God—that is what we say all the time to get [the DJ] to play it, which is the hardest thing in the world to do."

○ ○ ○ ○ ○ Pete Bennett was born in the Bronx, New York, on May 11, 1935. His said his career in the music business took hold when, as a teenager, "I bought a drum set for $22 at a pawnshop. I wanted to be a famous drummer, and won a Gene Krupa drum contest. So at 17, I worked with Tommy Dorsey on a reunion tour with [Frank] Sinatra. Well, I had shined Sinatra's shoes one time, and he remembered me. Later when we were on stage, he would say, 'Hey kiddo,' and introduce me as his former shoeshine boy. He embarrassed me, I hated it."

Pete also road-managed the Tommy Dorsey Orchestra and later formed his own Pete Bennett and the Embers, which scored a minor hit in 1961 with an instrumental version of "Fever." Pete also turned to record promotion, pushing releases for major acts like The Lettermen. For Nat King Cole, he helped turn Capitol recordings like "Ramblin' Rose" and "Those Lazy-Hazy-Crazy-Days of Summer" into hits. For Cambridge Distributors, he promoted records by Motown artists such as the Supremes and

Mary Wells, and for Scepter Records artists like the Shirelles. A Republican activist, Pete secured Bobby Vinton to sing at President Richard Nixon's 1969 inauguration.

Rolling Stone described Pete on a typical promotion day as being "[m]anicured, cologned, pinky-ringed and form fit in a top coat of Spanish leather," with a voice in "slightly heliumized Buddy Hackett tones." Austin, Texas, entertainment attorney Mike Tolleson knew Pete well in the 1980s, after meeting him at a music conference in Acapulco, Mexico, and through Texas music seminars. "Pete was the stereotypical old-school record guy," Tolleson said. "Not at all shy, he was quick to let you know he was the greatest record promo man in the world."

Lon Van Eaton, who with his brother Derrek recorded an album for the Beatles' Apple label in the early 1970s, said Pete once told him that record promotion "was about dropping a bag of money on a radio station desk on Fridays. In his office, he had photos all over the walls of himself with famous people like Frank Sinatra. Pete wanted a picture of himself with the Pope so that he could use it for the cover of a photo book he wanted to publish titled *Who's That Standing Next to Pete Bennett?*"

○ ○ ○ ○ ○ One Thursday evening in November 1975, Pete Bennett arrived home to find an urgent message waiting for him from Sam Weiss, a well-known record distributor in the New York area to whom Pete had sold the undrilled promotional copies of the Beatles' *Let It Be* album. Pete said that when he phoned Weiss the next morning, Weiss told him there were "a couple of agents, government people, that came into his place and picked up the checks. So I says, 'What checks?'"

"Well, of the Beatles, of the records that I was buying from ABKCO of the Beatles," the anxious Weiss supposedly replied. "The agents told me not to say anything to you about it. I want to tell you because I want you to explain it to them and let them know the story, what's going on."

"Tell Allen Klein and I hope there is no problem," Weiss said before his phone conversation with Pete Bennett ended.

But there was a problem. Internal Revenue Service agents were investigating whether this was income that should have been reported on Bennett's federal tax returns. The agents had already examined the accounting books and cancelled checks of several record distributors. When Pete went down to ABKCO on Friday afternoon, his first stop was at in-house counsel Alan Kahn's office. Kahn, however, was out playing tennis with Klein. When the two ABKCO executives returned, Pete began telling them Weiss's story.

"Don't talk here," Kahn cautioned. "Probably the whole place is bugged."

So Bennett, Klein and Kahn went downstairs to the Stage Delicatessen, where they sat at a back table. According to Pete, Allen told him, "Look, don't involve me in this. You can't do that, mention my name at all. That would be the end of my $20 million Beatles suit [against John Lennon, George Harrison, and Ringo Starr for firing Klein as their manager in 1973]." In addition, the IRS investigation into unreported income from Bennett's sales to distributors involved a federal crime.

"If anybody asks you anything, just tell them that you cashed the checks and you gave the money back to Sam Weiss," Klein directed Bennett.

∘ ∘ ∘ ∘ ∘ But Pete Bennett quit ABKCO the following Tuesday. A little over a year later, on December 16, 1976, he was indicted by a federal grand jury on criminal tax charges. The indictment, handed up in the Southern District of New York, charged Pete personally with six counts: evading taxes on at least $84,000 in income from the sale of promotional records to wholesalers and distributors in 1970, 1971, and 1972, and for filing false federal tax returns for those years. This included money from sales of promotional copies of George Harrison's charity album *Concert for Bangladesh*. Pete pleaded guilty to one count — filing a false tax return for 1970 — and agreed to be a government witness against Allen Klein.

In April 1977, Allen was indicted on three counts of evading federal taxes on over $216,742 in income from promotional record sales from 1970 to 1972, and on three counts for filing false tax returns during those years. If convicted, he faced a maximum of five years in jail for each tax evasion count and three years for each false tax return count, plus a total maximum fine of $45,000. But he pleaded not guilty on all counts and the federal court set his bail bond at $50,000.

This wasn't Allen Klein's first time in court on a criminal tax charge. In January 1971, a New York federal district jury found him guilty of willfully failing to file ten federal quarterly returns between 1959 and 1962, related to employee withholding taxes. Klein pleaded not guilty in that case, too, by claiming the Internal Revenue Service lost or misplaced the returns ABKCO did file. Federal prosecutors argued, however, that the "copies" of those returns that Klein retained were "highly suspicious," and that his "evasive conduct and contradictory statements" were proof that he "intentionally failed to file the required returns." The district court fined Klein $15,000 on the misdemeanor conviction and the Second Circuit appeals court affirmed.

27 "Believe PB's Testimony?"

The trial on Allen Klein's 1977 indictment began in Manhattan federal court on October 11 of that year. Klein didn't learn until a few days before the trial that Pete Bennett was cooperating with federal prosecutors against him. That was because after Bennett was indicted, his attorney Martin Schwartz claimed there were "clear indications of threats against" Pete and his family "on the part of some people who were perhaps in the employ of Mr. Klein." For example, Schwartz contended, a private investigator working for Klein had been to Hartsdale, New York, where Pete lived, asking neighbors about Pete's children, "Where were they? Where did they go to school? What time did they come home from school?"

Schwartz said his client was seeking help from the federal witness protection program, which offered bodyguards and new identities, though Pete scoffed at this as "nonsense."

Klein's case was assigned to US district judge Charles M. Metzner, a former US attorney general executive assistant appointed to the federal bench in 1959 by President Dwight D. Eisenhower. Klein's lead defense counsel was Gerald Walpin, a former chief of special prosecutions at the US Attorney's Office whose government work had included shutting down the avant-garde Living Theater in Manhattan, and the arrest of its director Julian Beck and cast for failing to pay withholding and amusement-ticket taxes. Later, in private practice, Walpin had defended Allen Klein in the 1971 tax-withholding case.

Robert N. Shwartz, assistant US attorney in the promotional records case, said to the twelve-member jury in opening, "During this trial you will learn how the defendant, Allen Klein, set up a scheme that put almost $220,000 in cash in his own pocket over the course of three years' time. He was able to do this while he was the manager of the Beatles and their music empire."

Shwartz continued, "The proof will show that Mr. Klein's record-selling scheme had two essential dimensions. The first, of course, is that he produces cash in large quantities. You will see through the course of this trial just how successful [he] was at doing that. But the second dimension of the scheme that he devised was just as important and that was that he be able to get this cash in a way that could not be traced back to him. . . . And the front that Allen Klein used is someone by the name of Pete Bennett."

Gerald Walpin told the jury that Klein chose Pete Bennett to work for him because Bennett was "the top promotion man in the country" whom Klein gave "almost a free hand in the promotion end of the business." Walpin noted the industry practice of giving undrilled promotional copies of records to distributors — who then sold those copies as regular stock — as an incentive to stock labels' record releases was used, too, by Apple Records' parent label Capitol. But Walpin insisted Allen Klein hadn't known that Pete Bennett was *selling* the promotional copies to distributors. Behind the government's prosecution of Klein, Walpin argued to the jury, was that Bennett was trying to frame his former boss, to make him the fall guy for Bennett.

∘ ∘ ∘ ∘ ∘ The government's evidence against Allen Klein was also based on testimony from record distributors with whom Bennett had dealt, and from ABKCO employees who said they knew that Pete had passed large amounts of cash to Allen Klein. Joel Silver, ABKCO's vice president in charge of royalties, was among these latter witnesses. Though he still worked at Klein's company, Silver testified that several times Pete Bennett had handed him money saying it was earmarked for Klein.

Bennett took the witness stand on the trial's second day. He described himself as, at the time, a self-employed executive producer of records, TV programs, and movies. He said he had midwifed artist contracts with the Atlantic, Epic, and Warner Bros. labels, and been involved in projects by such acts as Laverne & Shirley, Rick Nelson, and Emerson, Lake & Palmer.

Bennett testified that as early as when he promoted Sam Cooke's posthumous 1965 single "Shake," Allen Klein asked him to sell the 5,000 promotional copies of the record that RCA sent to ABKCO's office. To give the jurors an idea of how much space an equivalent number of albums would take up, the government's cocounsel, Assistant US Attorney Thomas E. Engel, asked about the Beatles' 1969 album *Abbey Road*, "From the end of the jury box to the witness stand and from the [court] clerk's desk to the wall?"

"Right," Bennett replied, adding that the *Abbey Road* promotional copies were kept in an ABKCO conference room in a stack that was about five feet high. He then testified that he sold those discs for two dollars each and gave the money to Klein. Pete added that he sold the 5,000 promotional copies of the *Let It Be* album to a local distributor [i.e., Sam Weiss] for three dollars each and also sold promotional copies of the Beatles' "Hey Jude" single, and of the solo albums *Beaucoups of Blues* by Ringo Starr and *All Things Must Pass* by George Harrison.

Pete claimed that when Capitol Records sent unsalable "drilled" promotional copies of John Lennon's *Imagine* and Paul McCartney's Wings *Wild Life* albums to ABKCO, Klein "got on the phone and called Capitol and said he — starts yelling and says he wants no holes in the records."

During cross-examination, however, Klein's lawyer Gerald Walpin charged, "Isn't it a fact that you lied when you told the government that you had turned over all of the money to Mr. Klein?"

"Yes, I did," Bennett admitted to lying.

⚬ ⚬ ⚬ ⚬ ⚬ It was during the second week of the trial that now former ABKCO executive Harold Seider testified to confirm the incident in which he had seen Allen Klein counting a large amount of cash at his desk. Seider said he also remembered an incident in which he saw a wholesaler's truck driver at ABKCO with a fully loaded dolly whom Pete Bennett "was directing to get the records into the elevator."

For Klein, Seider was a particularly troubling witness, because he had been a trusted all-around ABKCO executive. Allen once described Harold as "in-house counsel. He was a member of the board. He was an officer. And he was the number two man at ABKCO." This made Gerald Walpin's cross-examination of Seider crucial to Klein's defense.

Walpin set out to damage Seider's credibility by raising whether Seider had been caught in an attorney/client conflict of interest between his relationships with Klein and with the Beatles.

"You first met the Beatles, did you not, through your association with ABKCO?" Walpin asked.

"That's correct," Seider replied.

"When the dispute first arose between the Beatles and ABKCO [i.e., when the band terminated the management agreement with Klein in March 1973], you advised Mr. Klein and the board of directors on that subject, isn't that right?"

"I don't believe that is a fairly accurate statement," answered Seider, who had resigned from ABKCO in 1971.

Walpin continued, "Isn't it a fact that you were advising Mr. Lennon during the same period [i.e., June 1973 to January 1977] ABKCO and Klein were litigating with Mr. Lennon and the Beatles?"

"Come up here and tell me what that has to do with this lawsuit," Judge Metzner interrupted.

At the judge's bench, outside the jury's hearing, Walpin said, "The fact is, as I will attempt to show, that what happened was that it was improper for him to be advising Lennon during the litigation which was between Lennon and Klein."

But Metzner didn't agree that could establish bias by Seider against Klein in the tax-evasion case and cut off Walpin's line of questioning.

∘ ∘ ∘ ∘ ∘ Federal prosecutors also brought in Bhaskar Menon, Capitol Records president/CEO since April 1971, to testify against Allen Klein. While Menon was on the witness stand, Thomas Engel handed him a copy of a Capitol memo from that year sent by the label's vice-president of marketing to the vice president of operations. Menon noted the memo discussed Capitol's sales representative in Buffalo, New York, who discovered that a local distributor "had many more Badfinger albums than Capitol sold him. And it suggests that the sales representative believed that this was an outlet for Apple non-drilled albums."

Menon verified that he wrote on the memo himself, back to the marketing executive, "[C]an we place any absolutely secret markings on labels or sleeves or somewhere on some of these Apple non-drilled albums experimentally to check on them, at this stage known to yourself, me and whoever you entrust the job to?"

But the record industry was beset by corrupt practices, such as gifts to radio DJs and program directors — in exchange for airplay — of drugs, paid trips, and arrangements for sexual favors. The sale of copies of records intended for promotional uses was but another of these crooked traditions.

Menon testified that when he discussed the promotional records issue with Allen Klein in the summer of 1971, Klein assured him Apple Records' reason for wanting undrilled copies was that they were to be "giveaways to the radio stations, to customers, to dealers for a variety of promotional purposes." Menon admitted he had then approved Klein's demand that Capitol send only undrilled promotional copies to the Beatles' record company.

∘ ∘ ∘ ∘ ∘ With Seider's and Menon's testimonies completed, Allen Klein began his testimony on October 25, 1977, two weeks into the trial. While his wife Betty looked on, Klein detailed his record industry career. Gerald Walpin asked him to describe the success of the Beatles albums that were released while ABKCO managed the group (i.e., *Abbey Road, Let It Be,* and two greatest hits albums). When Walpin asked Klein to "describe the success or lack of success of the Beatles solo releases," Allen coyly responded, "[T]here are members of the press here. I don't want to speak disparagingly."

"Don't give me this 'members of the press.' Answer his question," Judge Metzner ordered Klein. Klein then discussed a litany of Beatles solo releases, from George Harrison's *All Things Must Pass* ("a very big hit") and *John Lennon/Plastic Ono Band* ("under a million [sold], but it was in my mind a hit") to Paul McCartney's Wings *Wild Life,* "which did about a half a million, was not a hit for Paul McCartney or for the Beatles."

Klein did recall that when Bhaskar Menon told him "one of their people up in the Buffalo area had been into a one-stop or a dealer, and he appeared to have albums in quantities that were larger than they had purchased, I asked him how he knew that they were ours. He said, 'Allen they were in the same boxes. They are not even opened.' That ended the conversation."

But when Walpin asked, "Did you ever, in connection with the promotional records received from Capitol on the Beatles, did you ever, or Apple, did you ever tell Pete Bennett to go out and sell them?" Klein claimed no.

Klein did acknowledge that he stored a large reserve of cash in his office safe. He said that he used the money to buy gifts and named John Lennon, George Harrison, Klein's secretary Iris Keitel, and his nephew (and future ABKCO lawyer) Michael Kramer among the recipients. Klein claimed the substantial sums Pete Bennett had given him were to repay monies that Klein loaned to Bennett. But prosecutor Thomas Engel argued "there were no cash expenditures by Mr. Klein during that period that anywhere equate or proximate what the government has proven."

Engel read the jury an excerpt from a lengthy interview Klein gave *Playboy* magazine in 1971. In the interview, reporter Craig Vetter asked Klein, "Short of destroying a man, would you do literally anything to accomplish what you felt you have to do for a client?"

"Yes, I think so," Klein had responded.

"Would you lie?"

"Oh, sure."

"Would you steal?"

"Probably. Look, you have to survive and you do whatever it takes because if you don't stay alive in this business you can't help anybody. And then all the discussions about ethics and morals don't mean a thing. Yoko told me when she and John came to me they were looking for a real shark, someone to keep the other sharks away. Now she says I am too moral."

But Klein claimed *Playboy* quoted him out of context. Rather, Klein testified, he had been referring to how parties negotiate deals, with each telling other they can't give any more ground, when they can.

∘ ∘ ∘ ∘ ∘ The trial took 17 days, 33 witnesses — 29 for the government — nearly 450 exhibits in evidence and 2,500 reported pages of trial testimony. Jury deliberations began on November 3, 1977. The jurors certainly weren't Beatles aficionados. In a note to Judge Metzner that day, the foreperson asked, "[M]ay we have a ruling as to whether the Beatle single 'The Long and Winding Road,' released 5/11/70, recalled by a juror as a Lennon recording, may be *assumed* to be the Lennon album" *Imagine*. "The Long and Winding Road" was written and sung by Paul McCartney, and appeared on the Beatles' *Let It Be* album.

But after considering all the testimony they had heard, the jurors struggled over a verdict. On the sixth day of jury deliberations, the trial judge wrote them, "Are you still deadlocked?" The response was yes.

Metzner wrote back, asking "is there a possibility that you can reach a verdict as to any count in the indictment?"

The foreperson responded, "9 — No 3 — Yes."

Without a needed unanimous response Judge Metzner immediately declared a mistrial. But it had been unlikely since the first day of deliberations that the jury would reach a unanimous guilty verdict against Allen Klein, for when the jurors pondered among themselves in the jury room on November 3 whether to "Believe PB's testimony?," one juror had already concluded, "No" about Pete Bennett's credibility.

However, the jury deadlock didn't end the federal government's pursuit of Allen Klein. It meant there would be a retrial. The case was reassigned to federal judge Vincent L. Broderick, who previously served as New York City police commissioner. Klein moved to dismiss the case on the ground that trying him twice on the same criminal charges would amount to double jeopardy in violation of the US Constitution's Fifth Amendment. But Judge Broderick denied Klein's motion.

Several months later, on April 28, 1978, Klein was slapped with the second criminal indictment. This one charged him with the same six criminal tax counts as in the original indictment. But now the amount Klein allegedly received from the promotional records sales was lowered from $216,742 to $175,472. Klein's counsel claimed the government had reduced the figure "clearly to avoid the embarrassment it experienced in front of the jury during the first trial — an embarrassment that dramatically demonstrated the basic flaw in the Government's case, which was that, in reality, the Government's case rested entirely on the uncorroborated testimony" of Pete Bennett that he gave all the money from the sale of the promotional records to Klein.

° ° ° ° ° Trial two began on February 20, 1979. It, of course, featured many of the same witnesses who testified at the first trial. A key point of contention for Klein was to have his relationship with Iris Keitel, who began working for him as an assistant in 1966, excluded from jury consideration. According to the US attorneys, by 1969, when Keitel stopped regularly showing up at ABKCO's offices, "her relations with the defendant were intimate, and it is not seriously contested that she was, in plain words, his mistress."

Keitel had remained a salaried ABKCO employee until late 1975, the government said, which was when Allen Klein learned the IRS was investigating him. The prosecutors argued Klein's relationship with Keitel would establish that "a person of enormous financial wealth but also one saddled with substantial obligations and debts, had a reason that he needed cash — to support a mistress in the style to which she had become accustomed."

Assistant us Attorney Steven Shatz agreed, however, the jury would only be told that from 1970 to 1972, Klein "made gifts of cash or gifts which he purchased or caused to be purchased with cash in the approximate amount of $15,000 to $20,000 to a personal friend."

◦ ◦ ◦ ◦ ◦ The second trial ran until April 23, 1979. During their three days of deliberation, the jurors' requests to Judge Broderick included for them to be sent a bottle of Mylanta and a package of Gelusil antacid medicine, to quell stomach indigestion.

The jury found Allen Klein guilty, but only on one count: filing false tax returns for 1970. Still, Klein faced a maximum sentence of three years in jail on the one tax-return conviction. (For testifying as a government witness, Pete Bennett was ordered by Judge Broderick to pay only a $2,000 fine and placed on one-year unsupervised probation.) Desperate for leniency, Allen submitted letters of support to Judge Broderick from family, colleagues, and doctors.

Among these, Klein's sister Anne wrote: "I personally will give my life for my brother please don't put him away I just can't plead enough my heart is filled with horror I am sincerely upset to the point that I fear for him."

Artist Sam Cooke's father, the Reverend Charles Cooke, who received monthly payments from Klein, wrote, "Allen Klein was my son's manager. The two of them were good friends, and I know that Mr. Klein was always forthright in dealing with my son."

Psychiatrist Jerry Weisfogel, who met with Allen and Betty Klein three times a week over their troubled marriage, reported to the judge that Allen developed "claustrophobic anxiety" from his "incarceration" at a New Jersey orphanage as a child. As a result, Dr. Weisfogel determined, Betty Klein's "strong emotional dependency on Allen which takes the form of a demanding need to be with him most of the time" had driven him into the relationship with Iris Keitel. Sending Klein to jail "would seriously aggravate" this claustrophobia, Weisfogel claimed.

At the August 9, 1979, sentencing hearing, Judge Broderick said he concluded that Klein "lied during the trial" but did give him a reduced sentence: two months of confinement and a $5,000 fine. Gerald Walpin filed an appeal the same day, but on December 17, 1979, the us Court of Appeals for the Second Circuit affirmed Judge Broderick's ruling. In June

1980, the US Supreme Court turned down Klein's petition for the high court to consider his tax case.

In the end, the federal government proved what Paul McCartney charged in his infamous 1969 *Abbey Road* song "You Never Give Me Your Money," recorded three days before the other Beatles signed their May 9, 1969, management agreement with Klein. "This was me directly lambasting Allen Klein's attitude to us," Paul had said.

Allen Klein began his two-month jail term on July 14, 1980, in the minimum-security section of Manhattan's Metropolitan Correctional Center with its private rooms for prisoners. The man who had once managed the high-powered financial affairs of the Beatles now had a new obligation: he was assigned to work in the prison kitchen, where he was given the delicate task of preparing fruit salads for his fellow inmates.

Epilogue
The Law & Winding Road

fter the tax-evasion case, both Allen Klein and Pete Bennett stayed in the entertainment industry for the remainder of their careers. Bennett continued working in music promotion, though his most successful years had passed. He also promoted fashion models and developed a "How to Become a Star" seminar. Bennett's friend, artist manager Sal Vasi, said that only two weeks before Pete died of a heart attack in November 2012, "I played him a new artist from Nashville. Pete thought he was great and met with him and plotted out an entire campaign we were going to do together."

Bennett's defection from ABKCO in the 1970s didn't dampen the loyalty that many ABKCO staffers, working at the company for decades, had for Allen Klein. Attorney Barry Slotnick, who litigated against ABKCO in recent years on behalf of Herman's Hermits, joked that the ABKCO employees he saw in court "looked like they were 142 years old."

But Klein continued to be a lightning rod for litigation in his post-tax-conviction years. In 1981, a new legal conflict burst out of his long-running relationship with the Rosenman Colin law firm. The firm sued Klein for $350,000 in allegedly unpaid legal fees and costs related to Rosenman Colin's representation of him in the second tax trial. Klein said he paid the firm a total of more than $1 million for the 1977 and 1979 tax trials, and "millions of dollars in fees over the past five years." He countersued Rosenman Colin by claiming that for the 1979 retrial, "I was overbilled because of undue turnover of [Rosenman Colin] personnel who worked on the trial."

Rosenman Colin asked the New York state court for an early ruling in its favor. But after the court denied the motion in June 1982 (though it dismissed Klein's counterclaims), a state appellate court affirmed. Klein and the law firm then settled their differences.

Later, in the 1980s and 1990s, Allen Klein aggressively asserted ABKCO's music rights by filing lawsuits over unauthorized karaoke uses of music from his company's catalog and over the sampling of Rolling Stones music.

In 2007, Klein sued his longtime ally Phil Spector. Allen had funded Phil's defense in two music-royalty suits, one by singer Darlene Love, who sang lead on Crystals records Phil produced, and the other by Phil's former wife Ronnie Spector and the other members of the 1960s vocal group the Ronettes, whose hits included "Be My Baby." (Love won $132,000 in back royalties; the Ronettes lost their claim for royalties from Phil's licensing of their recordings in video commercials, TV shows, and movies.) Klein's suit, in New York federal court, accused Spector of failing to repay $1.67 million Allen Klein allegedly loaned him to cover legal fees and costs in the Love and Ronettes litigations.

The ABKCO/Spector case was also settled, in February 2009. In April of that year, a California jury convicted Phil Spector of murdering actress Lana Clarkson at his California home. Allen Klein died on July 4, 2009, from complications of Alzheimer's disease. In its obituary, the British *Mail on Sunday* recalled Klein's "bad language and abrasive management style." The Associated Press wire story memorialized him as a music manager "who bulldozed his way into and out of deals."

○ ○ ○ ○ ○ In their post-Klein era, John Lennon, Paul McCartney, and Ringo Starr all stabilized their management teams. Working out of her office downstairs from the Lennons' apartment at the Dakota next to New York's Central Park, Yoko Ono cultivated John's money through such investments as real estate and cattle into tens of millions of dollars by the time he died in December 1980 — criminally by the gun of crazed fan Mark David Chapman.

The team of Lee and John Eastman that Paul had wanted to manage Apple Corps guided him into becoming one of the largest independent music publishers in the world with his MPL Music Publishing, founded in 1971, and its vast array of song-copyright acquisitions, from Buddy Holly's tunes and the catalog of Broadway musicals composer Frank Loesser to Paul's solo compositions. Ringo, meanwhile, retained business manager Hilary Gerrard and Los Angeles lawyer Bruce Grakal, who have represented him for four decades.

George Harrison was the odd Beatle out. Soon after firing Allen Klein in April 1973, George signed a management contract with lawyer/financial adviser Denis O'Brien, who went on to manage him for the next twenty years. But in 1993, Harrison learned that his finances, parked in a complex web of companies O'Brien had created, were in serious trouble.

George sued Denis in Los Angeles Superior Court alleging in part that O'Brien had "enriched himself and lived on a lavish scale at Harrison's expense, buying yachts and villas in various parts of the world, while Harrison suffered enormous losses and liabilities as a result of O'Brien's improper and inept management and deceitful conduct." In 1995, the trial judge awarded George $11 million from O'Brien to help repay more than $20 million of a loan that Handmade Films, the Harrison/O'Brien partnership that produced Monty Python films, owed American Express Bank.

George never collected on the court judgment. In 2000, Denis O'Brien filed for bankruptcy in a St. Louis federal court to avoid paying George. George challenged the bankruptcy filing, but after he failed to show up for a July 2001 deposition — on the ground that he couldn't travel from England to St. Louis due to the vicious cancer rapidly spreading through his body — the court ruled in favor of O'Brien. Bankruptcy judge Barry Schermer emphasized that George Harrison had recently flown from England to Rhode Island to attend the college graduation of his son, Dhani Harrison. Unbelievably, Judge Schermer accused George of attempting "to fool this court. . . . Harrison's disregard of an order to answer questions was obviously willful."

Sadly, George died from cancer only a few weeks after the harsh decision was issued.

○ ○ ○ ○ ○ Even though the Beatles had reached a settlement in December 1974 that ended Paul McCartney's partnership-dissolution suit against the other three, their relations with Paul remained chilly for years. McCartney said in 1986, "I went at Yoko's request to New York recently. She said she wanted to see me." But when he called her after arriving at the reception area of her Dakota residence, "[S]he said she couldn't see me that day. I was 400 yards away from her," Paul claimed. "I said, 'Well, I'll pop over any time today; five minutes, ten minutes, whenever you can squeeze me in.' She said, 'It's going to be very difficult.' . . . So I felt a little humiliated."

McCartney added about George and Ringo, however, "I'm just starting to get back with them. It's all business troubles. If we don't talk about Apple then we get on like a house on fire."

But in the 1980s, Apple Corps was struggling financially, due in large part to the expense of music-royalty suits the Beatles had filed against Capitol-EMI Records in the United States and England. Apple Corps claimed the record companies underpaid the Beatles millions of dollars from the sales of the band's records. This allegedly included royalties from the sale of un-drilled promotional copies, the same practice that had landed Allen Klein in jail.

Lee Eastman worried that the Capitol-EMI litigation was costing Apple Corps "a million dollars a year." In addition, the legal dispute was holding up the lucrative release of Beatles product in the then new compact-disc format.

In the meantime, George, Ringo, and Yoko became furious when they learned that McCartney had obtained an "override" — an increased royalty rate for himself on Beatles product — when he signed a solo artist deal with Capitol-EMI in 1985, in the middle of Apple Corps' litigation against the record company.

"You've got a problem, you better sue us," Paul told Harrison, Ono, and Starr, who began preparing, but never filed, the legal complaint against McCartney.

Instead, Apple Corps regained its financial footing after settling the dispute with Capitol-EMI in 1989 in exchange for an $80 million payment. Since then Apple Corps' business has flourished through its repackaging of all things Beatles, from sound recordings in physical and digital configurations to Beatles films, *The Beatles Anthology* book, video and audio series, and, since 2006, the Cirque du Soleil Beatles production *Love* in Las Vegas.

But some grudges die hard. In December 2009, six months after Allen Klein died — and decades after Paul McCartney had sued the other Beatles to rid Apple Corps of him — McCartney was again preparing to go to court over Klein's business interests. The complaint by McCartney's MPL Music Publishing claimed Klein's ABKCO had mishandled money owed MPL. MPL alleged ABKCO owed MPL $100,000 in back royalties from the exploitation of records by the Rays, a now-obscure doo-wop group that scored a number three *Billboard* hit with "Silhouettes" in 1957. ABKCO had acquired ownership of the Rays' master recordings through its purchase of the Cameo-Parkway record company in 1967.

MPL, which bought the royalty rights of the company that produced the Rays, alleged breach of contract against ABKCO. ABKCO countered that it "without fail paid every royalty owed" to MPL and that, in suing Klein's company, McCartney's MPL "evinces a high degree of moral turpitude and wanton dishonesty."

Allen Klein's nephew, ABKCO lawyer Michael Kramer, complained he hadn't been able to reach MPL's lawyer to discuss the suit. "I have made at least five (5) phone calls in an effort to have you confirm that the facts were as I had expressed to you." But, Kramer claimed, "Not one of those phone calls were [*sic*] answered or returned."

In February 2014, the New York Appellate Division dismissed MPL's complaint. The court found that the only specified payment responsibility ABKCO acquired under the Cameo-Parkway agreement was to account to MPL for sales of Rays 78 rpm and 45 rpm singles sales, markets that are practically nonexistent today.

But MPL did establish one major point: More than four decades after the Beatles broke up, Allen Klein was still a financial thorn in Paul McCartney's side.

ACKNOWLEDGMENTS

Many thanks to Steve Hull, my editor at University Press of New England, for his receptiveness to the proposal for this book and insightful suggestions for making the book manuscript stronger.

Susan Barone for being there with an open ear while I deliberated over how to transform a massive amount of Beatles litigation materials into a cohesive tome.

The staffs at archives I traveled to: the British Library Newspaper Archives, British National Archives, California Court of Appeal, Los Angeles Superior Court, New York Appellate Division, New York County Lawyers' Association Library, Palm Beach County Civil Court, US District Court for the Southern District of New York, and the US National Archives in Philadelphia.

Special thanks for the extensive assistance provided me by the staffs while I researched on-site at the New York Supreme Court in New York City and at the US National Archives in Kansas City.

For their hospitality while I was in Kansas City, my niece, Jenny, her husband, James, and children, Rebecca and Nathan.

Music faculty colleagues at University of Colorado Denver: Chris Daniels, Leslie Gaston-Bird, and Sam McGuire.

George Krieger for his perspectives on Beatles history and G. Brown for taking over the Music Business Senior Seminar at CU Denver while I was on my book-research sabbatical.

Very special thanks to Austin entertainment attorney Mike Tolleson for his invaluable help with this project.

Additional thanks to Alexis Grower, Ted Nussbaum, Richard Palik, and Steve Ruggier.

Finally, thanks to those individuals who were interviewed on or off the record for this book.

APPENDIX OF BEATLES-RELATED COURT DOCUMENTS

This appendix offers a sampling of some historic Beatles-related legal documents. Original documents included in the appendix are: the summons served on George Harrison in February 1971 via his manager Allen Klein's ABKCO office in New York, when Harrison was sued for copyright infringement over his song "My Sweet Lord"; the court summons signed by John Lennon's immigration lawyer Leon Wildes in October 1973, when Wildes was filing Lennon's Freedom of Information Act suit against the US government during Lennon's battle to gain permanent residency in the United States; the handwritten verdict note from the jury to the trial judge in the US government's tax evasion case against Allen Klein; and the original letter from singer Sam Cooke's father asking the tax-evasion case judge for leniency in sentencing Klein.

Also in the appendix are copies of the Department of Justice grant that allowed John Lennon permission to temporarily enter the United States in August 1971, and the London magistrate court's 1968 drug conviction order against Lennon that the Nixon administration used as an excuse to try to bar the politically outspoken Lennon from staying in the United States.

U.S. MARSHALS SERVICE INSTRUCTION AND PROCESS RECORD	INSTRUCTIONS: See "INSTRUCTIONS FOR SERVICE OF PROCESS BY THE U.S. MARSHAL" on the reverse of the last (No. 5) copy of this form. Please type or print legibly, insuring readability of all copies. Do not detach any copies.

PLAINTIFF BRIGHT TUNES MUSIC CORP.	COURT NUMBER 71 C1V 602
DEFENDANT GEORGE HARRISON,	TYPE OF WRIT Summons

SERVE | NAME OF INDIVIDUAL, COMPANY, CORPORATION, ETC., TO SERVE OR DESCRIPTION OF PROPERTY TO SEIZE OR CONDEMN

George Harrison,

ADDRESS (Street or RFD, Apartment No., City, State and ZIP Code)

1700 Broadway, New York, N.Y.

AT

SEND NOTICE OF SERVICE COPY TO NAME AND ADDRESS BELOW:

Arthur Goodstein, Esq.
2 Pennsylvania Plaza
New York, N.Y. 10001

Show number of this writ and total number of writs submitted, i.e., 1 of 1, 1 of 3, etc. **NO. 2 TOTAL OF 7**

CHECK IF APPLICABLE:
☐ One copy for U. S. Attorney or designee and two copies for Attorney General of the U. S. included.

SHOW IN THE SPACE BELOW AND TO THE LEFT ANY SPECIAL INSTRUCTIONS OR OTHER INFORMATION PERTINENT TO SERVING THE WRIT DESCRIBED ABOVE.

SPECIAL INSTRUCTIONS:

The Office of Allen Klein and Afco Industries, Inc. maintains offices at 1700 Broadway, New York. All of the defendants are affiliated with the Beatles Company at that address, and may be served there.

NAME AND SIGNATURE OF ATTORNEY OR OTHER ORIGINATOR ARTHUR GOODSTEIN	TELEPHONE NUMBER 279-2424	DATE Feb. 1971

SPACE BELOW FOR USE OF U.S. MARSHAL ONLY – DO NOT WRITE BELOW THIS LINE

Show amount of deposit (or applicable code) and sign USM-285 for first writ only if more than one writ submitted.	DEPOSIT/CODE	DIST. OF ORIGIN 54	DISTRICT TO SERVE 57	LOCATION OF SUB-OFFICE OF DIST. TO SERVE
I acknowledge receipt for the total number of writs indicated and for the deposit (if applicable) shown.	SIGNATURE OF AUTHORIZED USMS DEPUTY OR CLERK		DATE 2/10/7/	

☒ I hereby certify and return that I have personally served, have legal evidence of service, or have executed as shown in "REMARKS," the writ described on the individual, company, corporation, etc., at the address shown above or on the individual, company, corporation, etc., at the address inserted below.

☐ I hereby certify and return that, after diligent investigation, I am unable to locate the individual, company, corporation, etc., named above within this Judicial District.

NAME AND TITLE OF INDIVIDUAL SERVED (If not shown above)
Paul Mozian adm. asst.

☐ A person of suitable age and discretion then abiding in the defendant's usual place of abode.

ADDRESS (Complete only if different than shown above)

| FEE (If applicable) $ 3 — | MILEAGE $ — |

DATE(S) OF ENDEAVOR (Use Remarks if necessary)	DATE OF SERVICE 2-23-7/	TIME 3:15 ☐AM ☒PM	SIGNATURE OF U. S. MARSHAL OR DEPUTY P. Sabatelli

REMARKS

U.S. MARSHALS SERVICE
INSTRUCTION AND PROCESS RECORD

INSTRUCTIONS: See "INSTRUCTIONS FOR SERVICE OF PROCESS BY THE U.S. MARSHAL" on the reverse of the last (No. 5) copy of this form. Please type or print legibly, insuring readability of all copies. Do not detach any copies.

PLAINTIFF JOHN WINSTON ONO LENNON
DEFENDANT ELLIOT RICHARDSON, et.al.

COURT NUMBER 73 Civ 4476
TYPE OF WRIT Summons+Complaint

SERVE NAME OF INDIVIDUAL, COMPANY, CORPORATION, ETC., TO SERVE OR DESCRIPTION OF PROPERTY TO SEIZE OR CONDEMN
ELLIOT RICHARDSON, Secty of State Attorney General.

AT ADDRESS (Street or RFD, Apartment No., City, State and ZIP Code)
Constitution Avenue bet. 9th + 10th St, N.W. Wash. D.C.

SEND NOTICE OF SERVICE COPY TO NAME AND ADDRESS BELOW:
Leon Wildes
515 Madison Avenue
N.Y., N.Y 10022

NO. 1 OF 5 TOTAL

One copy for U.S. Attorney or designee and two copies for Attorney General of the U.S. included. [X]

NAME AND SIGNATURE OF ATTORNEY OR OTHER ORIGINATOR
Leon Wildes

TELEPHONE NUMBER PL 3-3468 DATE 10/18/73

SPACE BELOW FOR USE OF U.S. MARSHAL ONLY - DO NOT WRITE BELOW THIS LINE

DEPOSIT/CODE
DIST. OF ORIGIN 254
DISTRICT TO SERVE 8

NAME AND TITLE OF INDIVIDUAL SERVED (If not shown above)
Mr. Elliot Richardson BY MAIL
FEE $3.00 MILEAGE $.36

DATE(S) OF ENDEAVOR DATE OF SERVICE 10/25/73 TIME 11:15 AM SIGNATURE Edward Brown

REMARKS
10/25/73 SERVED MR BRANNEN chief CLERK US ATTORNEY office RM 315 Foley SQ N.Y.C. AND BY MAILING A COPY TO ATTORNEY GEN. WASH. D.C. RECEIPT NO. 490300
Edward Brown

USM-285 (Ed. 7-1-70) **1. CLERK OF THE COURT** 490 300.

We have a
verdict.

EXHIBIT
U. S. DIST. COURT
S. D. OF N. Y.

25
4/26/79

1504 East 86th Street
Chicago, Illinois
May 31, 1979

Hon. Vincent L. Broderick
United States District Court
Southern District of New York
Foley Square
New York, N. Y. 10007

Dear Judge Broderick:

    I am writing this letter with regard to Allen Klein and
his current plight.

    I am the father of Sam Cooke, the singer, who died many years
ago. At the time of his death my son was paying me a monthly allowance.
Allen Klein was my son's manager. The two of them were good friends,
and I know that Mr. Klein was always forthright in dealing with my son.
After my son's death, Mr. Klein arranged that the monthly allowance
continue, and that arrangement and obligation has been paid promptly
and continuously from 1965 to date.

    Needless to say, these payments have been greatly appreciated
and should in some small way indicate the measure of the man. I would
hope, Sir, that you will show compassion.

                              Very truly yours,

                              Rev Charles Cooke

                              Reverend Charles Cooke

UNITED STATES DEPARTMENT OF JUSTICE
Immigration and Naturalization Service

FILE: A17 597 321   DATE: August 11, 1971

IN RE: John Winston Lennon

APPLICATION: Temporary admission to the United States pursuant to
section 212(d) (3) (A), Immigration and Nationality Act

[X] consular officer

The applicant(s) has (have) been found by a   to be ineligible to receive a nonimmigrant
[ ] immigration officer

visa under Section(s) 212(a)_____23_____ of the Act.

Nationality:	Date and Country of Birth:	Country of Residence:
Great Britain	9-10-40 - England	England

Occupation:	Employer:
Musician	Self-employed

Purpose in seeking entry into United States and destination:

To edit film and consult with business associates at ABKCO Industries, 17 Broadway,
New York City and Capital Records in New York City in connection with record release
in September 1971 and to attend custody hearing in St. Thomas, Virgin Islands on
September 16, 1971.

Plans regarding travel to United States and period of temporary stay:

One entry during August or September for six weeks.

Basis for favorable action:

To promote American Business Interests and for Humanitarian reasons.

ORDER: It is ordered that the application be granted for the above indicated purpose, subject to revocation
at any time, valid as set forth below.

ENTRY: One during August or September 1971

PERIOD OF TEMPORARY STAY: Six weeks on condition that the activities and
itinerary of the applicant shall be limited to those set forth above
and that no extension of stay or change in activities or deviation of
itinerary shall be authorized without prior approval of the District
Director, Washington, D. C.

Section 212(a) (28) cases only.   Assistant Commissioner, Adjudications
Basis of excludability

TO: MJM:hcm   Telephoned to Mrs. Gilchrist, Visa Office 2:30 PM, 8/11/71
Form I-194
(Rev. 1-15-71) Y

File Copy

-201-

IN THE INNER LONDON AREA AND IN THE METROPOLITAN POLICE DISTRICT

MEMORANDUM of a CONVICTION ORDER entered in the REGISTER of the

MARYLEBONE MAGISTRATES' COURT.

The 28th day of NOVEMBER 1968

Name of informant or of complainant	Name of defendant Age if known	Nature of offence or matter of complaint	Date of offence or matter of complaint	Plea or consent to order	Minute of Adjudication	Time allowed for payment and instalments
D.S. PILCHER C.O.C.I.	John Winston LENNON Age 28 Musician	(1) Having in his possession a dangerous drug to wit Cannabis Resin without being duly authorised, at 34 Montague Square W.1. on 18-10-68. Con to Regs. 3 Dangerous Drugs (No.2) Regs; Dangerous Drugs Act 1965. (2) Wilfully obstructing Norman Pilcher a constable of the metropolitan police force then exercising his powers under the Dangerous Drugs Act 1965 at 34, Montague Square, W.1. Con to Sec. 14(3) Dangerous Drugs Act 1965.	18/10/68	Est. Guilty E.ot. N.A. guilty	1 £150, 20gns costs. 2 No evidence offered dismissed (Signed) John PHIPPS Magistrate Adjudicating	7 days

M.C.A. 118—1.59

Extract from Register Proving Proceeding

I certify the above extract to be a true copy.

The 13th day of JANUARY 106 9 . 106 9

....
Clerk of the said Magistrates' Court.

NOTES

INTRODUCTION

ix   But during a recess: Author's courthouse discussion with Allen Klein, June 1998.

xi   "scared" and "I was going to have": Craig Vetter, "Playboy Interview: Allen Klein," Playboy, November 1971.

xi   "People were very scared": Richard Williams, "John & Yoko," *Melody Maker*, December 6, 1969.

xi   "influx of accountants, solicitors": Johnny Rogan, *Starmakers and Svengalis* (London: Futura Publications, 1989), 255.

xiii   "Would you do anything": Vetter, "Playboy Interview: Allen Klein."

1. DRIPPING WITH ENTHUSIASM

3   "looked around the room": Geoff Emerick, *Here, There and Everywhere: My Life Recording the Music of the Beatles* (New York: Gotham Books, 2006), 203.

3   "Well, Brian": Ibid., 204.

3   "a fait accompli": Ibid.

3   "an inspired song": Jade Wright, "Rock of Ages," *Liverpool Daily Echo*, July 21, 2012.

4   "stammered and stuttered": Tony Bramwell, *Magical Mystery Tours: My Life with the Beatles* (New York: St. Martin's Press, 2005), 211.

4   "was our first 'manager'": Hunter Davies, ed., *The John Lennon Letters* (New York: Little, Brown and Company, 2012), 299.

4   "a little Welshman": The Beatles, *The Beatles Anthology* (San Francisco: Chronicle Books, 2000), 41.

5   "Brian was artistic, temperamental": Ray Coleman, *The Man Who Made the Beatles: An Intimate Biography of Brian Epstein* (New York: McGraw-Hill Publishing Co., 1989), 30.

5   "I venomously hated": Deborah Geller, *The Brian Epstein Story* (London: Faber and Faber, 1999), 8.

5   Brian showed up at Joe's house: Ibid., 26.

5   "When I left RADA": Ibid., 23.

6   "Bert K et al thought": Davies, *John Lennon Letters*, 299.

6   "he'd seen this poster": Deborah Geller, "When Brian Met the Beatles," *Independent* (London), November 16, 1999.

6   "It took about half-an-hour": Ibid.

6   "a Liverpool group": Brian Epstein, interviewed by Larry Kane, summer 1964, accessed June 8, 2014, https://www.youtube.com/.

7   "I told John Lennon": "Allan, You're a Rich Man: Paddy Shennan Meets the Man Who Gave the Beatles Away—But Can Laugh About It," *Liverpool Daily Echo*, February 24, 2010.

7   "At that time, there were 300 groups": Norman Silvester, "These Beatles Kids? Don't Touch Them with a Bargepole," *Sunday Mail*, October 23, 2011.

7   "It made me look": Hunter Davies, *The Beatles* (New York: W.W. Norton & Co., 2009), 126.

7   "I had given my word": Ibid., 126-27.

7   "such was their utter faith": Bramwell, *Magical Mystery Tours*, 88.

7   "authority to negotiate": Affidavit of Brian Epstein, May 5, 1964, in *Remco Industries Inc. v. Goldberger Doll Mfg. Co. Inc.*, 64 C 430 (E.D.N.Y.).

8   "I'm very careful": Brian Epstein, interviewed on *UK Tonight*, 1964, accessed June 11, 2014, https://www.youtube.com/.

8   "always had disrespect": Emerick, *Here, There and Everywhere*, 74-75.

8   "I did everything that I could": Epstein, interviewed by Kane, summer 1964.

8   "He would kill for them": Ken Sharp, "Andrew Loog Oldham," *Goldmine*, June 2014.

9   "It was love at first sight": George Martin with Jeremy Hornsby, *All You Need Is Ears: The Inside Story of the Genius Who Created the Beatles* (New York: St. Martin's Press, 1979), 122.

9   "threaten[ing] to withdraw": Coleman, *Man Who Made the Beatles*, 108.

9   "EMI was as mean": Martin, *All You Need Is Ears*, 55.

9   "very critical": Ibid.

10   "The Beatles were prisoners": David Griffiths, "The Beatles: Backstage at the London Palladium," *Record Mirror*, December 21, 1963.

10   "From the beginning": Philip Norman, *Shout!—The Beatles in Their Generation* (New York: MJF Books, 1981), 203.

10   "did everything he could to find out": Geoffrey Ellis, *I Should Have Known Better: A Life in Pop Management—The Beatles, Brian Epstein and Elton John* (London: Thorogood, 2005), 16.

10   "trouble was": Bramwell, *Magical Mystery Tours*, 85-86.

10   "Walter came into my office": Author interview with Tom Levy, April 5, 2013.

11 "The money has got to be paid": "U.S. and British Taxers Vie to Shear Beatles," *New York Times*, January 3, 1965.

11 "no American visits": "Beatles to Shun U.S. Because of Tax Rift," *New York Times*, January 3, 1965.

11 "I'm not a commercial person": Brian Epstein interview on BBC TV program *Panorama*, March 30, 1964.

12 "Just make sure": Barry Miles, *Paul McCartney: Many Years from Now* (New York: Henry Holt and Company, 1997), 157.

12 "was Brian's most embarrassing failure": Andrew Loog Oldham, *Stone Free*, (Vancouver: Because Entertainment, 2012), 109.

12 three tons of court papers: Norman, *Shout!*, 253.

2. "start a scream team!"

13 "would be cheeky to predict": Clarence Newman, "The Beatles Craze Threatens Big Dent in Parents' Wallets," *Wall Street Journal*, February 12, 1964.

13 anagram for "Smart Acts": Ellis, *I Should Have Known Better*, 101.

14 It took Reliance only three days: Norman, *Shout!*, 217.

14 "We had almost a tongue-in-cheek attitude": Martin Arnold, "Beatleggers Trying to Capture a Share of Success, Moneywise," *New York Times*, February 17, 1964.

14 "widely recognized": *Remco Industries Inc.*, 64 C 430.

14 "dolls and parts of dolls": This and subsequent Saul Robbins quotes from Affidavit of Saul Robbins, April 24, 1964, in ibid.

17 "great and irreparable injury": *Remco Industries Inc. v. Goldberger Doll Mfg. Co. Inc.*, 141 U.S.P.Q. (BNA) 898 (E.D.N.Y. 1964).

17 "Settlement papers": Affidavit of David Kirschstein, July 3, 1964, in *Remco Industries Inc.*, 64 C 430.

17 In the settlement deal: Judgment and Decree, September 24, 1964, in ibid.

3. "outrageous irrelevancies and distortions"

18 "[W]e were besieged": Bramwell, *Magical Mystery Tours*, 140.

18 "generally on all matters": Letter of Brian Epstein to M. A. Jacobs & Sons, October 14, 1963.

18 "Overwhelmed by licensing requests": Oldham, *Stone Free*, 109.

19 "designed specially for Beatles people": Beatles program book quoted in Davies, *The Beatles*, 184.

19 "used to pop in": Bramwell, *Magical Mystery Tours*, 140.

19   "David came up with Nicky Byrne": Ibid.

19   "Write in what percentage": Norman, *Shout!*, 209.

19   "So I put down the first figure": Ibid.

20   "was concerned that poor-quality items": Bramwell, *Magical Mystery Tours*, 140.

20    $9,700 and "Nicky Byrne's personal income": Peter Brown and Steven Gaines, *The Love You Make: An Insider's Story of the Beatles* (New York: McGraw-Hill, 1983), 129.

20   "couldn't think of it without": Ibid.

20   "Royalty statements from Seltaeb": Affidavit of Brian Epstein, October 25, 1965, in *NEMS Enterprises Ltd. v. Seltaeb Inc.*, 18398/64 (N.Y. Sup. Ct., N.Y. County).

21   "the House the Beatles built": Ellis, *I Should Have Known Better*, 23.

21   "Walter had a considerable practice": Author interview with Tom Levy, April 5, 2013.

21   "willfully and deliberately": Complaint in *NEMS Enterprises Ltd.*, 18398/64.

21   "so replete with blatant lies": Affidavit of Louis Smigel, December 19, 1964, in ibid.

21   "to grab everything for itself": Affidavit of Nicky Byrne, June 3, 1966, in ibid.

21   Seltaeb contended NEMS was withholding: Defendants' Verified Answer, stamped January 21, 1965, in ibid.

21   others allegedly conflicted with merchandise licenses: merchandise list from Seltaeb Bill of Particulars, August 23, 1966.

22   "to franchise both a candy bar": Letter from Kingsley Chemical Laboratories to Brian Epstein, October 14, 1964.

22   "Large retailers and manufacturers": Affidavit of Nicky Byrne, June 3, 1966, in *NEMS Enterprises Ltd.*, 18398/64.

22   "that manufacturers who had been considering": Ellis, *I Should Have Known Better*, 103.

22   Both J. C. Penney and Woolworth: Brown and Gaines, *The Love You Make*, 162, and Norman, *Shout!*, 227.

22   "intense animosity": Affidavit of Brian Epstein, October 25, 1965, in *NEMS Enterprises Ltd.*, 18398/64.

22   Byrne went so far as to buy: Albert Goldman, *The Lives of John Lennon* (Chicago: A Cappella Books, 2001), 157.

22   "A great many heated and intemperate statements": Affidavit of Brian Epstein, October 25, 1965, in *NEMS Enterprises Ltd.*, 18398/64.

22   "This made Brian Epstein furious": Ellis, *I Should Have Known Better*, 102.

22 "promptly usurped all corporate profits": Nicky Byrne's business associates quoted in Affidavit of Brian Epstein, October 25, 1965, in *NEMS Enterprises Ltd.*, 18398/64.

22 "running up huge bills": Complaint in *Eliot v. Byrne*, 12941/64 (N.Y. Sup. Ct., N.Y. County), and Affidavit of Malcolm G. Evans, August 10, 1964, in *Eliot*.

23 "horrendous": Affidavit of Brian Epstein, October 25, 1965, in *NEMS Enterprises Ltd.*, 18398/64.

23 "mucking about": Steve Bird, "Heir found dead in bath," *Times* (London), April 18, 2006.

23 Seltaeb's May 1964 balance sheet: Prepared by Joseph S. Herbert & Co., CPAs, May 31, 1964.

23 "petty cash vouchers": Affidavit of Malcolm G. Evans, August 10, 1964, in *Eliot*, 12941/64.

23 "the continued existence" and "in jeopardy": Complaint in ibid.

24 "Epstein has been, and continues to come": Answering Affidavit of Douglas Anthony Nicholas Byrne, January 14, 1965, in *NEMS Enterprises Ltd.*, 18398/64.

24 "probably not as qualified": Affidavit of Brian Epstein October 25, 1965, in *NEMS Enterprises Ltd.*, 18398/64.

24 "I am familiar with all the facts": Affidavit of Brian Epstein, May 5, 1964, in *Remco Industries Inc.*, 64 C 430.

24 "cannot be tolerated": Order of Justice George Carney, *New York Law Journal*, May 11, 1965.

24 The appellate court instead let Epstein's company refile: *NEMS Enterprises Ltd. v. Seltaeb Inc.*, 24 A.D.2d 739 (N.Y. App. Div. 1st Dept. 1965).

25 "six months later we discovered": Affidavit of Walter Hofer, April 6, 1966, in *NEMS Enterprises Ltd.*, 18398/64.

25 "For all his business and negotiating skills": Ellis, *I Should Have Known Better*, 103.

25 "It's *terrible*": Coleman, *Man Who Made the Beatles*, 314.

26 "suffering from Infective Hepatitis": Affidavit of Dr. Norman Michael Cowan, December 7, 1965, in *NEMS Enterprises Ltd.*, 18398/64.

26 "had left his home": Seltaeb allegation in Report of Referee Jesse Friedman, June 3, 1966, in *NEMS Enterprises Ltd.*, 18398/64.

26 "he had to admit that he knew virtually nothing": Ellis, *I Should Have Known Better*, 106.

26 "There is no honest distinction": Affidavit of Nicky Byrne, June 3, 1966, in *NEMS Enterprises Ltd.*, 18398/64.

27   "no doubt at all": Geller, *The Brian Epstein Story*, 141.

27   "We got screwed for millions" and "It was all Brian's fault": Davies, *The Beatles*, 371.

4. THE REIGN ENDS

28   "biggest fear": Peter Asher, "Brian Epstein Inducted into the Rock and Roll Hall of Fame," *brianepstein.com*, April 10, 2014, accessed July 1, 2014, http://www.brianepstein.com/induction.html.

28   "To begin with, we needed": Richard Williams, "The Times Profile: Paul McCartney," *Times* (London), January 4, 1982.

29   "gnawed at his conscience": Bramwell, *Magical Mystery Tours*, 181.

29   "it was inevitable": Martin, *All You Need Is Ears*, 178.

29   "Brian, by his own design": Coleman, *Man Who Made the Beatles*, 379.

30   "George Harrison wanted me to stop by": Wayne Robins, "In Which This Jack-of-All-Jams Remembers the Stones, Beatles, Little Richard," *Creem*, May 1974.

30   "On the bedside table": Collin Willis, "At Last . . . The Truth about How the Man Who Made the Beatles Died," *Sunday Mirror*, December 27, 1998.

30   "John got particularly frightened": Jon Savage, "Jon Savage Describes How Brian Epstein Fell Victim to Drugs and the Pressures of Being a Secret Homosexual," *Guardian* (London), December 18, 1998.

5. "CHARISMATIC, ARROGANT—AMERICAN"

33   "Since Brian died": "The Beatles: You Never Give Me Your Money," *Rolling Stone*, November 15, 1969, 30.

33   "Brian's death opened the floodgates": Savage, "How Brian Epstein Fell Victim."

33   "[W]e *were* in a mess": Alan Smith, "Beatles Are on the Brink of Splitting: One Group Is Just Not Big Enough for All This Talent," *New Musical Express*, December 13, 1969.

33   "abandoned by his father": Cynthia Lennon, *John* (New York: Three Rivers Press, 2005), 212.

34   "moody and sensitive" and "insecure and ineffectual": Letter of Jerry Weisfogel, MD, to Lee Stoeker, US probation officer, June 12, 1979, in *U.S. v. Klein*, 77 Crim. 234 (S.D.N.Y.).

34   "I went on vacation to celebrate": Allen Klein personal and business autobiographical quotes from trial testimony of Allen Klein in *U.S. v. Klein*, 77 Crim. 234 (S.D.N.Y.), unless otherwise indicated.

36   "This was completely unheard of": "Ex-Beatles Manager Dies," *Geelong*

Advertiser (Australia), July 6, 2009. Not necessarily so. In 1961, ABC-Paramount Records had given Ray Charles an even better deal: a 5 percent artist royalty rate, *plus* 75 percent of the profits for Charles to produce his own records, and a right for Charles to own the sound recording masters.

36   "Allen would get you back": Oldham *Stone Free*, 298.

37   "any dishonest or improper conduct": Affidavit of Allen Klein, February 12, 1971, in *McCartney v. Lennon*, 1970 M. No. 6315, High Court of Justice, Chancery Division.

37   "Our habits then were": Dave Schulps, "Andrew Loog Oldham, the Rolling Stones," *Trouser Press*, June 1978.

37   "In walks this little fat American geezer": "Allen Klein: Beatles and Rolling Stones Manager Whose Lack of Financial Probity Led to Him Being Sued by Both Groups and Spending Time in Prison," *Times* (London), July 6, 2009.

38   "got heavily into drugs": A. E. Hotchner, *Blown Away: A No-Holds Barred Portrait of the Rolling Stones and the Sixties Told by the Voices of the Generation* (New York: Fireside, 1991) 170.

38   "a vehicle for diversion": Ibid., 196.

38   Oldham reportedly did this: Ray Connolly, "Monster of Rock: Allen Klein Swindled the Stones and Broke Up the Beatles and Is Still Rock 'n' Roll's Most Ruthless Svengali," *DailyMail.com*, July 5, 2009, accessed July 15, 2014, http://www.dailymail.co.uk/tvshowbiz/article-1197709/.

38   "Mick really hated him": Hotchner, *Blown Away*, 199.

38   "What did he want": "Brash Record Executive Managed the Beatles," *Washington Post*, July 8, 2009.

39   Hermusic sued Most, Klein: *Hermusic Ltd. v. Reverse Producers Corp.*, 65 Civ. 2714 (S.D.N.Y.).

40   pretrial judgment in favor of Peter Noone: *Hermusic Ltd. v. Reverse Producers Corp.*, 254 F. Supp. 502 (S.D.N.Y. 1966).

40   "every dilatory device": Affidavit of Robert C. Osterberg, August 5, 1966, in Support of Application for Contempt Order in *Hermusic Ltd.*, 65 Civ. 2714.

40   "completely stopped": Affidavit of Special Master Lewis Shapiro in ibid.

40   The parties settled: Order of Discontinuance, March 17, 1972, in ibid.

40   "The minute the audit report": This and subsequent Barry Slotnick quotes, author interview with Barry Slotnick, March 20, 2014.

40   "drastically diminished": Complaint in *ABKCO Music & Records Inc. v. Chimeron LLC*, 10 Civ. 3064 (S.D.N.Y.).

40   "You're unrecouped!": Allen Klein quoted in author interview with Barry Slotnick, March 20, 2014.

41   "scumbag" and subsequent Peter Noone quotes: Rich Calder and Bruce

Golding, "Herman's Hermits Singer Admits He Called Music Mogul a 'Scumbag,'" *New York Post*, January 26, 2012.

41   in February 2013 the Second Circuit affirmed: *ABKCO Music & Records Inc. v. Chimeron LLC*, 517 Fed. Appx. 3 (2d Cir. 2013).

6. "don't you want it now?"

42   "sipped beer, flicked ashes": "Enterprise: Beatles, Inc.," *Newsweek*, May 27, 1968, 68.

42   "The aim of this company": Ibid.

42   "I wrote it down": Davies, *The Beatles*, 286.

42   "I don't go around reading": Trial testimony of John Lennon in *Big Seven Music Corp. v. Lennon*, 75 Civ. 1116 (S.D.N.Y.).

42   "umbrella where people": Davies, *The Beatles*, 308.

43   "The largesse of the Beatles": Brown and Gaines, *The Love You Make*, 328.

43   "These get-togethers": Pete Shotton and Nicholas Schaffner, *John Lennon in My Life* (New York: Stein and Day 1983), 158.

43   "Apple was a complete fiasco": Martin, *All You Need Is Ears*, 171.

43   "Brian's death left us": Coleman, *Man Who Made the Beatles*, 383.

43   "hardheaded, sophisticated": Charles Tillinghast, *How Capitol Got the Beatles* (Denver: Outskirts Press, 2008), 46.

43   "very patriarchal": Miles, *Paul McCartney*, 507.

43   "I think [Lee] wanted": Ibid.

44   "Obviously everyone worried": Chris Salewicz, "Paul McCartney: An Innocent Man?" *Q*, October 1986.

44   "seemed to be interested": Brian Southall with Rupert Perry. *Northern Songs: The True Story of the Beatles Song Publishing Empire* (London: Omnibus Press, 2007), 64.

44   "John and Paul meeting": Bramwell, *Magical Mystery Tours*, 179.

44   "at some length": Coleman, *Man Who Made the Beatles*, 265.

44   "Klein said that he heard": John McMillian, "Baby You're a Rich Man, Too," *Newsweek*, December 19, 2013, accessed June 21, 2014, http://www.newsweek .com/baby-youre-rich-man-too-244952.

44   "It was like I was clairvoyant": Vetter, "Playboy Interview: Allen Klein."

45   "I think he's a sentimental": Peter McCabe and Robert D. Schonfeld, *Apple to the Core: The Unmaking of the Beatles* (New York: Pocket Books, 1972), 132.

45   "Look, the Eastmans": John Lennon quoted in Allen Klein Deposition excerpt in case file of *ABKCO Industries Inc. v. Lennon*, 2598/74 (N.Y. Sup. Ct., N.Y. County).

45   "I was really trying to remain": Allen Klein Deposition excerpt in case file of
      ABKCO Industries Inc., ibid.

45   "It was plain to me": Affidavit of John Lennon in Support of Motion to
      Dismiss, May 27, 1974, in *ABKCO Industries Inc.*, ibid.

45   "Apple was/is": Davies, *John Lennon Letters*, 237.

45   "Klein was the primary beneficiary": Author interview with Nat Weiss,
      November 27, 1989.

45   "the Beatles should not meet": Pattie Boyd, *Wonderful Tonight: George
      Harrison, Eric Clapton, and Me* (New York: Three Rivers Press, 2007), 134.

46   "[T]here was no alternative": The Beatles, *The Beatles Anthology*, 324.

46   "Neither ABKCO nor Klein": Affidavit of John Eastman in Support of Motion
      to Dismiss or Stay, January 30, 1974, in *ABKCO Industries Inc. v. Lennon*,
      19258/73 (N.Y. Sup. Ct., N.Y. County).

46   "We were kind of all in it": Mat Snow, "The Beatles: 'We're a Damn Good
      Little Band,'" *MOJO*, October 1996.

46   "the most powerful man": "Allen Klein," *Times* (London), July 6, 2009.

46   "Allen tends to be masochistic": Letter of Jerry Weisfogel, MD, June 12, 1979.

47   "sharp, but young": Bramwell, *Magical Mystery Tours*, 312.

47   "launched an attack": Affidavit of Allen Klein, February 12, 1971, in *McCartney
      v. Lennon*.

48   "the reason which sparked": Affidavit of Allen Klein, February 12, 1971, in ibid.

48   "fallen under the influence": "Judge Refuses 'Freeze' on Beatles' £1m," *Times*
      (London), April 2, 1969.

48   "There might be a grave danger": Jeremiah Harmon quoted in ibid.

49   McCartney told Klein: Affidavit of Allen Klein, February 12, 1971, in
      McCartney v. Lennon.

49   Peter Howard determined: Details of *Magical Mystery Tour* monies from
      Letter of Rosenman Colin lawyer Larry Eno to Michael Kramer at ABKCO,
      July 7, 1971.

50   "It was a unique set-up": Southall, *Northern Songs*, 21.

50   "I learned that people": Trial testimony of George Harrison in *Bright Tunes
      Music Corp. v. Harrisongs Music Ltd.*, 71 Civ. 602 (S.D.N.Y.).

50   "The stock exchange seems": quoted in "I Wanna Hold Your Stock,"
      Newsweek, March 1, 1965, 70.

50   "Demand for the stock": Ibid.

50   "We honestly have no idea": Ibid.

51   "It emerged that the amounts": Affidavit of Allen Klein, February 12, 1971, in
      McCartney v. Lennon.

51　"James had made his fortune": McCabe and Schonfeld, *Apple to the Core*, 142.

51　"was a very sore point": Allen Klein Deposition excerpt in case file in *ABKCO Industries Inc. v. Lennon*, 2598/74.

52　Lennon "and I both considered": Ibid.

52　"insisted that Paul": John Eastman quoted in ibid.

52　"Look, the more and more": Ringo Starr quoted in ibid.

52　"Lennon and McCartney's biggest resentment": Southall, *Northern Songs*, 95.

53　getting the Beatles almost $10 million: "Allen Klein: 'I Cured All Their Problems," *Rolling Stone*, November 29, 1969, 6.

53　"In March 1969": The Beatles, *The Beatles Anthology*, 328.

53　"It would have been cheaper": Anne L. Trebbe, "Personalities," *Washington Post*, January 15, 1982.

53　"called Lee Eastman": Southall, *Northern Songs*, 129.

53　"I'm not interested in buying": Williams, "The Times Profile: Paul McCartney."

7. "EACH AND EVERY WORD"

54　"the biggest bulltwaddler": McCabe and Schonfeld, *Apple to the Core*, 49.

54　"all the petty shit": Davies, *John Lennon Letters*, 209.

54　"Apple, Beatles, Eastman and Klein": Apple press release quoted in Richard DiLello, *The Longest Cocktail Party: An Insider's Diary of the Beatles, Their Million-Dollar Empire and Its Wild Rise & Fall* (Edinburgh: Canongate, 2005), 219.

54　"the Rolling Stones complained": Affidavit of Richard Starkey in Support of Motion to Dismiss or Stay, January 24, 1974, in *ABKCO Industries Inc. v. Lennon*, 19258/73.

54　"Fuck McCartney": McCabe and Schonfeld, *Apple to the Core*, 196.

55　"like Mussolini": Ibid., 133.

55　"The Hells Angels' arrival": Chris O'Dell with Katherine Ketcham, *Miss O'Dell: My Hard Days and Long Nights with the Beatles, the Stones, Bob Dylan, Eric Clapton and the Women They Loved* (New York: Touchstone, 2009), 65.

55　"The short, round business manager": Emerick, *Here, There and Everywhere*, 308.

55　"practically *married* to": DiLello, *Longest Cocktail Party*, 207.

55　"Neil had a better idea": David Fricke, "Neil Aspinall, Beatles' Closest Adviser, Headed Apple Corps," *Rolling Stone*, April 17, 2008, 14.

55　"wanted to cancel": Southall, *Northern Songs*, 64.

56 "had been writing to Capitol": Affidavit of Allen Klein, February 12, 1971, in *McCartney v. Lennon.*

56 "seemed interminable" and subsequent Charles Tillinghast quote: Tillinghast, *How Capitol Got the Beatles*, 51.

57 "noticed that the Beatles": Williams, "John & Yoko."

57 "Capitol had the right": Trial testimony of Allen Klein in *U.S. v. Klein*, 77 Crim. 234.

57 "prior to the contract expiring": Trial testimony of George Harrison in *ABKCO Music Inc. v. Harrisongs Music Ltd.*, 71 Civ. 602 (S.D.N.Y.).

57 "Other than that": Trial testimony of Allen Klein in *U.S. v. Klein*, 77 Crim. 234.

58 "Each and every word": Trial testimony of Allen Klein in *Big Seven Music Corp.*, 75 Civ. 1116.

58 "I have no clue": Trial testimony of John Lennon in ibid.

58 "to manufacture and distribute": Trial testimony of Allen Klein in ibid.

58 "[I]t got a little bit": Miles, *Paul McCartney*, 561.

58 "Well, I wasn't gonna tell you": Ibid.

58 "So that was it": Ibid.

58 "how many records Capitol had sold": Allen Klein Deposition excerpt in case file of *ABKCO Industries Inc. v. Lennon*, 2598/74.

59 "took place completely behind": McCartney counsel David Hirst from transcript of hearing in *McCartney v. Lennon.*

59 "made an absolute fortune": "Beatles' Assets 'Not in Jeopardy,'" *Times* (London), February 25, 1971.

59 "The day before I became": Harold Bronson, "The Producers: Peter Asher," *Hit Parader*, September 1972.

59 "We intend to start recording": Apple Records internal memo reproduced in album notes for 2010 rerelease of *James Taylor.*

59 "Who needs the Iveys": John Lennon quoted in Bronson, "The Producers: Peter Asher."

60 "I still have the [press] clipping": Ibid.

60 "When the album didn't set": Bramwell, *Magical Mystery Tours*, 359.

60 "I decided that both": Bronson, "The Producers: Peter Asher."

60 "'We like you'": Miles, *Paul McCartney*, 547.

60 "You kidding?": Ibid.

60 "after my writing": Jerry Hopkins, "James Taylor on Apple: 'The Same Old Craperoo,'" *Rolling Stone*, August 23, 1969, 8.

60 Peter Asher made sure: David Browne, *Fire and Rain: The Beatles, Simon & Garfunkel, James Taylor, CSNY, and the Lost Story of 1970* (Cambridge, MA: Da Capo Press, 2011), 61.

61 The complaint that Rosenman Colin drafted: *Apple Records S.A. v. Warner Bros. Records Inc.* The New York County Court clerk's office has no record that the complaint was filed.

8. "TO STOP KLEIN"

62 "very anxious": David Hirst from transcript of hearing in *McCartney v. Lennon.*

62 "She came into the Manchester Square offices": Southall, *Northern Songs*, 63.

62 "to stop Klein": Trial testimony of George Harrison in *ABKCO Music Inc. v. Harrisongs Music Ltd.*, 71 Civ. 602.

62 "like Atilla [*sic*] the Hun": Al Aronowitz, "Why Is George in New York?" *Rolling Stone*, June 11, 1970, 34.

63 "was a terrible decision": Davies, *The Beatles*, 373.

63 "Imagine, seriously": Salewicz, "Paul McCartney: An Innocent Man?"

63 "I think really when Klein": Snow, "The Beatles: 'We're a Damn Good Little Band.'"

63 "willful and persistent breaches": Statement of Claim of Paul McCartney, served July 16, 1971, in *McCartney v. Lennon.*

64 "called me": Trial testimony of Allen Klein in *Greenfield v. Philles Records Inc.*, 0763/88 (N.Y. Sup. Ct., N.Y. County).

64 "fall over if you said": Trial testimony of George Harrison in *Bright Tunes Music Corp.*, 71 Civ. 602.

64 "A perfectly honest and competent attempt": Morris Finer from transcript of hearing in *McCartney v. Lennon.*

64 "When I told Paul": Affidavit of Richard Starkey in *McCartney v. Lennon.*

65 "So insecure": Salewicz, "Paul McCartney: An Innocent Man?"

65 "full of lawyers": Tim Cullen, "The End of the Beatles: Epstein's Death Started Trouble," Newspaper Enterprise Association syndicated report, April 1, 1971.

65 "one of the biggest ironies": Alan Smith, "It's Open Warfare," *New Musical Express*, March 6, 1971.

65 Starr jokingly asked his lawyer: "Peter Creightmore," *Times* (London), May 26, 1997.

66 "enthusiastic": Affidavit of Allen Klein, February 12, 1971, in *McCartney v. Lennon.*

67 "[I]f we didn't do what you wanted": Letter of John Lennon, *Melody Maker*, December 4, 1971.

67 "You just don't want to know": Williams, "The Times Profile: Paul McCartney."

67   "the receiver wasn't normal": John Lennon Deposition excerpt in case file in *ABKCO Industries Inc. v. Lennon*, 19258/73.

67   "we shall continue to avoid" and subsequent Malcolm Brown quotes: Letter of Malcolm Brown to J. D. Spooner, October 20, 1971.

67–68   the Beatles had yet to agree among themselves and "that they laid absolute claim": Letter of J. D. Spooner to Malcolm Brown, October 28, 1971.

68   "I cannot see that you can": Letter of Peter Howard to J. D. Spooner, October 11, 1971.

68   "received and satisfied": Affidavit of James Spooner November 25, 1971, in *McCartney v. Lennon*.

69   "having seen a press announcement": Statement of Stephen Marius Gray, January 16, 1974, in *McCartney v. Lennon*.

69   "the prolongation of the negotiations": Affidavit of Neil Aspinall, January 25, 1974, in *McCartney v. Lennon*.

69   "resulted in a certain measure": Letter of F. P. Caola to Stephen Gray, January 18, 1974.

69   "made it clear to me": Letter of Stephen Gray to F. P. Caola, January 18, 1974.

9. REMNANTS OF THE RELATIONSHIP

71   "The walls were decorated" and subsequent Lon Van Eaton quotes: Author interview with Lon Van Eaton, July 2, 2013.

71   "if I was interested in representing": *Sweet Music: Lon and Derrek*, accessed July 2, 2013, http://www.youtube.com/watch?v=lI9kAQC7ffU.

72   "staggeringly impressive": Stephen Holden, "Brother, Lon & Derrek Van Eaton," *Rolling Stone*, November 23, 1972, 62.

72   "grABKCO": Davies, *John Lennon Letters*, 258.

72   "There is a feeling that perhaps Klein": Judith Sims, "Beatles Meet, but Not for 'Reunion,'" *Rolling Stone*, April 26, 1973, 10.

73   "due to the presence of Lee Eastman": Stuart Werbin, "Lennons Discuss Deportation, Allen Klein, Beatles 'Reunion,'" *Rolling Stone*, May 10, 1973, 10.

73   "severed the remnants": "Ex-Manager Severs All Ties with Beatles," *New York Times*, April 3, 1973.

73   "I basically worked for John Lennon": Trial testimony of May Pang in *Big Seven Music Corp.*, 75 Civ. 1116.

74   "a form letter evidently addressed": Affidavit of Allen Klein in Opposition to Motions to Dismiss or Stay, April 29, 1974, in *ABKCO Industries Inc. v. Apple Corps Ltd.*, 456/74 (N.Y. Sup. Ct., N.Y. County).

74   ABKCO filed an action in Los Angeles Superior Court: *ABKCO Industries Inc. v. Harrison*, was moved to a California federal court before being

transferred to the Southern District of New York in Manhattan and docketed as 73 Civ. 4580.

74   In the trial-level New York Supreme Court: *ABKCO Industries Inc. v. Apple Films Ltd.*, 11088/73; *ABKCO Industries v. Apple Records Inc.*, 11496/73; and *ABKCO Industries Inc. v. Lennon*, 11558/73.

74   "the usual and some unusual": Letter of Lennon counsel David A. J. Richards to Robert Gottlieb at Rosenman Colin, November 5, 1973.

74   Lennon, Harrison, and Starr sued ABKCO: *Apple Corps Ltd. v. ABKCO Industries Inc.*, 1973-A-No. 4231, in the High Court of Justice, Chancery Division.

75   "to jump the gun": Affidavit of Allen Klein, April 29, 1974, in *ABKCO Industries Inc. v. Apple Corps Ltd.*

75   The November 8, 1973, filing: *ABKCO Industries Inc. v. Lennon*, 19258/73.

75   "tools of the trade": Vetter, "Playboy Interview: Allen Klein."

75   "To tell the truth": Anne Moore, "George Harrison on Tour—Press Conference Q&A," *Valley Advocate* (Northampton, MA), November 13, 1974.

75   "And then they would not": Allen Klein Deposition excerpt in case file in *ABKCO Industries Inc. v. Lennon*, 19258/73.

76   "as a payment against the sale": Letter of Richard Starkey to ABKCO Industries, October 29, 1971.

76   part of a plan Klein had: "Klein, 3 Beatles in Split," *Billboard*, April 14, 1973, 44.

76   "I have never had any business training": Affidavit of George Harrison in Support of Motion to Dismiss or Stay, January 18, 1974, in *ABKCO Industries Inc. v. Lennon*, 19258/73.

76   "never took part in negotiating": Affidavit of Richard Starkey, May 2, 1974, in ibid.

76   "Which one of them is which": John Lennon Deposition excerpt in appellate case file in ibid.

76   "They let me have": Ibid.

76   "involve essentially the same parties": Affidavit of John Eastman in Support of Motion to Dismiss or Stay, January 30, 1974, in ibid.

77   "I was in New York": Affidavit of George Harrison in Support of Motion to Dismiss or Stay, January 18, 1974, in ibid.

77   "the great majority": Affidavit of Allen Klein in Opposition to Motions to Dismiss or Stay, April 29, 1974, in ibid.

77   "pervasively, unmistakably, undeniably": Justice Jacob Markowitz quoted in *ABKCO Industries Inc. v. Lennon*, 52 A.D.2d 435 (N.Y. App. Div. 1st Dept. 1976).

77   In June 1976, that court affirmed: Ibid.

10. TO "BLEED" ABKCO

79   "without regard to money": Plaintiffs' Statement of Claim in *Apple Corps Ltd. v. ABKCO Industries Inc.*

80   "becoming most anxious": Letter of Peter Howard to Joynson-Hicks & Co., December 9, 1969.

80   "After a thorough review": Minutes of Special Meeting of Board of Directors of Apple Records Inc., January 28, 1970.

80   "afraid": Affidavit of George Harrison in Support of Motion to Disqualify, January 18, 1974, in *ABKCO Industries Inc. v. Lennon*, 19258/73.

81   "brilliant": Author interview with Peter Parcher, July 7, 2013.

81   "said that we had never had": Affidavit of George Harrison in Support of Motion to Disqualify, January 18, 1974, in *ABKCO Industries Inc. v. Lennon*, 19258/73.

81   "I received similar letters": Affidavit of John Ono Lennon in Support of Motion to Disqualify, January 30, 1974, in ibid.; "piracy case": *Harrison v. Audio Tapes Inc.*, 3126/73 (N.Y. Sup. Ct., N.Y. County).

81   "I don't recall ever being told": Affidavit of John Ono Lennon in Support of Motion to Disqualify, January 30, 1974, in *ABKCO Industries Inc. v. Lennon*, 19258/73.

81   "to make it as expensive": Affidavit of Max Freund, April 29, 1974, in ibid.

81   "'bleed' ABKCO": Affidavit of Allen Klein, May 15, 1975, in ibid.

82   "While plaintiff's counsel represented": *ABKCO Industries Inc. v. Lennon*, 52 A.D.2d 435.

82   In one suit, seeking management commissions: *ABKCO Industries Inc. v. Apple Corps Ltd.*

82   ABKCO also filed the fourth suit: *ABKCO Industries Inc. v. Lennon*, 2598/74.

82   "Simply as a matter of arithmetic": Affidavit of Richard W. Hulbert, June 16, 1975.

83   "[I]s it not true": Apple Records attorney George Grumbach cross-examining witness Allen Klein during trial of *Big Seven Music Corp.*, 75 Civ. 1116.

83   "It's very hard": Bob Woffinden, "Ringo Starr: Everyone One of Us Has All We Need," *New Musical Express*, April 12, 1975.

83   "It's going to be awful": Peter Doggett, *You Never Give Me Your Money: The Beatles After the Breakup* (New York: HarperCollins, 2009), 252–53.

83   "When I arrived": Bob Gruen, *John Lennon: The New York Years* (New York: Stewart, Tabori & Chang, 2005), 120.

84   "It wasn't her money": Joan Goodman, "Interview: Paul and Linda McCartney, *Playboy*, December 1984.

84   "I single-handedly saved": Miles, *Paul McCartney*, 580.

11. "IN A SECRET VAULT"

87 "I saw him removing" and immediately following Leon Wildes quotes: Affidavit of Leon Wildes, May 1, 1972, in *Lennon v. Marks*, 72 Civ. 1784 (S.D.N.Y.).

87 "kept in a secret vault": Petition for Review of Deportation, September 6, 1974, in *Lennon v. Immigration and Naturalization Service*, 74–2189 (S.D.N.Y.).

87 "fact that we may have expressed views": Affidavit of John Winston Ono Lennon and Yoko Ono Lennon, May 1, 1972, in *Lennon v. Marks*.

88 "If I say that it's mine": John Lennon quoted in hearing testimony of Allen Klein in *Matter of Lennon*, A17 597 321 (I.N.S.).

89 "a headhunter": *The Dick Cavett Show*, May 11, 1972 broadcast.

89 "The impact of the proceedings": Letter of Martin Polden to Leon Wildes, March 14, 1972.

89 "If you want to end up": "Peter Creightmore," *Times* (London), May 26, 1997.

89 "Look what Yogi, our dog" and "Are you mad?": Boyd, *Wonderful Tonight*, 128–29.

89 "I had to go through rigorous tests" and "most humiliating": Ibid.,131.

90 "I'm not sure I understand": Bramwell, *Magical Mystery Tours*, 172.

90 "She's very pushy": Ibid.

90 "the elite school": "Yoko Ono Brief Biography" attached to Petition to Classify Preference Status of Alien on Basis of Profession or Occupation, February 29, 1972.

90 "being based on 'Event'": Ibid.

91 "edit film and consult": *In Re: John Winston Lennon*, August 11, 1971 Visa Application, File # A 17 597 321.

92 "I got myself voted": Charles Moritz, ed., *Current Biography 1965* (New York: H.W. Wilson Co., 1965-66), 255.

92 "I haven't got time for politicians": Ibid., 257.

92 "asked Lennon about": Larry Kane, *Ticket to Ride: Inside the Beatles' 1964 Tour that Changed the World* (Philadelphia: Running Press, 2003), 28.

93 In his article, Riesel discussed: In *Subject: The Beatles*, FBI File Number: 62–52493-A.

93 *Los Angeles Times* article by Art Berman: In *Subject: The Beatles*, FBI File Number: 66-28-7118.

94 "Oldtimers around the Cow Palace": Bob Foster, "Hysteria Heaven Rocks Cow Palace," *San Mateo Times*, August 20, 1964.

95 "The saddest part": The Beatles, *The Beatles Anthology*, 192.

95 "I've seen those famous": Ibid.

95 "The President then indicated": Bud Krogh, "Memorandum for: the

President's File, Subject: Meeting with Elvis Presley," December 21, 1970, accessed July 5, 2013, www.preslaw.info/4-meeting-notes.html.

12. "GET THE HELL OUT OF THE COUNTRY"

97   "In the U.S.": Ritchie Yorke, "Boosting Peace: John and Yoko in Canada," *Rolling Stone*, June 28, 1969, 1.

97   "He's not a radical lawyer": *The Dick Cavett Show*, May 11, 1972.

97   "Because it's you": Sol Marks quoted in author interview with Leon Wildes, June 17, 2013.

97   "had impressive economic implications": Letter of Leon Wildes to the Immigration and Naturalization Service, March 2, 1972.

98   "would be a kind of artistic": Letter of Dick Cavett to US Immigration Service, February 28, 1972.

98   "immediately revoke": Sol Marks memorandum quoted in Jack Anderson, "Beatle John Lennon Wins Stay in U.S.," June 14, 1975, syndicated column.

98   "didn't find out until": Author interview with Leon Wildes, June 17, 2013.

98   "One morning we woke up": Jonathan Karp, "Yoko Ono: How We Were Almost Deported," ABC News, September 5, 2006.

99   "acted as if she despised": Bramwell, *Magical Mystery Tours*, 244.

99   "If he's fallen in love": "Yoko's Husband Files for Divorce," *The Stars and Stripes*, November 10, 1968.

99   Tony filed for a divorce: *Cox v. Cox*, 20-1969 (D.V.I.).

99   "incompatibility of temperament": Answer of Yoko Ono quoted in *Cox v. Cox*, 457 F.2d 1190 (3d Cir. 1972).

99   "no arrangement made": *The Dick Cavett Show*, May 11, 1972.

100   "had not earned a living" and next John Lennon quote: Hearing testimony of John Lennon in *Matter of Lennon*.

100   Sometimes, John and Yoko were accompanied: *ABKCO Industries Inc. v. Lennon*, 19258/73.

100   Yoko filed a child custody motion: *Cox v. Cox*, 71-1946 (D.V.I.).

100   "At the last minute": *The Dick Cavett Show*, May 11, 1972.

101   "elaborate": Motion of Anthony D. Cox to Stay Order Pending Appeal, filed October 18, 1971, in *Cox*, 20-1969.

101   "In your opinion": *Ex parte Cox*, 479 S.W.2d 110 (Tex. App. Houston, 1st Dist. 1972).

101   "What we have now": "Lennons Seek Haven in U.S., Possession of Yoko's Child," *Oakland Tribune*, April 29, 1972.

101   "[W]e only got": Hearing testimony of John Lennon in *Matter of Lennon*.

101   the Third Circuit upheld: *Cox v. Cox*, 457 F.2d 1190.

13. "NATIONAL SECURITY RISKS"

102 "in identical black suits": Jon Wiener, *Come Together: John Lennon in His Own Time* (Urbana: University of Illinois Press, 1984), 229.

103 "distinguished, knowledgeable": Author interview with Leon Wildes, June 17, 2013.

103 "MASH prevents the alien": Paul L. Montgomery, "U.S. Streamlines Alien Deportation," *New York Times*, January 29, 1972.

103 "national security risks" and next quote: Affidavit of Leon Wildes, February 19, 1974, in *Lennon v. Richardson*, 73 Civ. 4476 (S.D.N.Y.).

103 "a liberal": Nick Ravo, "Charles Gordon, 93, I.N.S. Counsel," *New York Times*, May 2, 1999.

103 "I don't see any point": Letter of Charles Gordon to Leon Wildes, April 7, 1972.

104 lawsuit to stop the government's pursuit: *Lennon v. Marks.*

105 "I carefully prepared affidavits": Author interview with Leon Wildes, June 17, 2013. Sol Marks approved the deferrals for John and for Yoko differently. Marks checked a box in Yoko's petition acknowledging her application for permanent residency, while in John's case, the district director only recognized a temporary visa, which Leon Wildes complained to Ira Fieldsteel at the May 12, 1972, hearing was a "prejudgment" that "Mr. Lennon had no right whatsoever to apply for residence."

105 "might be viewed": Letter of Jon Hendricks, May 11, 1972.

105 "It may be that there is a theory": Letter of Lord Harlech, May 11, 1972.

105 "[T]o the shame of the whole world of rock": Ralph J. Gleason, "Perspectives: Fair Play for John and Yoko," *Rolling Stone*, June 22, 1972, 34.

106 "political idiots": Victor Lasky, "Lennons Spouting Off on U.S. Acts," May 13, 1972, syndicated column.

106 "found it almost impossible": Wiener, *Come Together*, 235.

106 "It's ironic": *The Dick Cavett Show*, May 11, 1972.

106 "urging John and Yoko" and next quote: Author interview with Leon Wildes, June 17, 2013.

107 "never took out American citizenship": *The Dick Cavett Show*, May 11, 1972.

107 "She had dropped off": Author interview with Leon Wildes, June 17, 2013.

14. "SKULLDUGGERY WAS AFOOT"

112 "one of the major factors" and "That's all right": Werbin, "Lennons Discuss Deportation, Allen Klein, Beatles 'Reunion.'"

112 "substantial evidence": Brief for Petitioner in *Lennon v. Immigration and Naturalization Service.*

112   "I had a difficult time": Author interview with Leon Wildes, June 17, 2013.

112   "There were instances of people": Ibid.

113   "Yoko advised me": Pam Zimmerman, "The Ballad of John Lennon and Leon Wildes," *jweekly.com*, December 9, 2010.

113   "defects fatal": Ruling of Ira Fieldsteel, September 12, 1973, in *Re: Lennon*, A17 597 321 (I.N.S.).

113   "shrouded in secrecy": Leon Wildes, "The Deferred Action Program of the Bureau of Citizenship and Immigration Services: A Possible Remedy for Impossible Immigration Cases," *San Diego Law Review* 41, no. 2 (Spring 2004).

113   "district directors are required" and "full and fair hearing": Letter of Leon Wildes to E. A. Loughran, August 1, 1973.

114   A new lawsuit by John Lennon: *Lennon v. Richardson*.

114   companion complaint: *Lennon v. United States*, 73 Civ. 4543 (S.D.N.Y.).

114   "We have been apart more": Chris Charlesworth, "John Lennon: Lennon Today," *Melody Maker*, November, 3, 1973.

115   "I remember someone yelling": Doggett, *You Never Give Me Your Money*, 218.

115   "Pilcher guilty of perjury": Telegram of Martin Polden to Leon Wildes.

115   "provocative" and "no showing": *Lennon v. Richardson*, 378 F.Supp. 39 (S.D.N.Y. 1974).

116   "They were not filed chronologically": Letter of Leon Wildes to Paul J. Curran, December 10, 1974.

116   "is not provided for": Respondent's Brief in *Lennon v. Immigration and Naturalization Service*.

15. "i'm a doctrine now"

117   The Board of Immigration Appeals issued its ruling: *In re: Lennon*, A17 597 321, July 10, 1974 (B.I.A.).

117   "This country was founded" and "If John Lennon is deported": "Comments: Let Him Be," *Rolling Stone*, August 29, 1974, 27.

118   "speeding up hearings": "Marks Is Retiring as District Director for Immigration," *New York Times*, May 19, 1974.

118   "[T]hey'd get me for spitting": Ralph Blumenthal, "Ex-Chief Immigration Trial Attorney Quits Abruptly," *New York Times*, December 8, 1973.

118   "the United States harbors": Jack Anderson's August 1974 report quoted in Jack Anderson, "Beatle John Lennon Wins Stay in U.S.," June 14, 1975, syndicated column.

119   "We met with": Author interview with Leon Wildes, June 17, 2013.

119   Owen dismissed: *Lennon v. United States*, 387 F.Supp. 561 (S.D.N.Y. 1975).

120   "I can last out": Pete Hamill, "Long Night's Journey into Day: A Conversation with John Lennon," *Rolling Stone*, June 5, 1975, 70.

120   "there was no illegal surveillance": Respondent's Brief in *Lennon v. Immigration and Naturalization Service.*

120   "the record indicates": Ibid.

120   *Rolling Stone* published a full copy: Chet Flippo, "Lennon's Lawsuit: Memo from Thurmond," *Rolling Stone*, July 31, 1975, 16.

120   The Second Circuit issued its appellate ruling: *Lennon v. Immigration and Naturalization Service*, 527 F.2d 187 (2d Cir. 1975).

121   In a major music case: *Berlin v. E.C. Publications Inc.*, 329 F.2d 541 (2d Cir. 1964).

122   "Yesterday, all of John Lennon's troubles": Leslie Maitland, "John Lennon Wins His Residency in U.S.," *New York Times*, July 28, 1976.

122   "It's great to be legal again": Chris Charlesworth, "John Lennon Gets His Ticket to Ride," *Melody Maker*, August 7, 1976.

122   "I have on a number of occasions": Letter of Leon Wildes to Mary P. Maguire, December 8, 1976.

122   "John immediately called me up": Author interview with Leon Wildes, June 17, 2013.

16. SAY YOU WANT A REVELATION
123   "I remember shaking his hand": Davies, *John Lennon Letters*, 311.

123   "withdrawal from activist politics": Wiener, *Come Together*, xix.

124   "carr[ied] the government's burden": Judge Robert M. Takasugi quoted in *Wiener v. Federal Bureau of Investigation*, 943 F.2d 972 (9th Cir. 1991).

124   "If Peeping Tom surveillance": "Seeing F.B.I. Files on Lennon: A Hard Day's Night," David Margolick, *New York Times*, Sept. 6, 1991.

124   Ninth Circuit reinstated the FOIA lawsuit: *Wiener*, 943 F.2d 972.

124   "using delay tactics": Jon Wiener, *Gimme Some Truth: The John Lennon FBI Files* (Berkeley: University of California Press, 1999), 270.

124   religious sect known as the Walk: Jim Calio, "Yoko Ono's Ex-Husband, Tony Cox, Reveals His Strange Life Since Fleeing with Their Daughter 14 Years Ago," *People*, February 3, 1986, accessed December 29, 2014, www.people.com/people/archive/article/0,,20092860,00.html.

124   "It was just like we were all in a big giant cosmic car accident": "Last Lost Lennon Tape," *Legendary Auctions Spring 2004 Catalog*, accessed January 1, 2015, www.legendaryauctions.com/lot-35648.aspx.

125   "We were getting calls": Neil Spencer, "Ono Speaks Softly about Past," *Pacific Stars and Stripes*, July 26, 1997.

125   "there is nothing": Andrew Gumbel, "The Lennon Files," *Independent* (London), December 21, 2006.

125   Jon Wiener found no evidence: Jon Wiener e-mail to author, October 24, 2013.

125   "It had become almost like a paranoia": Philip Norman, *John Lennon: The Life* (New York: HarperCollins, 2008), 718.

125   "I wish somebody would bug me": Robert Palmer, "The Pop Life," *New York Times*, June 17, 1981.

126   "The use of the Freedom of Information Act": Leon Wildes, "The Deferred Action Program of the Bureau of Citizenship and Immigration Services: A Possible Remedy for Impossible Immigration Cases."

126   "That case was a complete win": Author interview with Leon Wildes, June 17, 2013.

126   didn't know of any John Lennon–type deportation efforts: Jon Wiener e-mail to author, October 24, 2013.

126   "was 100 percent" and "The free speech aspect": Author interview with Leon Wildes, June 17, 2013.

17. "I'VE CAUGHT THE BEATLES!"

129   "It's something I've been wanting": Chris Charlesworth, "John Lennon: Rock On!", *Melody Maker*, March 8, 1975.

129   "It was a weird day" and subsequent John Lennon quotes, unless otherwise indicated: Trial testimony of John Lennon in *Big Seven Music Corp.*, 75 Civ. 1116.

129   "had a helluva mug": Walter Yetnikoff with David Ritz, *Howling at the Moon: The Odyssey of a Monstrous Music Mogul in an Age of Excess* (New York: Broadway Books, 2004), 61.

131   "I used to book talent" and subsequent Morris Levy quotes, unless otherwise indicated: Trial testimony of Morris Levy in *Big Seven Music Corp.*, 75 Civ. 1116.

131   Morris Levy originally sued: *Big Seven Music Corp. v. Maclen Music Inc.*, 70 Civ. 1348 (S.D.N.Y.).

132   "Freed got the rights": This and subsequent William Krasilovsky quotes, from author interview with William Krasilovsky, April 5, 2013, unless otherwise indicated.

132   "It's wonderful!": Morris Levy quoted in ibid.

132   "dynamic success": Trial Memorandum of Defendants in *Big Seven Music Corp.*, 70 Civ. 1348.

132   "especially the similarities": Expert Report of Harold Barlow, May 25, 1970, in ibid.

133   "a more accurate comparison": Memorandum of William L. Dawson, in ibid.

133   "Tell your detectives": Allen Klein quoted in author interview with William Krasilovsky, April 5, 2013.

133   Lennon claimed sole authorship: In their October 8, 1970, answer to Big Seven's complaint, Apple Records lawyers mistakenly stated "the words and the music for the musical composition 'Come Together' were written by John Lennon and Paul McCartney," though this was Lennon and McCartney's traditional credit on Beatles songs.

134   "I had created many extra verses": Chuck Berry, *Chuck Berry: The Autobiography* (New York: Harmony Books, 1987), 100.

134   "overtaken by some dudes": Berry, *Autobiography*, 147–48.

134   "used the phrase": Affidavit of John Lennon, October 1971, in *Big Seven Music Corp.*, 70 Civ. 1348.

134   "approximately 10 to 11 years prior": Ibid.

134   "attacked me years later": David Sheff, *Last Interview: All We Are Saying— John Lennon and Yoko Ono* (London: Sidgwick & Jackson, 2000), 201.

134   "a very perky little song": Miles, *Paul McCartney*, 553.

135   "a surrealistic stream of consciousness": Affidavit of John Lennon, October 1971, in *Big Seven Music Corp.*, 70 Civ. 1348.

135   "in 1969 Paul McCartney and I": Ibid.

135   "a small, middle-aged, but boyish-looking": "American Grandstand: Sue You, Sue Me Blues," Dave Marsh, *Rolling Stone*, June 17, 1976, 22.

136   "I am calling the shots": Morris Levy quoted in ABKCO Internal Memorandum of Harold Seider to Allen Klein, November 8, 1971.

136   "to tell the Big Seven attorney": Ibid.

18. "I AM ALWAYS WORRIED"

138   "Phil was running around": Mick Brown, *Tearing Down the Wall of Sound: The Rise and Fall of Phil Spector* (New York: Alfred A. Knopf, 2007), 272.

138   "It got a little out of hand": Mick Brown, "Pop's Last Genius: Phil Spector," *Telegraph Magazine*, February 4, 2003.

138   "I remember Phil's mother": Mick Brown, *Tearing Down the Wall of Sound*, 274.

139   "Listen, Phil, if you're gonna kill me": Norman, *John Lennon: The Life*, 721.

139   "I didn't know that until" and subsequent John Lennon quotes, unless otherwise indicated: Trial testimony of John Lennon in *Big Seven Music Corp.*, 75 Civ. 1116.

139   "[W]e wholeheartedly approved" and subsequent Bhaskar Menon quote: Deposition of Bhaskar Menon, May 28, 1975, in ibid.

139   "What happened was": "John Lennon's 'Lost Weekend' with Phil Spector," *Uncut*, September 2008, accessed June 29, 2014, www.uncut.co.uk/phil -spector/john-lennons-lost-weekend-with-phil-spector-interview.

139   "Harry told me": Norman, *John Lennon: The Life*, 731.

140   "I [didn't] know whether": Ibid.

140   "Look, whatever, Richard Perry got" and subsequent Harold Seider quotes: Trial testimony of Harold Seider in *Big Seven Music Corp.*, 75 Civ. 1116.

141   "hyperventilating" and subsequent Bob Mercer quote: Brown, *Tearing Down the Wall of Sound*, 276.

141   "more time-consuming": May Pang, *Instamatic Karma: Photographs of John Lennon* (New York: St. Martin's Press, 2008), 93.

142   "there would be some difficulties": Memo of William Krasilovsky to John Feigenbaum at Marshall, Bratter, Greene, Allison & Tucker, October 4, 1974.

143   "should be cleared": Ibid.

143   "After we sat down in the booth" and subsequent May Pang quotes, unless otherwise indicated: Trial testimony of May Pang in *Big Seven Music Corp.*, 75 Civ. 1116.

144   "Unbearably pretentious": Jon Landau, "*Mind Games*," *Rolling Stone*, January 3, 1974, 61.

144   "just a small business": and details of the Harry Fox audit: "Mail-Order Gold: Where's the Money from TV Oldies?," *Rolling Stone*, November 9, 1972, 16.

146   "set up like a luxury resort": Author interview with William Schurtman, October 4, 2013.

146   "In which wing": Pang, *Instamatic Karma*, 94.

147   "Nobody gets in John's sessions": Trial testimony of Jesse Ed Davis in *Big Seven Music Corp.*, 75 Civ. 1116.

147   The Beatles and Capitol Records did file suit: *Harrison v. Audiotape Inc.*, 3126/73 (N.Y. Sup. Ct., N.Y. County).

148   "We got the boys increased royalties": Vetter, "Playboy Interview: Allen Klein."

148   "I hear you are doing an album" and subsequent Allen Klein quotes, unless otherwise indicated: Trial testimony in *Big Seven Music Corp.*, 75 Civ. 1116.

150   "I was a bit nervous": Chris Charlesworth, "John Lennon: Rock On!"

151   "I was home with John": Pang, *Instamatic Karma*, 98.

151   "George blew his cool": Salewicz, "Paul McCartney: An Innocent Man?"

151   That night, according to May Pang: Pang, *Instamatic Karma*, 98.

19. EXPEDIENCE ON ALL SIDES

152   "because I was so worn out": This and subsequent John Lennon quotes: Trial testimony of John Lennon in *Big Seven Music Corp.*, 75 Civ. 1116.

258 | Notes to Pages 152–66

152   "one of the kids": This and subsequent Harold Seider quotes: Trial testimony of Harold Seider in ibid.

152   "What was happening": Morris Levy quoted in trial testimony of Harold Seider in ibid.

153   "in Disneyworld": Charlesworth, "John Lennon: Rock On!"

154   "Otherwise," Lennon told Levy: John Lennon quoted in author interview with William Schurtman, October 4, 2013.

154   "Levy reluctantly agreed" and subsequent William Schurtman quotes, unless otherwise indicated: Author interview with William Schurtman, October 4, 2013.

154   "breeched": Letter of Morris Levy to David Dolgenos, January 9, 1975.

155   "a brilliant mind": Tillinghast, *How Capitol Got the Beatles*, 38.

155   "I just think": Allen Klein quoted in Deposition of Bhaskar Menon, May 28, 1975, in *Big Seven Music Corp.*, 75 Civ. 1116.

155   "strange and inexplicable" and subsequent Bhaskar Menon quotes: Ibid.

156   "all bets are off": Harold Seider quoted in trial testimony of Morris Levy in ibid.

156   "some profanity" and subsequent Morris Levy quotes, unless otherwise indicated: Trial testimony of Morris Levy in ibid.

156   "Don't worry": Bob Gruen, *John Lennon*, 114.

157   The complaint in Manhattan federal court: Levy originally initiated suit in New York state court, then filed a federal complaint so he could charge the defendants with trying to monopolize the market for the Lennon oldies album in violation of federal antitrust law. The Big Seven plaintiffs moved their state law causes of action, including breach of contract, to the federal court, but subsequently dropped the antitrust claim.

158   "It is Lennon": Plaintiffs' Memorandum in Opposition to Motion to Dismiss, March 25, 1976, in *Big Seven Music Corp.*, 75 Civ. 1116.

158   "They didn't think I'd show": Chet Flippo, "Lennon in Court Again: $24 Million of Old Gold," *Rolling Stone*, April 8, 1976, 12.

159   "said he liked the way": William Schurtman e-mail to author December 12, 2013.

160   "All this started": Flippo, "Lennon in Court Again: $24 Million of Old Gold."

160   "Half the table swore": Videotape interview of Barrett Prettyman, April 12, 2012, at Robert H. Jackson Center, Jamestown, New York.

20. "EXTRAORDINARY NOISE"

166   Judge Griesa ruled: *Big Seven Music Corp. v. Lennon*, 409 F.Supp. 122 (S.D.N.Y. 1976).

166   In March 1976, Griesa granted: *Rolls-Royce Motors Ltd. v. Custom Cloud Motors Inc.*, U.S.P.Q. (BNA) 80 (S.D.N.Y. 1976).

167   "As soon as the needle": This and subsequent Dave Marsh quote: Author interview with Dave Marsh, April 8, 2013.

168   The appeals court issued its ruling: *Big Seven Music Corp v. Lennon*, 554 F.2d 504 (2d. Cir. 1977).

169   Levy was convicted: *U.S. v. Levy*, 86–301 (D.N.J. 1988).

169   "When Morris was dying" and subsequent William Krasilovsky quotes: Author interview with William Krasilovsky, April 5, 2013.

169   "self-conscious musical attitudinizing": Jon Landau, "Lennon Gets Lost in His Rock & Roll," *Rolling Stone*, May 22, 1975, 66.

169   "was such a mess": David Sheff, *Last Interview*, 206–7.

21. HERE COMES THE SUMMONS

173   "a simple one": Allen Klein quoted in Affidavit of David Braun, May 15, 1975, in *ABKCO Industries Inc. v. Harrison*, 19282/74 (N.Y. Sup. Ct., N.Y. County).

174   "enormity, complexity": Ibid.

174   "left the room": Affidavit of George Harrison in Support of Motion to Disqualify, January 18, 1974, in *ABKCO Industries Inc. v. Lennon*, 19258/73.

174   "In walks two of Klein's thugs": Author interview with Joseph Santora, April 4, 2014.

175   "four policemen arrived": This and subsequent John Loiacono quotes in Affidavit of Service of Peter F. Nadel, December 27, 1974, in *ABKCO Industries Inc. v. Harrison*, 19282/74.

175   "Get that guy": Barry Imhoff quoted in ibid.

176   "I have summonses here": William Ward and Denis O'Brien quoted in ibid.

177   "refused to deny or admit" and "No reply": Affidavit of Allen Klein, April 25, 1975, in ibid.

177   "Internal Revenue Service and other tax agencies": Complaint in ibid.

177   "ABKCO refused" and "to send all payments": Affidavit of David Braun, May 15, 1975, in ibid.

177   "had the sole power": Affidavit of Allen Klein, April 25, 1975, in ibid.

177   By June 1975, George admitted: Consent Judgment, June 17, 1975, in ibid.

177   "told me I did not own": Deposition testimony of George Harrison, August 22, 1974, quoted in Affidavit of Allen Klein, April 25, 1975, in ibid.

22. "AN UNMISTAKABLE SIMILARITY"

178   Bright Tunes' complaint: *Bright Tunes Music Corp. v. Harrisongs Music Ltd.*, 71 Civ. 602 (S.D.N.Y.).

178   "When 'My Sweet Lord' came out" and subsequent Jay Siegel quote: Author interview with Jay Siegel, February 4, 2014.

178   "Very limited" and "It was no event": Trial testimony of George Harrison in *Bright Tunes Music Corp.*, 71 Civ. 602.

179   The complaint also named: But the "My Sweet Lord" case wasn't the first Bright Tunes suit against Apple Records. The Brute Force release may have led Bright Tunes to file a lawsuit against the Beatles label in September 1969. (*Bright Tunes Productions Inc. v. Apple Records*, no case index number available [N.Y. Sup. Ct., N.Y. County].) That complaint in New York state court sought $202,226 for an alleged unauthorized record release.

       In a September 8, 1969, memorandum, ABKCO vice president Harold Seider recommended to Peter Howard—an attorney for ABKCO at Joynson-Hicks & Co. in London whom Allen Klein installed at Apple Corp's offices—that the New York law firm Rosenman Colin handle the case for Apple. John Lennon approved hiring Rosenman Colin to defend Apple Records against the Bright Tunes' suit.

       But details of the case are sketchy. Neither Bright Tunes co-principal Jay Siegel nor Harrison "My Sweet Lord" counsel Joseph Santora could recall the suit, and a recent search for the case file by the New York court clerk's office came up empty-handed. In January 1974, Albert Pergam, a lawyer from Cleary, Gottlieb, Steen & Hamilton, the US firm that Apple Corps hired after breaking away from Allen Klein in 1973, noted, "We have been unable to obtain information either from the court records or from [Rosenman Colin] concerning this action." It's possible, though, that the suit arose over a license to use the "King of Fuh" composition, which hadn't otherwise been released on record. That would have required Apple Records to negotiate with Bright Tunes for permission to distribute the Brute Force recording.

179   "I was starting to try": Trial testimony of George Harrison in *Bright Tunes Music Corp.*, 71 Civ. 602.

180   "it was humorous": Trial testimony of Alan Pariser in ibid.

180   "five acoustic guitars": Trial testimony of George Harrison in ibid.

180   "an unmistakable similarity": Comparative Analysis by David Greitzer in ibid.

180   "the similarity is in my opinion": Report of Joseph Murrells, February 16, 1971, in ibid.

180   "I had no contact with Lennon": Author interview with Joseph Santora, April 4, 2014.

181   "told George" and subsequent John Barham quotes: Author interview with John Barham, May 8, 2013.

182   "that we could defend": Trial testimony of Allen Klein in *Bright Tunes Music Corp.*, 71 Civ. 602.

182   "No one had ever told me" and immediately following George Harrison quotes: Affidavit of George Harrison in Support of Motion to Disqualify, January 18, 1974, in *ABKCO Industries Inc. v. Lennon*, 19258/73.

182   "we narrowly avoided": Howard Kaylan with Jeff Tamarkin, *Shell Shocked: My Life With the Turtles, Flo & Eddie, and Frank Zappa, etc.*. . . . (Milwaukee: Backbeat Books, 2013), 203.

183   "Assuming for purposes": Letter of Joseph J. Santora to J. B. Broadie at Frere Cholmeley, September 30, 1975.

23. THE RHYTHM OF THE WATER PUMP

184   "Owen was a bright, no-nonsense judge": Author interview with Gideon Cashman, January 15, 2014.

185   "the same as his stage persona": Author interview with Jay Siegel, February 4, 2014.

187   "Harrison looked like he was thinking": This and next Gideon Cashman quote from author interview with Gideon Cashman, January 15, 2014.

24. "FUN KNOCKING HIM OVER THE HEAD"

190   Judge Richard Owen handed down his ruling: *Bright Tunes Music Corp. v. Harrisongs Music Ltd.*, 420 F.Supp. 177 (S.D.N.Y. 1976).

190   "avoided the central issue": Author interview with John Barham, May 8, 2013.

190   "helps get rid of": George Harrison, *I Me Mine* (San Francisco: Chronicle Books, 2002), 36.

191   "After that we never had a radio": Boyd, *Wonderful Tonight*, 80.

191   "We probably owed over $400,000": Author interview with Jay Siegel, February 4, 2014.

191   "It's a joke": Harrison, *I Me Mine*, 63.

191   "I had messages": Trial testimony of George Harrison in *ABKCO Music Inc. v. Harrisongs Music Ltd.*, 71 Civ. 602, which was the damages trial of the case.

192   "George called to tell me": Author interview with Joseph Santora, April 4, 2014.

192   "Klein had terminated our services" and subsequent Gideon Cashman quotes: Author interview with Gideon Cashman, January 15, 2014.

193   When he issued the damages judgment: *ABKCO Music Inc. v. Harrisongs Music Ltd.*, 508 F.Supp. 798 (S.D.N.Y. 1981).

194   "I couldn't believe Klein": Author interview with Joseph Santora, April 4, 2014.

194 "This is one of the few cases": Stan Soocher, *They Fought the Law: Rock Music Goes to Court* (New York: Schirmer Books, 1999), 92.

195 "Harrison astonishingly creates": Plaintiff's Post-Trial Reply Memorandum of Law, filed June 17, 1986, in *ABKCO Music Inc. v. Harrisongs Music Ltd.*, 71 Civ. 602.

195 "Dracula-like" and "Whenever defendants feel": Defendant's Reply Memorandum, June 16, 1986, in ibid.

195 "true-meaning": *ABKCO Music Inc. v. Harrisongs Music Ltd.*, 944 F.2d 971 (2d Cir. 1991).

25. "THE LARGEST REFUGEE FLIGHT IN HISTORY"

196 "The civil war created": Letter of C. Lloyd Bailey to IRS chief counsel Meade Whitaker, January 29, 1974.

196 "I was in Los Angeles": Harrison, *I Me Mine*, 59.

196 "they say a lot of these charities": Davies, *The Beatles*, 325.

196 "would pay the expenses": Affidavit of George Harrison in Support of Motion to Disqualify in *ABKCO Industries Inc. v. Lennon*, 19258/73.

197 "[W]e have to go to": Alan Smith, "John Lennon & Yoko Ono: Doing the Rounds for Publicity," *New Musical Express*, July 31, 1971.

197 "to make sure": Trial testimony of Allen Klein in *U.S. v. Klein*, 77 Crim. 234.

197 "Pattie and I leaped": O'Dell, *Miss O'Dell*, 201.

197 "100 per cent" and "The question of recording": Trial testimony of Allen Klein in *U.S. v. Klein*, 77 Crim. 234.

198 "one album will be deemed": Letter of Len Wood to Apple Records Inc., September 30, 1971.

198 under the terms of the deal: Trial testimony of Allen Klein in *U.S. v. Klein*, 77 Crim. 234. Also see, Peter McCabe, "Some Sour Notes From the Bangladesh Concert," *New York*, February 28, 1972, 46–49, in which McCabe tallies the figures one way and Klein in two additional ways.

198 "We estimated": Trial testimony of Allen Klein in *U.S. v. Klein*, 77 Crim. 234.

198 "literally just covering": McCabe and Schonfeld, *Apple to the Core*, 48.

199 "It is important that you let us": Letter of Len Wood to Apple Records Inc., September 30, 1971.

199 "the largest contribution": Letter of Guido Pantaleoni Jr., US Committee for UNICEF president, to Allen Klein, May 31, 1972.

199 "There is no reason to think": McCabe, "Some Sour Notes From the Bangladesh Concert," 47.

199 ABKCO Industries filed: *ABKCO Industries Inc. v. New York Magazine*, 4355/72 (N.Y. Sup. Ct., N.Y. County).

200 "Klein's figures": Ben Fong-Torres, "Did Allen Klein Take Bangla Desh Money?", *Rolling Stone*, March 30, 1972, 6.

200 "we think you might": Harrison, *I Me Mine*, 61.

200 "did not give me a definite answer": Harrison Affidavit in Support of Motion to Disqualify, January 18, 1974, in *ABKCO Industries Inc. v. Lennon*, 19258/73.

201 "that there will be no adverse tax": Letter of Henry Newfeld to Peter Howard, April 21, 1972.

201 "before any such arrangement is finalized": Letters of James Spooner to George Harrison and P. J. Howard, July 27, 1971.

201 "This does place me in some difficulty": Letter of James Spooner to George Harrison, July 27, 1971.

202 "Would you please refer this": Letter of P. J. Howard to J. D. Spooner, August 20, 1971.

202 "would have no objection whatsoever": Letter of M. R. Lampard to J. D. Spooner, September 9, 1971.

202 "I have still not heard from you": Letter of P. J. Howard to J. D. Spooner, October 4, 1971.

202 "a taxation liability": Affidavit of J. D. Spooner, November 25, 1971, in *McCartney v. Lennon*; "onerous": Letter of J. D. Spooner to Peter Howard, September 13, 1971.

203 In the complaint, UNICEF charged: *United States Committee for UNICEF v. Apple Records Inc.*, 15299/77 (N.Y. Sup. Ct., N.Y. County).

203 But the complaint was quickly withdrawn: Notice of Voluntary Discontinuance, filed August 11, 1977.

203 "large percentage": Deposition of Denis O'Brien, September 15, 1979, in *ABKCO Music v. Harrisongs Music Ltd.*, 71 Civ. 602.

203 "they have now almost": Harrison, *I Me Mine*, 61; "I'm afraid": Graeme Thomson, "The Coming of Age of George," *British GQ*, November 18, 2013, accessed February 9, 2014, www.gq-magazine.co.uk/entertainment/articles/2013-11/18/george-harrison-the-beatles-concert-for-bangladesh-pictures.

204 "more calls": Hearing testimony of Allen Klein in *Matter of Lennon*.

26. IN THE BAG

205 "pile" and "a lot of money": Trial testimony of Harold Seider in *U.S. v. Klein*, 77 Crim. 234 (S.D.N.Y.). Except for the 1971 tax prosecution case against Allen Klein, all *U.S. v. Klein* endnotes in this and the next chapter are from this case, which was assigned different docket numbers at various stages of the litigation, and from court rulings on *U.S. v. Klein*, 77 Crim. 234.

205   "I stood there" and subsequent Pete Bennett quotes: Trial testimony of Pete Bennett in ibid.

206   "Free, no holes": Capitol Records memo confirmed in trial testimony of Allen Klein in ibid.

207   "unless, of course, he had performed": Ibid.

207   "I bought a drum set": Bonnie King, "Pete Bennett Presents: An Evening of Classic British Rock and Roll with Denny Laine," *Salem-News.com*, October 1, 2008, accessed August 4, 2014, www.salem-news.com/articles/october012008/.

208   "[m]anicured" and "slightly heliumized": Tim Crouse, "A Day in the Life of the Beatle Promo Man," *Rolling Stone*, December 9, 1971, 1, 6.

208   "Pete was the stereotypical": Author interview with Mike Tolleson, April 5, 2013.

208   "was about dropping": Author interview with Lon Van Eaton, July 2, 2013.

208   "a couple of agents": Sam Weiss quotes from trial testimony of Pete Bennett in *U.S. v. Klein.*

208   When Pete went down to ABKCO on Friday afternoon: Details from ibid.

210   "highly suspicious" and prosecution's other quotes: Brief of United States, filed September 7, 1971, in the US Court of Appeals for the Second Circuit in *U.S. v. Klein*, 71-1464 (S.D.N.Y.)

210   the Second Circuit appeals court affirmed: *U.S. v. Klein*, 448 F.2d 1399 (2d. Cir. 1971).

27. "BELIEVE PB'S TESTIMONY?"

211   "clear indications of threats": Jerry Knight, "Tax Trial Centers on Former Beatles' Manager and Aide," *Washington Post*, October 11, 1977.

211   "nonsense": Steven Clark, "Bennett to Promote Elvis," *Herald Statesman* (Yonkers, NY), January 12, 1979.

216   "[M]ay we have a ruling": This and the following jury-deliberation quotes from author's examination of original handwritten exchanges between the jury and Judge Metzner, and original internal notes from the jurors' deliberations. Some of these quotes also appear in the appellate opinion *U.S. v. Klein*, 582 F.2d 186 (2d Cir. 1978).

217   But Judge Broderick denied: *U.S. v. Klein*, 442 F.Supp. 1164 (S.D.N.Y. 1977), affirmed, *U.S. v. Klein*, 582 F.2d 186.

217   "clearly to avoid": Supplementary Brief on Behalf of Appellant in *U.S. v. Klein* 78-1052.

217   "her relations with": Memorandum in Opposition to Defendant's Motion to

Preclude Reference to Iris Keitel and Defendant's Prior Conviction, January 10, 1978, in *U.S. v. Klein.*

218   "I personally will give": Letter of Anne Klein to Judge Vincent L. Broderick, May 28, 1979.

218   "Allen Klein was my son's manager": Letter of Rev. Charles Cooke to Judge Vincent L. Broderick, May 31, 1979.

218   "claustrophobic anxiety" and other Jerry Weisfogel quotes: Letter of Jerry Weisfogel, MD, to Lee Stoeker, US probation officer, June 12, 1979.

218   Second Circuit affirmed: *U.S. v. Klein,* 97-1292 (2d Cir. 1979).

219   the US Supreme Court turned down: *Klein v. U.S.,* 79-1342, on Petition for Writ of Certiorari.

219   "This was me": Miles, *Paul McCartney,* 556.

EPILOGUE: THE LAW AND WINDING ROAD

220   "I played him a new artist": Fred Bronson with additional reporting by Jem Aswad, "Pete Bennett, Legendary Promotion Man for Beatles, Stones, Many More, Dead at 77," *Billboard,* November 27, 2012, accessed April 27, 2014, http://www.billboard.biz/bbbiz/industry/record-labels/pete-bennett-legendary -promotion-man-for-1008028872.story.

220   "looked like they were": Author interview with Barry Slotnick, March 20, 2014.

220   The firm sued Klein: *Rosenman Colin Freund Lewis & Cohen v. Klein,* 19912/81 (N.Y. Sup. Ct., N.Y. County).

220   "millions of dollars" and "I was overbilled": Affidavit of Allen Klein, November 4, 1981, in *Rosenman Colin Freund Lewis & Cohen,* 19912/81.

220   a state appellate court affirmed: *Rosenman Colin Freund Lewis & Cohen v. Klein,* 92 A.D.2d 1093 (N.Y. App. Div. 1st Dept. 1983).

221   Klein sued his longtime ally: *ABKCO Music Inc. v. Spector,* 07 CV 1235 (S.D.N.Y.).

221   "bad language": Will Davies, "Allen Klein, the Manager Fans Blamed for the Beatles Break-Up, Dies at 77," *Mail on Sunday,* July 5, 2009.

222   "enriched himself": *Harrison v. O'Brien,* BC120397 (L.A. Sup Ct., L.A. County).

222   Denis O'Brien filed for bankruptcy: *In re: O'Brien,* 02-3716 (Bankr. E.D.Mo.).

222   "I went at Yoko's request": Salewicz, "Paul McCartney: An Innocent Man?"

223   "I'm just starting to get back": Ibid.

223   music royalty suits the Beatles had filed: The New York case was *Apple Records Inc. v. Capitol Records Inc.,* 08041/79 (N.Y. Sup. Ct., N.Y. County).

223   "a million dollars": Lee Eastman quote from a mid-1980s tape recording of a meeting of Lee and John Eastman, and Paul and Linda McCartney.

223   "You've got a problem": Ibid.

223   after settling the dispute with Capitol-EMI: Apple Corps again sued Capitol-EMI in 2005 over the alleged underpayment of $55 million in record royalties from 1994 to 1999 but settled, with confidential terms, in 2007.

224   MPL, which bought the royalty rights: MPL filed the suit but around the time of the litigation against ABKCO sold its Rays royalty rights to the Artist Rights Enforcement Corp., the music company that coordinated the Ronettes' royalty litigation against Phil Spector. According to Artist Rights, ABKCO had been paying compact disc and digital exploitation royalties to MPL, but at too-low amounts, for a number of years.

224   "evinces a high degree": Defendant's Answer and Counterclaims, August 30, 2010, in *MPL Music Publishing Inc. v. ABKCO Music & Records Inc.*, 650794/09 (N.Y. Sup. Ct., N.Y. County).

224   "I have made at least five": Letter of Michael B. Kramer to Oren J. Warshavsky August 6, 2010.

224   New York Appellate Division dismissed: *MPL Music Publishing Inc. v. ABKCO Music & Records Inc.*, 114 A.D.3d 598 (N.Y. App. Div. 1st Dept. 2014). In its ruling, the state court cited the 2002 opinion by the New York Court of Appeals, the state's highest court, that had limited the Ronettes' royalty recovery against Phil Spector. *Greenfield v. Philles Records*, 98 N.Y.2d 562 (2002).

BIBLIOGRAPHY

"Allan, You're a Rich Man: Paddy Shennan Meets the Man Who Gave the Beatles Away — But Can Laugh about It." *Liverpool Daily Echo*, February 24, 2010.

"Allen Klein: Beatles and Rolling Stones Manager Whose Lack of Financial Probity Led to Him Being Sued by Both Groups and Spending Time in Prison." *Times* (London), July 6, 2009.

"Allen Klein: 'I Cured All Their Problems.'" *Rolling Stone*, November 29, 1969.

Anderson, Jack. "Beatle John Lennon Wins Stay in U.S." June 14, 1975, syndicated column.

Arnold, Martin. "Beatleggers Trying to Capture a Share of Success, Moneywise." *New York Times*, February 17, 1964.

Aronowitz, Al. "Why Is George in New York?" *Rolling Stone*, June 11, 1970.

Asher, Peter. "Brian Epstein Inducted into the Rock and Roll Hall of Fame." *brianepstein.com*, April 10, 2014. Accessed July 1, 2014. http://www.brianepstein .com/induction.html.

The Beatles. *The Beatles Anthology*. San Francisco: Chronicle Books, 2000.

"The Beatles: You Never Give Me Your Money." *Rolling Stone*, November 15, 1969.

"Beatles' Assets 'Not in Jeopardy.'" *Times* (London), February 25, 1971.

Berman, Art. "Beatles' Visit Posing Top Security Problem." *Los Angeles Times*, August 9, 1964.

Berry, Chuck. *Chuck Berry: The Autobiography*. New York: Harmony Books, 1987.

Bird, Steve. "Heir Found Dead in Bath." *Times* (London), April 18, 2006.

Blumenthal, Ralph. "Ex-Chief Immigration Trial Attorney Quits Abruptly." *New York Times*, December 8, 1973.

Boyd, Pattie. *Wonderful Tonight: George Harrison, Eric Clapton, and Me*. New York: Three Rivers Press, 2007.

Bramwell, Tony. *Magical Mystery Tours: My Life with the Beatles*. New York: St. Martin's Press, 2005.

"Brash Record Executive Managed the Beatles." *Washington Post*, July 8, 2009.

Bronson, Fred, with additional reporting by Jem Aswad. "Pete Bennett, Legendary Promotion Man for Beatles, Stones, Many More, Dead at 77." *Billboard*, November 27, 2012.

Bronson, Harold. "The Producers: Peter Asher." *Hit Parader*, September 1972.

Brown, Mick. "Pop's Last Genius: Phil Spector." *Telegraph Magazine*, February 4, 2003.

———. *Tearing Down the Wall of Sound: The Rise and Fall of Phil Spector*. New York: Alfred A. Knopf, 2007.

Brown, Peter, and Steven Gaines. *The Love You Make: An Insider's Story of the Beatles*. New York: McGraw-Hill, 1983.

Browne, David. *Fire and Rain: The Beatles, Simon & Garfunkel, James Taylor, CSNY, and the Lost Story of 1970*. Cambridge, MA: Da Capo Press, 2011.

Calder, Rich, and Bruce Golding. "Herman's Hermits Singer Admits He Called Music Mogul a 'Scumbag.'" *New York Post*, January 26, 2012.

Calio, Jim. "Yoko Ono's Ex-Husband, Tony Cox, Reveals His Strange Life Since Fleeing with Their Daughter 14 Years Ago." *People*, February 3, 1986. Accessed December 29, 2014. www.people.com/people/archive/article/0,,20092860,00 .html.

Charlesworth, Chris. "John Lennon Gets His Ticket to Ride." *Melody Maker*, August 7, 1976.

———. "John Lennon: Lennon Today." *Melody Maker*, November 3, 1973.

———. "John Lennon: Rock On!" *Melody Maker*, March 8, 1975.

Clark, Steven. "Bennett to Promote Elvis," *Herald Statesman* (Yonkers, NY), January 12, 1979.

Coleman, Ray. *The Man Who Made the Beatles: An Intimate Biography of Brian Epstein*. New York: McGraw-Hill Publishing Co., 1989.

"Comments: Let Him Be." *Rolling Stone*, August 29, 1974.

Connolly, Ray. "Monster of Rock: Allen Klein Swindled the Stones and Broke Up the Beatles and Is Still Rock 'n' Roll's Most Ruthless Svengali." *DailyMail.com*, July 5, 2009. Accessed July 15, 2014. http://www.dailymail.co.uk/tvshowbiz/article -1197709/.

Crouse, Tim. "A Day in the Life of the Beatle Promo Man." *Rolling Stone*, December 9, 1971.

Cullen, Tim. "The End of the Beatles: Epstein's Death Started Trouble." Newspaper Enterprise Association syndicated report, April 1, 1971.

Davies, Hunter. *The Beatles*. New York: W.W. Norton & Co., 2009.

———, ed. *The John Lennon Letters*. New York: Little, Brown and Company, 2012.

Davies, Will. "Allen Klein, the Manager Fans Blamed for the Beatles Break-Up, Dies at 77." *Mail on Sunday*, July 5, 2009.

DiLello, Richard. *The Longest Cocktail Party: An Insider's Diary of The Beatles, Their Million-Dollar Empire and Its Wild Rise & Fall*. Edinburgh: Canongate, 2005.

Doggett, Peter. *You Never Give Me Your Money: The Beatles after the Breakup.* New York: HarperCollins, 2009.

Ellis, Geoffrey. *I Should Have Known Better: A Life in Pop Management — The Beatles, Brian Epstein and Elton John.* London: Thorogood, 2005.

Emerick, Geoff. *Here, There and Everywhere: My Life Recording the Music of the Beatles.* New York: Gotham Books, 2006.

"Enterprise: Beatles, Inc." *Newsweek*, May 27, 1968.

"Ex-Beatles Manager Dies." *Geelong Advertiser* (Australia), July 6, 2009.

"Ex-Manager Severs All Ties with Beatles." *New York Times*, April 3, 1973.

Flippo, Chet. "Lennon in Court Again: $24 Million of Old Gold." *Rolling Stone*, April 8, 1976.

———. "Lennon's Lawsuit: Memo from Thurmond." *Rolling Stone*, July 31, 1975.

Fong-Torres, Ben. "Did Allen Klein Take Bangla Desh Money?" *Rolling Stone*, March 30, 1972.

Foster, Bob. "Hysteria Heaven Rocks Cow Palace." *San Mateo Times*, August 20, 1964.

Fricke, David. "Neil Aspinall, Beatles' Closest Adviser, Headed Apple Corps," *Rolling Stone*, April 17, 2008.

Geller, Deborah. *The Brian Epstein Story.* London: Faber and Faber, 1999.

———. "When Brian Met the Beatles." *Independent* (London), November 16, 1999.

Gleason, Ralph J. "Perspectives: Fair Play for John and Yoko." *Rolling Stone*, June 22, 1972.

Goldman, Albert. *The Lives of John Lennon.* Chicago: A Cappella Books, 2001.

Goodman, Joan. "Interview: Paul and Linda McCartney." *Playboy*, December 1984.

Griffiths, David. "The Beatles: Backstage at the London Palladium." *Record Mirror*, December 21, 1963.

Gruen, Bob. *John Lennon: The New York Years.* New York: Stewart, Tabori & Chang, 2005.

Gumbel, Andrew. "The Lennon Files." *Independent* (London), December 21, 2006.

Hamill, Pete. "Long Night's Journey into Day: A Conversation with John Lennon." *Rolling Stone*, June 5, 1975.

Harrison, George. *I Me Mine.* San Francisco: Chronicle Books, 2002.

Holden, Stephen. "*Brother*, Lon & Derrek Van Eaton." *Rolling Stone*, November 23, 1972.

Hopkins, Jerry. "James Taylor on Apple: 'The Same Old Craperoo.'" *Rolling Stone*, August 23, 1969.

Hotchner, A. E. *Blown Away: A No-Holds Barred Portrait of the Rolling Stones and the Sixties Told by the Voices of the Generation.* New York: Fireside, 1991.

"I Wanna Hold Your Stock." *Newsweek*, March 1, 1965.

"John Lennon's 'Lost Weekend' with Phil Spector." *Uncut*, September 2008. Accessed June 29, 2014. www.uncut.co.uk/phil-spector/john-lennons-lost-weekend-with -phil-spector-interview.

"Judge Refuses 'Freeze' on Beatles' £1m." *Times* (London), April 2, 1969.

Kane, Larry. *Ticket to Ride: Inside the Beatles' 1964 Tour That Changed the World.* Philadelphia: Running Press, 2003.

Karp, Jonathan. "Yoko Ono: How We Were Almost Deported." ABC News, September 5, 2006.

Kaylan, Howard, with Jeff Tamarkin. *Shell Shocked: My Life With the Turtles, Flo & Eddie, and Frank Zappa, etc. . . .* Milwaukee: Backbeat Books, 2013.

King, Bonnie. "Pete Bennett Presents: An Evening of Classic British Rock and Roll with Denny Laine." *Salem-News.com*, October 1, 2008. Accessed August 4, 2014, www.salem-news.com/articles/october012008/.

"Klein, 3 Beatles in Split." *Billboard*, April 14, 1973.

Knight, Jerry. "Tax Trial Centers on Former Beatles' Manager and Aide." *Washington Post*, October 11, 1977.

Krogh, Bud. "Memorandum for: the President's File, Subject: Meeting with Elvis Presley," December, 21, 1970. Accessed July 5, 2013. www.preslaw.info/4-meeting -notes.html.

Landau, Jon. "Lennon Gets Lost in His Rock & Roll." *Rolling Stone*, May 22, 1975.

———. "*Mind Games.*" *Rolling Stone*, January 3, 1974.

Lasky, Victor. "Lennons Spouting Off on U.S. Acts." May 13, 1972, syndicated column.

"Last Lost Lennon Tape." *Legendary Auctions Spring 2004 Catalog.* Accessed January 1, 2015. www.legendaryauctions.com/lot-35648.aspx.

Lennon, Cynthia. *John.* New York: Three Rivers Press, 2005.

"Lennons Seek Haven in U.S., Possession of Yoko's Child." *Oakland Tribune*, April 29, 1972.

"Mail-Order Gold: Where's the Money from TV Oldies?" *Rolling Stone*, November 9, 1972.

Maitland, Leslie. "John Lennon Wins His Residency in U.S." *New York Times*, July 28, 1976.

Margolick, David. "Seeing F.B.I. Files on Lennon: A Hard Day's Night." *New York Times*, September 6, 1991.

"Marks Is Retiring as District Director for Immigration." *New York Times*, May 19, 1974.

Marsh, Dave. "American Grandstand: Sue You, Sue Me Blues." *Rolling Stone*, June 17, 1976.

Martin, George, with Jeremy Hornsby. *All You Need Is Ears: The Inside Story of the Genius Who Created the Beatles.* New York: St. Martin's Press, 1979.

McCabe, Peter. "Some Sour Notes From the Bangladesh Concert." *New York*, February 28, 1972.

McCabe, Peter, and Robert D. Schonfeld, *Apple to the Core: The Unmaking of the Beatles*. New York: Pocket Books, 1972.

McMillian, John. "Baby You're a Rich Man, Too." *Newsweek*, December 19, 2013. Accessed June 21, 2014. http://www.newsweek.com/baby-youre-rich-man-too -244952.

Miles, Barry. *Paul McCartney: Many Years from Now*. New York: Henry Holt and Company, 1997.

Montgomery, Paul L. "U.S. Streamlines Alien Deportation." *New York Times*, January 29, 1972.

Moore, Anne. "George Harrison on Tour — Press Conference Q&A." *Valley Advocate* (Northampton, MA), November 13, 1974.

Moritz, Charles, ed. *Current Biography 1965*. New York: H.W. Wilson Co., 1965–66.

Newman, Clarence. "The Beatles Craze Threatens Big Dent in Parents' Wallets." *Wall Street Journal*, February 12, 1964.

Norman, Philip. *John Lennon: The Life*. New York: HarperCollins, 2008.

———. *Shout! – The Beatles in Their Generation*. New York: MJF Books, 1981.

O'Dell, Chris, with Katherine Ketcham. *Miss O'Dell: My Hard Days and Long Nights with the Beatles, the Stones, Bob Dylan, Eric Clapton and the Women They Loved*. New York: Touchstone, 2009.

Oldham, Andrew Loog. *Stone Free*. Vancouver: Because Entertainment, 2012.

Palmer, Robert. "The Pop Life." *New York Times*, June 17, 1981.

Pang, May. *Instamatic Karma: Photographs of John Lennon*. New York: St. Martin's Press, 2008.

"Peter Creightmore." *Times* (London), May 26, 1997.

Riesel, Victor. "Inside Labor: Rallies Against Beatles." Undated article clipping in 1964, *Subject: The Beatles*, FBI File Number: 62-52493-A.

Robins, Wayne. "In Which This Jack-of-All-Jams Remembers the Stones, Beatles, Little Richard." *Creem*, May 1974.

Rogan, Johnny. *Starmakers and Svengalis*. London: Futura Publications, 1989.

Salewicz, Chris. "Paul McCartney: An Innocent Man?" *Q*, October 1986.

Savage, Jon. "Jon Savage Describes How Brian Epstein Fell Victim to Drugs and the Pressures of Being a Secret Homosexual." *Guardian* (London), December 18, 1998.

Schulps, Dave. "Andrew Loog Oldham, the Rolling Stones." *Trouser Press*, June 1978.

Sharp, Ken. "Andrew Loog Oldham." *Goldmine*, June 2014.

Sheff, David. *Last Interview: All We Are Saying – John Lennon and Yoko Ono*. London: Sidgwick & Jackson, 2000.

Shotton, Pete, and Nicholas Schaffner. *John Lennon in My Life*. New York: Stein and Day 1983.

Sims, Judith. "Beatles Meet, but Not for 'Reunion.'" *Rolling Stone*, April 26, 1973.

Silvester, Norman. "These Beatles Kids? Don't Touch Them with a Bargepole." *Sunday Mail*, October 23, 2011.

Smith, Alan. "Beatles Are on the Brink of Splitting: One Group Is Just Not Big Enough for All This Talent." *New Musical Express*, December 13, 1969.

——. "It's Open Warfare." *New Musical Express*, March 6, 1971.

——. "John Lennon & Yoko Ono: Doing the Rounds for Publicity." *New Musical Express*, July 31, 1971.

Snow, Mat. "The Beatles: 'We're a Damn Good Little Band.'" *MOJO*, October 1996.

Soocher, Stan. *They Fought the Law: Rock Music Goes to Court*. New York: Schirmer Books, 1999.

Southall, Brian, with Rupert Perry. *Northern Songs: The True Story of the Beatles Song Publishing Empire*. London: Omnibus Press, 2007.

Spencer, Neil. "Ono Speaks Softly about Past." *Pacific Stars and Stripes*, July 26, 1997.

Thomson, Graeme. "The Coming of Age of George." *British GQ*, November 18, 2013. Accessed February 9, 2014. www.gq-magazine.co.uk/entertainment/articles/2013 -11/18/george-harrison-the-beatles-concert-for-bangladesh-pictures.

Tillinghast, Charles. *How Capitol Got the Beatles*. Denver: Outskirts Press, 2008.

Trebbe, Anne L. "Personalities." *Washington Post*, January 15, 1982.

"U.S. and British Taxers Vie to Shear Beatles." *New York Times*, January 3, 1965.

Vetter, Craig. "Playboy Interview: Allen Klein." *Playboy*, November 1971.

Werbin, Stuart. "Lennons Discuss Deportation, Allen Klein, Beatles 'Reunion.'" *Rolling Stone*, May 10, 1973.

Wiener, Jon. *Come Together: John Lennon in His Own Time*. Urbana: University of Illinois Press, 1984.

——. *Gimme Some Truth: The John Lennon FBI Files*. Berkeley: University of California Press, 1999.

Wildes, Leon. "The Deferred Action Program of the Bureau of Citizenship and Immigration Services: A Possible Remedy for Impossible Immigration Cases." *San Diego Law Review* 41, no. 2 (Spring 2004).

Williams, Richard. "John & Yoko." *Melody Maker*, December 6, 1969.

——. "The Times Profile: Paul McCartney." *Times* (London), January 4, 1982.

Willis, Collin. "At Last . . . The Truth about How the Man Who Made the Beatles Died." *Sunday Mirror*, December 27, 1998.

Woffinden, Bob. "Ringo Starr: Everyone One of Us Has All We Need." *New Musical Express*, April 12, 1975.

Wright, Jade. "Rock of Ages." *Liverpool Daily Echo*, July 21, 2012.

Yetnikoff, Walter, with David Ritz. *Howling at the Moon: The Odyssey of a Monstrous Music Mogul in an Age of Excess*. New York: Broadway Books, 2004.

"Yoko's Husband Files for Divorce." *The Stars and Stripes*, November 10, 1968.

Yorke, Ritchie. "Boosting Peace: John and Yoko in Canada." *Rolling Stone*, June 28, 1969.

Zimmerman, Pam. "The Ballad of John Lennon and Leon Wildes." *jweekly.com*, December 9, 2010.

INDEX

and Brian Epstein, 3; and Concert
for Bangladesh, 197, 201–2; drug
possession plea, 88–89; early years,
33–34; on Eastmans, 54; immigration
dispute, xii, 87–95, 96–101, 102–10,
111–16, 117–22, 123–26; on James Taylor,
59–60; in McCartney's Beatles
partnership suit, 62, 64–65, 67–70,
141, 150; on meeting McCartney, 163;
and Morris Levy, xii, 129–30, 131–37,
138–49, 151, 152–61, 162–70, 180, 182;
and 1969 UNICEF concert, 196; and
Northern Songs, 49–53; Yoko Ono,
separation from, 131, 139, 150, 152, 169.
See also Cox, Kyoko; Ono, Yoko
Lennon, Julia, 33–34
Lennon, Julian, 19, 142–43, 152–53, 154
Lennon, Sean, 120, 123
Let It Be (album), 58, 63, 64, 67, 68, 75,
138, 149, 216; promotional copies, 205,
208, 213, 215
Let It Be (film), 30, 58, 59, 66, 67, 74,
142, 179
Lettermen, The (vocal group), 207
Levy, Adam, 146, 152
Levy, Morris, 182; background of,
130–31; "Come Together" suit, xii, 130,
131–32, 135–36; Lennon oldies sessions
litigation, 129, 138, 140–49, 151, 152–61,
162–70
Levy, Tom, 10–11, 21
Liberace, 18
Lindsay, John, 105
Liverpool College of Art, 92
Living in the Material World (album),
199
Living Theater, 211
Lockwood, Sir Joseph, 46, 164
Loden, Barbara, 98

Loesser, Frank, 221
Loiacono, John, 174–76
"Long and Winding Road, The," 63, 216
Los Angeles Superior Court, 40, 74, 222
Los Angeles Times (newspaper), 93
Loughran, E. A., 113
Love, Darlene, 221
Love (musical revue), 223
"Love Me Do," 7, 9
Lowell Toy Company, 13
Lulu (singer), 36

Machat, Marty, 39, 140, 141
Machonic, Irv, 144
Mack, Ronald, 178, 184, 191
Maclen Music Inc., 51, 58
Maclen Music Ltd., 51
MacMahon, Lloyd, 159–60
Madison Square Garden, xii, 150, 173–76,
196–99, 200–201
Magical Mystery Tour (movie), 28, 49, 73
Magistrate's Court, Marylebone, 89
Mail on Sunday (newspaper), 221
Makin, Rex, 5
managers. *See* Epstein, Brian; Klein,
Allen; NEMS Enterprises
Manhattan School of Music, 184
Marcos, Imelda, 4
Margo, Phil, 181
Markowitz, Jacob, 77, 82
Marks, Sol, 96, 97–98, 102, 104–5,
106, 107, 113, 117–18, 252n105; press
conference, 111
Marro, Joseph, P., 116
Marsh, Dave, 135, 166–67, 169
Marshall, Paul, 15
Marshall, Bratter, Greene, Allison &
Tucker, 142, 162
Martin, George, 8–9, 29, 43, 49, 130